PHILIP K. DICK

EXHILARATION AND TERROR OF THE POSTMODERN

CHRISTOPHER PALMER

LIVERPOOL UNIVERSITY PRESS

First published 2003 by
LIVERPOOL UNIVERSITY PRESS
4 Cambridge Street
Liverpool L69 7ZU

Reprinted 2007

British Library Cataloguing-in-Publication Data
A British Library CIP record is available

ISBN 978–0–85323–618–4 (hardback)
ISBN 978–0–85323–628–3 (paperback)

Typeset in 10/12.5pt Meridien by
Servis Filmsetting Ltd, Manchester
Printed by MPG Books Ltd, Bodmin

PHILIP K. DICK
EXHILARATION AND TERROR
OF THE POSTMODERN

Liverpool Science Fiction Texts and Studies
General Editor DAVID SEED

Series Advisers: I.F. Clarke, Edward James, Patrick Parrinder and Brian Stableford

Contents

Preface

This book discusses the science fiction of Philip K. Dick, both short stories and novels. The discussion is from two points of view: historical and formal. The first considers the fiction as a depiction of and a response to postmodernity, and investigates a clash between humanism and postmodernism, which is seen as the inscription of Dick's own historical predicament—a predicament which might also be ours. The second considers matters of genre and form. Dick is an enthusiastic rather than a conventional writer of SF, so that he exploits the conventions of the genre rather than obeying them. Not that his version of SF is simply playful: the clash between humanism and postmodernism is played out in the complex forms of the fiction; the tension between realism and fantasy, endemic to SF, is exacerbated in this case. The focus on genre opens up issues of representation, which can otherwise be overlooked when texts are considered as responses to historical conditions, though no one has ever argued that Dick's novels are simply mimetic or straightforwardly extrapolative, given the wild mixture of satire, metaphor, fantasy, and reflection on the fake and fictional that they present. The focus on history puts into question both the nature of postmodernity and issues of agency, as regards the postmodern subject and as regards the postmodern text.

Because our ideas of authors and their agency and autonomy in history—or lack of it—have changed, the writing of a monograph is no longer a simple business. Indeed, in the case of Dick, it never was a simple business, as a perusal of previous efforts, by Hazel Pierce, Douglas Mackey, Patricia Warrick and Kim Stanley Robinson, will confirm: all are insightful and I have learnt from them all, especially the last, but all struggle with Philip K. Dick's prolific output. Thirty-five SF novels, half a dozen (roughly) realist novels, and more than a hundred stories: such a large and dazzlingly varied production does not lend itself to a steady chronological exposition. One can spend more time summarizing the invariably tangled plots and specifying the crowded cast lists than actually commenting on and interpreting the novels. I have not tried to discuss all of Dick's novels in detail, or even all his major ones. The first part of the book (Chapters 1–3) ranges generally over his SF, introducing the historical and formal questions touched on above. The second part (Chapters 4–12) concentrates on specific stories and novels. I have included extensive discussions of *The Man in the High Castle, Martian Time-Slip, A Scanner Darkly, Valis* and the short stories, but referred only briefly to novels such as *Ubik, The Three Stigmata of Palmer Eldritch* and *The Transmigration of Timothy Archer*, which the emerging consensus agrees are major works; and I would love to have offered detailed discussions of a few others that would reward more consideration than they have been given so far, especially *A Maze of Death* and *Lies, Inc.*

Most chapters range widely back and forth in Dick's *oeuvre*, which is treated as a megatext within—or on the margins of—the wider megatext of SF. The primary focus is on the historical and formal issues, and I rely on the spiky quirkiness and wit of Dick's fictions to defeat any temptation to smooth them out for the sake of neat argument. Chapters more particularly devoted to a single novel (the discussion of *Martian-Time Slip* is divided between a pair of chapters) should correct any remaining tendency to subject the fiction to a simplifying or patronising thesis, but in these cases I have begun each chapter with a survey ('Wide Angle') of relevant aspects of his SF as a whole.

Like that of many contemporary critics, my approach is eclectic, though it draws heavily on the Marxism of Fredric Jameson. I view literary criticism as an active dialogue between the critic, who must argue with the courage of his or her theoretical convictions, and the text, which is best regarded as an intelligent piece of discourse about (in the case of Dick) the conditions of contemporary society, one that practises its own discipline of truth-production—a discipline that is necessarily supple to the point of elusiveness. Critics can no longer expect to serve the text and transmit a transparent truth from it to their readers, but nor should they expect the text to illustrate their theory, or to be demolished and triumphed over if it doesn't illustrate their theory. Philip K. Dick is a humorous, exaggerating, excessive, restless, gloomy, unquenchable writer, affectionate and cynical, empathetic and paranoid, pontificating and undecided; moreover, his texts are hospitable to a vast amount of the schlock, dross and fad of popular culture and popular literature, from Barbie dolls and the folklore of Coca-Cola to psychokinesis and alien invasion. They are responsive not only to the epochal currents carrying us all from modernity to postmodernity, but to the local but pressing differences between the fifties and the sixties, and all this in California, where the fever of postmodernity reaches its most spectacular crises.[1]

There is, then, much to accommodate, interpret and argue about. Theory is here treated as a kit of more or less delicate tools, not as an

---

[1] Or so I assume, joining a consensus and a tradition, but see David Reid's introduction to *Sex, Death and God in LA* (1994).

edifice. The aim is to apply it, not to perfect it. So much by way of manifesto—a manifesto whose air of confidence probably fails to disguise its
moderation. The usefulness of characterizing the author as if he were an
agent, as I have just done, may best be assessed in the light of later discussions of his texts' complex, quirky and exacerbated relations to SF as a
megatext. The usefulness of reference to the now fruitfully controversial,
but dangerously general, term 'humanism' may be assessed in the light of
later discussions of the clashes between Dick's ethical ideals and the
responses to postmodernity which shape and misshape his texts. As for
postmodernity, it is like a game that is only half over: why write as if one
already knew the outcome? Besides, the rules are uncertain and shifting,
bluff serves for authority, spectators and commentators are periodically
transformed into players, and, when they are, their fumbles are apt to
make their earlier barracking from the stands look foolish or parochial:
much generalizing about the postmodern is too closely tied to a decade
(the 1980s) or to a brief roster of allegedly symptomatic events (for
instance, the Gulf War, symptomatic perhaps, but certainly not a typical
contemporary war).

There is a sentence in Don DeLillo's *Mao II* which runs like this:

> Bill opened the door in the middle of traffic, the thick choked blast
> of yellow metal, and he walked out into it. (1991: 94)

The quiet hum of the word processor faces us as we write, but at our back
is always the growl of traffic, 'the thick choked blast of yellow metal', and
we sometimes need to get up from the desk and walk out into it—though
the experience of Bill Grey (a writer and recluse) is not very reassuring in
this connection, since he is knocked down by an Athenian taxi in the terminal stages of the novel.

My discussion is intended to broaden our understanding of Dick's
fiction, and of our age—where we are and where we have just recently
come from. It is true that everything conceivable comes within the ambit
of fiction, and of theory. Ilya Prigognine has studied the complexities of
traffic flow in the light of chaos theory (Prigognine and Herman 1971),
and Fredric Jameson (1993) has used Kevin Lynch's study of the quotidian experience of moving through city streets as model for his theory of
'cognitive mapping'; in Chapter 3 below I discuss the devolution of the
kinetic into blockage and stasis in Dick's novels, noting in passing his particular depiction of vehicles and journeys. The particular subtle and
adventurous textualities of theory and fiction can sometimes crowd the
scene of perception, reassuringly blocking out 'the thick choked blast'
which DeLillo evokes—in a text, of course. Caught in the pleasures of
conceptual overview and control, the cold snows of the contemporary

dream, we can lose the fact that this stuff can make us sick or knock us down.

I have tried to remain aware of this pressure of the actual when drawing on recent theories in order to define the relations of Dick's fiction to history. Yet the best of Dick's fiction is science fiction, and its qualities of textuality, intertextuality, and, as I shall argue, its relations with megatextuality surround us like a thicket and entice us like a garden. Thence the second focus of this discussion, that on genre. How do the protocols of realism and of fantasy shape the stories, and how are they defied? How does Philip K. Dick, who imagines worlds that are wholly constructed, that are fakes or illusions—*this* being the predominant form of his relation to history, to what I have just been emphatically evoking in its uncouth actuality—himself construct his fictions out of the materials and procedures of genre? If recent criticism is a battle between the political and the textual —between those who see the textual as the ultimate horizon of our attention and those who see the social and historical as the ultimate horizon of our attention, or rather, when it is most interesting, a battle between those visions within a single critic—that battle is fought out in Dick's fiction, with the difference that with Dick it is as often the ethical as the political that is the second contestant, since he is strongly humanist in his commitments. This difference is itself the mark of history, reminding us that Dick is not our contemporary. My suggestion is that we must recognize the immediacy of genre—of what SF has imagined and how it has imagined it—in Dick's texts, yet acknowledge how they make a response—and a provocation—to a history that floods through the tropes of genre and often imperiously bends or drowns them as it does so.

There are two published bibliographies of Philip K. Dick, by Daniel J.H. Levack (1988) and by Phil Stephensen-Payne and Gordon Benson, Jr (1990); in addition, Lawrence Sutin and Paul Williams provide useful chronologies at the conclusions of their discussions of Dick's life (Sutin 1989: 290–312; P. Williams 1986: 178–84).

Christopher Palmer
La Trobe University, Melbourne
2002

Acknowledgments

I would like to thank the following for help and inspiration: my students Gerard Wood, Simon Whithear and Ross Farnell; Damien Broderick; Eric Rabkin and George Slusser; Samuel J. Umland; the meticulous Helen Tookey; Damaris, Eddie and Sam Palmer. I would also like to thank La Trobe University for granting me two periods of study leave, and California State University, Fullerton (especially Willis McNelly and Sharon Parry) and Duke University for their hospitality while I was a visitor.

The following chapters have been published in somewhat different forms: Chapter 12 as 'Postmodernism and the Birth of the Author in Philip K. Dick's *Valis*' in *Science-Fiction Studies*, 18 (1991); Chapter 11 as '*A Scanner Darkly* and Postmodern Society' in *Arena* (Melbourne) (1988); Chapter 5 as 'Philip K. Dick and the Nuclear Family' in *Philip K. Dick: Recent Critical Studies*, edited by Samuel J. Umland (Greenwood Press, 1995); Chapter 6 as 'Critique and Fantasy in Two Novels by Philip K. Dick' in *Extrapolation*, 32, number 1 (Fall 1991).

Abbreviations

The following short titles are used for novels by Philip K. Dick:

Androids	*Do Androids Dream of Electric Sheep?*
Clans	*Clans of the Alphane Moon*
Confessions	*Confessions of a Crap Artist—Jack Isidore (of Seville, Calif.). A Chronicle of Verified Scientific Fact 1949–1959*
Dr Bloodmoney	*Dr Bloodmoney or How We Got Along After the Bomb*
Flow My Tears	*Flow My Tears, the Policeman Said*
Frolix 8	*Our Friends from Frolix 8*
Palmer Eldritch	*The Three Stigmata of Palmer Eldritch*
Puttering About	*Puttering About in a Small Land*
Teeth	*The Man Whose Teeth Were All Exactly Alike*
Time-Slip	*Martian Time-Slip*
Timothy Archer	*The Transmigration of Timothy Archer*

For short stories by Philip K. Dick, reference is to volumes of the *Collected Stories of Philip K. Dick* (1987), abbreviated as CS.

Part I

1. Philip K. Dick and the Postmodern

Today we live in the epoch of the postmodern, and are subject to the condition of postmodernity. This book concerns the science fiction writer Philip K. Dick (1928–1982), whose fiction gives a sometimes frightening, often funny rendition of the condition of postmodernity, and also struggles with its implications for humanist ethics.

The postmodern is related to the modern, and in discussion of the latter it is customary to make use of a trio of terms: 'modernization' (the economic process); 'modernity' (the consciousness that accompanies, facilitates and results from modernization); and 'modernism' (the artistic style that constitutes a response to the modern, and sometimes a critique of it). This book mostly uses 'modernity' and 'modernism', and their equivalents, 'postmodernity' and 'postmodernism'. For the purposes of discussion of science fiction in general and Philip K. Dick in particular, it is important to recognize that a text can reflect and reflect on a condition of society and consciousness (call it postmodernity, assuming that it continually overlaps and interrelates with postmodernization) without necessarily being postmodernist in style (and thence, importantly, in its view of the subject). The relations between reflection and representation, and the question of whether an intense reflection of, or let us say an immersion in, postmodernity itself involves postmodern*ism*, will need be examined later.

There is a great deal about the concept and the periodization that is vexed: for instance, is postmodernity a complete break from modernity or an intensification and development of it? It is interesting that Henry Ford, so indelibly associated with modernization that his name has been given to one aspect of it (Fordism), also set up a kind of theme park that anticipates postmodernism in its blurring of the boundaries between the replica and the real thing (see Wills 1987: 373–75). It is certainly useful to distinguish between the dominant and the emergent in thinking about culture and society, but that the emergent postmodern should pitch its tent so close to the dominant modern challenges strict periodizations. Again, the discussion in this chapter about androids, robots, deities and aliens in Philip K. Dick, and their implications for human subjecthood, has been stimulated by essays on dolls and marionettes by Von Kleist, Baudelaire and Rilke (1994 [1810, 1853, 1913–14]): these meditations from the

Romantic and modernist periods are a reminder that thought about consciousness has led to scepticism about its privileged location in humans
throughout the modern epoch.[1]

The relations of the cultural situation to the economic are often uncertain, and so are the relations between the general social and—in postmodernity—emphatically cultural condition, and the aesthetic style and
philosophical position. As Perry Anderson has argued (1992, ch. 2), it is
an implication of Marshall Berman's account of 'the experience of modernity' that the writers who most vividly expressed this experience were the
great nineteenth-century realists, such as Dickens. This underlines the
question of representation, but it certainly complicates the relations
between modernity and modernism, as a literary style.

As regards the *post*modern, attempts to answer the corresponding questions are subject to an ironic twist. The term 'postmodern' is introduced
partly in response to the preoccupation of late capitalism with the fabrication, exchange and sale of images rather than artifacts; the commodifica-
tion of culture. The economic and the cultural have become intermingled.
Further, it is often alleged that postmodernity does something quite drastic
and unprecedented to history: it erases it. This is not just another period
in a succession of periods, it is the period to end periods, or, at least, the
sense of history is now decisively abrogated.[2] (Dick's dealings with history
and the sense of history are discussed in Chapter 6.)

Then again, while it may be unfair to label postmodernism as the genre
of theorizing about the postmodern, as has been done, the concept does
come with built-in mechanisms that prevent resolution of the problems to
which it gives rise.[3] There can be no post-postmodernism: that would be
ridiculous; the very name attempts to pre-empt historical discussion in a
fashion that must arouse suspicion and resistance. Turning our attention
more specifically to Philip K. Dick, we find that grand epochal categories
such as 'the modern' and 'the postmodern' do not help us with precise
periodization; what is most characteristically Dickian in Dick's fiction

---

[1] For Dick's romanticism in the context of his treatment of children, see Chapter 9 below;
for robots and subjecthood, see Chapter 12.

[2] It is certainly impossible to prove that contemporary culture as a whole has abrogated
the sense of history. Think of such excellent and sophisticated historical novels as A.S. Byatt's
Possession (1990), Margaret Atwood's *Alias Grace* (1996), and David Malouf's *The Conversations
at Curlow Creek* (1996). Notice that in obvious ways E.L. Doctorow's *The Waterworks* (1994) is
less postmodernist than his earlier *Ragtime* (1975), and the same is true of Thomas Pynchon's
Mason and Dixon (1998 [1997]) as compared to *Gravity's Rainbow* (1973); yet *The Waterworks*
and *Mason and Dixon* are both challenging historical novels.

[3] Postmodernism is 'a class which is a member of its own class', as Jameson more moderately puts it (1993: x); it is John Frow (1991) who says that postmodernism is the name for
the genre of theorizing about the postmodern.

emerges in the sixties and is emphatically of the sixties, but the nuances of difference between, say, the sixties and the eighties, so obvious to us as we live through the decades, are not always illuminated by the concept of the postmodern.[4]

Yet the concept of the postmodern is clearly a useful one. Once it is introduced, a whole set of phenomena and styles is brought into view and relation: ways of producing truths or plausibilities, and ways of being a person or personality, or acting as a person or personality, as well as economic and cultural conditions and styles. And if the boundaries of this set become blurred, then needless to say the blurring of boundaries is itself a theme of postmodernism. There is a further problem, which can be defined in two ways. One is, if we grant that the postmodern is, in Marxist terms, dominant, how do we assess residual or resistant phenomena? And if we grant that postmodern society is uniform *and* heterogeneous at the same time, then there is likely to be a good deal of confusion between the uniform on the one hand and the fragmented, decentred and heterogeneous on the other hand. What kind of heterogeneity is a given phenomenon actually left with if we insist that the phenomenon is postmodern, given that heterogeneity is characteristic of the postmodern, and given that the postmodern is dominant? Can something be heterogeneous to the general heterogeneity that is postmodernity only on condition that it is itself postmodern in its lineaments, and, if so, how heterogeneous is that?

The other aspect of the problem is that of finding a point of detachment or independence, dialectical, no doubt, both inside and outside what we wish to assess—a standpoint that enables us to be other than mouthpieces of the condition which encompasses us. Fredric Jameson at this point looks towards an as yet 'unimaginable' art (1993: 54; 1988: 347), but we need not be so poignantly bereft. Any discussion which starts from postmodernity as a historical condition attempts detachment by ignoring postmodernism's own tendency to elide history.[5] The problem of critical distance, and the related problem of historical change (which appears to require notions of sequence rather than notions of flux) nonetheless remain important. There is a danger that postmodern theory will smooth away aesthetic and experiential difficulties, by producing a unified, seamlessly dominant postmodernity, not a mixed, impure one of the sort that its emphasis on heterogeneity might have led to. The instability and

---

[4] Chapter 7 offers an account of the difference between the fifties and the sixties in Dick's changing imagination of consumption.

[5] Which is not to deny that postmodernist writers have often shown how history is itself a fabricated thing.

uncertainty—not to say violent change and intense anxiety—that characterize the cultural situation are elegantly assimilated into a theoretical discourse, and the possibility of a lack of fit between society and culture, or individual and historical situation—not to say a bruising collision between them—is discounted.

Rather than pursuing the theoretical issues, I want at this point to introduce into the discussion our subject, Philip K. Dick. Dick wrote science fiction stories and novels in the fifties and sixties and (at a lesser rate of production) in the seventies. In addition, in the late fifties he wrote a series of non-SF novels, sometimes rather misleadingly called 'mainstream' novels, though no one would publish them at the time. He was a popular writer, paid by the word, churning out stories (28 published in 1954) and novels (four published in 1964, along with 10 stories; two of these novels are discussed below in Chapter 8), improvising, recycling material, making use of current story forms and stereotypes, embracing the paranoia of the fifties, and the sixties' enthusiasm for altered states of consciousness. At his best, and quite often when he is not at his best, his fiction creates a particular blend of hysteria and entrapment, fragmentation and high anxiety, one that begins by seeming zany, off the wall, but soon prompts in the reader a desire to think about what is going on, what sort of experience or situation is being caught by the fiction.

Dick's writing situates itself on territory contested between politics and religion: politics, wherein a certain cultural practice or way of explaining the world can be seen as ideological, that is, an invention or production helpful to those in power; and religion, wherein the same thing can be seen as illusory, that is, the sign that secular, experienced reality is not really real. Behind a social ideology there may be nothing more than another fabrication, but behind a secular illusion there is, perhaps, a spiritual reality. If so, politics and religion crucially diverge, but for the moment we note that in both realms ordinary experience is taken to be fragile and deceptive, and the social, the basis and conditioner of ordinary experience, is seen as a fabrication or a fake. (In addition religion is often itself a fabrication in Dick's novels, yet not necessarily less consolatory for being a fabrication.[6])

Further, Dick writes about both industrial society (that is, a society in which *objects* are produced and consumed) and post-industrial society (that is, one in which *images and information* are produced and consumed).

---

[6] There are instances in *Solar Lottery*, *Androids*, *A Maze of Death* and *Counter-Clock World*. Given that behaviour in Dick's imagined societies is usually brutal and calculating, and that a mechanistic materialism is dominant in them, Marx's definition of religion as 'the soul of a soulless world' is very relevant here.

For him, the important historical break is between modernity and what-ever preceded it, which is now receding into invisibility, not that between modernity and what we now call postmodernity. The things that we might now call postmodern, implying by this a supersession of the modern, he depicts as a thickening or worsening of the modern.[7]

Dick's fiction constitutes a critique of modernity: of postwar America, split between a suburban society and a national security state,[8] divided between producers threatened with obsolescence and powerless consu-mers. It also develops an anticipation of what has now been defined as postmodernity, although the concept was not available to him: the regime of images and simulacra, the fading of the natural, the possibil-ity that social institutions and ruling conditions are imaginary, fabri-cated things, and that there is no objective ground of reality. To speak very approximately, his novels and especially his short stories of the fifties emphasize the former (the critique of modernity), and his novels of the sixties and seventies emphasize the latter (the anticipation of postmodernity), but it is the overlap between the two emphases that is challenging, not the shift, because it implies the links between moder-nity and postmodernity. Dick's fiction certainly does not establish a standpoint from which these conditions can be detachedly judged, but it sets going fluctuations of distaste and enthusiasm for them. It stimulates frissons of anxiety, as solid ground seems to melt away, and temptations of indulgence, as reality comes to seem wonderfully trans-formable.

Dick is a gameplayer in fiction; he delights in trying every combina-tion, in trumping each possibility or explanation with its contrary. If we think of modernity and thence postmodernity in Deleuzian terms as a libidinal release and a decoding, in which clear structures are dissolved (see Patton 1988), then in his fictions Dick enthusiastically indulges this aspect of modernity, because he wants to shock and transform. In fact, transformation is the engine, the pulsion of his fiction. It is not too much of a simplification to say that all the fun and liberatory release that post-modernity offers is reserved for the writer (so madly and comically inven-tive) and the reader (so bewildered but so entertained). Meanwhile the characters in the fiction are faced with the grim and frightening disorien-tation, the dissolution not merely of certainty but of purpose in the world

---

[7] A relevant text here is Guy Debord's *The Society of the Spectacle* (1967), especially in its contention (see paragraphs 100–13) that communism as well as capitalism is (what we would call) postmodern. All this for Debord is an extension of the alienated rationality of industrial production, not a departure from it.

[8] 'Half welfare and half garrison society' is the way Irving Howe put it in 1959 (1992: 24).

and connection with others. If the condition for making a text is a gap, a blindness even, then this illogical distribution of pleasure and pain is that gap and blindness in Dick's fiction. His characters suffer in one society, his readers enjoy in another society—a society consisting of the group that he tries to draw out of the larger, but still eccentric, group of SF readers. Meanwhile the relations between the two subcultures, as between the experiences of characters and of readers, are unstable. It is significant that his novels very often involve a beleaguered group of ordinary people, able to attain solidarity and community, yet split by suspicions and enmities.

Dick's fiction is certainly not comfortably euphoric, then. In fact one of its fascinations is that he affirms a set of values and views of reality that would seem contrary to *all* the diverse things the concept of the postmodern stands for. This is here called humanism, in order to underline the valuation of the individual subject, especially as vessel of ethical response and, potentially, action, though in most discussions of postmodernism it is reason that is the antagonist.[9] Whether this valuation, in Dick, implies a notion of universal human nature, a human essence, is less certain, though it is clear from remarks in interviews and speeches that he thought it did. He saw the question of what makes us truly human as central to his work—assuming that we are truly human, which is debatable in many cases.

Much about Dick's humanism is problematic precisely because of the context in which it attempts to operate; if it is best to think in terms of a will to value the individual subject, rather than a settled conviction of its essence, then this more embattled position still leads to a challenging collision between humanism and what undermines it.

Apart from being intriguing in itself, this collision has personal relevance to most of us today. Stigmatizing this or that worry as gauche and unsophisticated is a frequent resort of the intellectually evasive, and a good deal of the conceptual dazzlement and machismo assertiveness of contemporary cultural theory is evasive in this way. Simple questions such as 'What is to be done?' are often overlooked. Terms such as 'humanist' and 'liberal humanist', whether offered as descriptions or as charges, are occasionally used to postpone consideration of a matter which is, indeed, difficult to settle, the nature of the ethical foundations of political and social action in postmodern times.[10]

Dick is a writer who is warmly and confidingly candid, and also

---

[9] See for instance Lovibond 1989 for a good exposition of the issues.

[10] For attempts to confront these issues, see for instance the recent work of Christopher Norris, Habermas's *oeuvre*, Arac (ed.) (1986), Siebers 1993, and Lovibond 1989.

violently sceptical and disruptive of commonsense assumptions.[11] His humanism opens out questions of the nature and value of postmodernity and postmodernism in challenging ways, and indeed, even for him, the result is a contortion. In this chapter this vexed, contorted but refreshing quality of Dick's work will be approached through the complex situation of science fiction as a genre.

Science fiction (henceforth SF) is itself a split and unstable literary form, as we can see from critical discussions of its affiliations to fantasy and to realism, two literary modes which set up a force field whose energies and stresses shape the genre.[12] In Dick's case, the ideological potentials of the literary modes can be related to humanism and postmodernism, respectively, without assuming that these potentials are historically constant.[13] In his writing, the contest and interaction of realism and fantasy is a contest and interaction of humanism and postmodernism. This contest and interaction can be historicized; we can define it as reflex of and reflection on the passage of history since the fifties, a troubling and disorienting history.

In this cultural and literary context there are two striking things about Dick's work. One is that his anticipation of the condition of postmodernity, which develops out of a critique of the society, politics and psychology of modernity, is radical and spectacular. The other is that Dick's humanism is itself an active, self-questioning and developing aspect of his writing. By no means does it amount to an un-thought-out, assumed status quo; in fact his achievement as a writer is to extend the range of SF both by a more complex, less naïve humanism *and* by an enthusiastic imagination of the conditions of postmodernity. To accomplish either of these things is interesting, to accomplish both at once is bound to be fascinating, but also paradoxical, or perhaps contradictory. Chapter 3 delineates the political unconscious of Dick's SF; that is, as 'political unconscious' is defined here, the recurrent images and forms that speak an imaginative resolution—or irresolution—of real, historical contradictions. This discussion establishes the shaping force of the postmodern: a

[11] This is itself a humanist sentence, implying autonomy and continuity in its subject; this makes it necessary for me to shuttle back and forth between the texts that Dick produced—which are readily identifiable as idiosyncratic—and the history and textuality that produced him. And if, in turn, my reader feels that this recourse implies that I, like Dick, write as if the subject position of the writer were less embattled than those of his characters, then she or he is right.

[12] Other modes might be considered; that of horror is particularly relevant to Dick. But two makes enough complication for the moment.

[13] And neither realism nor fantasy is easily defined, as discussions and renominations of the latter have underlined. For the fantastic, as distinguished from fantasy, see for instance R. Jackson 1981; for the fantasmatic, as opposed not to the realistic but to the 'noematic', see Clayton 1982, or sample the flourishing subgenre of discussion of the uncanny.

particular imagination of the subjectivized and disintegrated is found to be at the heart of Dick's political unconscious; but first the historical interest of a more conscious and explicit side of his writing is defined.

* * * * *

The rest of this chapter surveys what happens to subjects in Dick's novels, and then what happens to objects. Subjects and objects are interdependent: each ought to have its own distinctness, let's say. If either seems to lack it, the other is jeopardized. They share the same fate. This chapter mainly describes the dimensions and qualities of Dick's representation of postmodernity. These dimensions and qualities are so sweeping and so densely layered that to take them for granted and proceed briskly to the formal and political problems that Dick's work presents would be to miss much of its interest. It is necessary to discuss what Dick's fiction represents as well as what it does, precisely because both representation and process, signification and production, are problematized in his fiction. It might seem that to follow this plan is to pre-empt important questions of form, implying that fictions are mere containers full of 'contents', and in addition to simplify the position of the reader and the condition of textuality. A novel is not a kind of zoo which the reader observes from outside, strolling, safe from the caged denizens, but an energetic event that involves reader, writing and written. What might be represented, 'out there' in American society of the fifties, or postmodern society, is worth investigation, but what is going on, in the fiction and as one reads, needs to be given weight.

Dick's fiction constitutes a radical representation of the conditions of contemporary society, conditions that affect the sense of time, the sense of self which an individual is required to attain in order to be an agent in contemporary society, the sense of objects as they are produced by contemporary society. He is in fact a writer who continually complicates, elides, or evaporates any implied definition of the objective and 'out there', emphasizing that actuality is something imagined or fabricated, like one of the fakes or simulacra that populate his novels. There is no difference, such as may be measured by a reality principle, between the interlocked vision and explanation advanced by a lone paranoiac, and the systematized ideology which provides worldview and structure to a society. In Dick's fictions, we all, rulers and ruled, practise the 'paranoiac-critical' activity which Breton endorsed in Dali's surrealism (see Breton 1978: 136–37). The world is simultaneously being produced and disowned by all those involved. Such difference as there is between the lone weirdo and the order of society is to be measured politically; it is a matter of who has the power. Several of Dick's novels dramatize the convergence of the worldview entertained by some lonely neurotic (definable as schizophrenic or autistic) and the world-views of various competing power groups headed by apparently ratio-nal individuals.

And if things in the texts are fabrications, so, it is acknowledged in the texts, are the texts themselves. How else could the author testify to his sense of the validity of what he is seeing in social life? His text, by which he frames that seeing, must participate in the conditions seen, so that the frame must dissolve, or admit that it is a frame-up in the colloquial sense. There is certainly a postmodernist *aspect*, at least, to Dick's writing, and it might be argued that regardless of the author's intentions and values, this will pervade the rest. Like a virus exuberantly on the loose in the network, the postmodernity of content (decentred or destabilized subjects, simula-cral environments, fabricated political set-ups) begins to capture the nar-rative form, which after all is the way the text produces meaning. The text in turn gets the point: it acknowledges that it is also a simulacrum. This happens increasingly in Dick's *oeuvre*.

And we might leave it at that; the more radical, subversive and disturb-ing, the better. But the matter also has implications for the politics of writing. It has frequently been assumed that the average reader exists in a state of complacency so dense that it cannot be upset and undermined sufficiently often. Thence the formally subversive text is privileged. It is not criticism of this or that aspect of reality that is required, but critique of the very way we take things for real in bourgeois society. Realism is suspect, unleash the potential of fantasy. But this notion of the subversive text and the smug reader (Jackson 1981: 82–91) has been undermined by postmodernist theory. If there is no longer an avant garde, because high culture has been subsumed in the popular, there is no longer a separate, inertial public to be galvanized or dismayed. The audience of, for instance, a rock video is presumably as thoroughly immersed in 'total flow', affect-less, apprised of the irrelevance of core meaning, as the form 'itself' is. This audience will be too savvy to entertain assumptions and would be too cool to allow them to be subverted if it did entertain them. But in Dick the case is altered, and not only because he writes in a popular genre; in his novels people are very commonly sunk in guilt, impotence and depression, and contemplate suicide, and this does in turn have implications for the reader, although, as was mentioned earlier, her or his position is much freer and more enjoyable. Dick feels that we all have plenty of self-subverting inner resources of gloom and negativity, so his relations with his readers will be different from relations between the avant-garde text and the complacent bourgeois reader. Continuous centred subjectivity is not really a strait-jacket for the reader of Dick, insofar as her or his reading position is prescribed by the call for empathy with Dick's characters; it's more a fleetingly glimpsed refuge.[14]

1. Mutations and Migrations of Subjectivity

In Dick's imaginary societies, one has no choice but to be a person (autonomous, integral, capable of decisions for which one takes responsibility); whether or not this is an ideal, it is certainly prescribed by social conditions, which the author takes care to tighten, by inventing some pressing crisis of survival for the main characters to face. His societies are both modern (prescribing autonomous centred subjectivity, or, at the very least, identity), and postmodern (prescribing, or enforcing, floating, decentred adaptiveness) (see Eagleton 1990: 377). Postmodernity is experienced as problematic when its elements conflict with modernity, and the problematic, by leading to disequilibrium, motivates the narrative.

The modern ethical subject is a bounded subject; at a certain point, physically and psychologically, she comes to an end and things and people that are not her begin. Thus bounded, she may decide, vote, compete, write articles and so on. It has certainly been suggested that an unbounded, decentred subject may act ethically, but the concept of boundedness is useful for appreciating what is problematic about persons in Dick's fiction, where boundaries are very uncertain.

It is true that from a broad perspective on narrative there is nothing remarkable about this. Most narratives blur the distinction between self and not-self. The self is shown to be incomplete, either by glimpses of fluctuating inner life, or by the way the story is about a transformation from one phase of life to another. The self never faces the outside world as a distinct thing, but always as an inchoate thing, and the facing, as soon as it enters crisis, makes you wonder whether there is a self there to do the facing. Dick's fictions simply exacerbate this common situation, after the mode of postmodernism, which works by exacerbation rather than invention.[15]

Nonetheless the exacerbation is spectacular. In a given work the range of active, purposeful and opinionated beings may include any—or almost all—of the following: robots, androids (artificial humans that seem to have the bodies of 'normal' humans), 'sims' (which are like androids, but usually radio controlled), animals, aliens, actors, fakes and pretenders.[16]

---

[14] On the embattled position of the individual in postmodernity, and indeed in modernity, see Eagleton 1990: 157–59.

[15] Brooke-Rose (1981) gives a good account of this.

[16] In all this, Dick is pillaging contemporary SF, rather than inventing for himself; consideration of the theoretical implications of the relations of Dick's SF to the larger SF 'megatext' is postponed to Chapter 3.

Their behaviour may range from the trivial to the menacing: they imitate the human rather than offering an alternative to it. Frequently they think they *are* human, in the conventional, consensual meaning of the term. They tend continually to collapse into *each other*, as if the non-human world provided a differentiated range of possibilities and there were no need of a human centre by which to classify this range of possibilities. The creature we thought was a Martian animal (that is, as readers we would like a few moments to assimilate the arrival of this unusual creature on the scene of the text) is rapidly revealed as a fake, a sort of android-Martian. In the novel in which this is a minor discovery, *The Simulacra* (1964), the major discovery is that the ruler of the novel's America, 'the First Lady', is actually played by an actress; then it is revealed that she is not actually the ruler anyway, since power is in the hands of a secret committee. Moreover, it becomes clear that she is better seen as the projection of the neurotic needs of her subjects; she exists in their collective psyche, not as a distinct entity who is working to deceive them. (And at this point conventional narrative procedures *are* breaking down; we infer that the First Lady's power is something conferred on her by her 'victims', because the idea that she is deceiving and manipulating them, which the narrative had encouraged us to entertain, has come to seem implausible.) Meanwhile time is dissolving, because the operation of a time machine brings about periodic visits of personalities from the Nazi era, and—in another part of the wood—a small group of, in effect, prehistoric humans is observed to be preparing to re-enter history after a very long absence, thus curving the future back towards the distant past. Even given that the novel has an improvised feel which verges on the ridiculous, the effect for the reader of this ever-shifting mélange is a kind of vertigo.

To speak of a category which might be expected to serve as 'the Other' and thus clarify what 'the Human' is: aliens may disguise themselves as humans, or they may be huge and capable of absorbing humans into their 'mentation' to form a collective entity, or they may exist not as individuals but as part of a collective mental life, or they may be just as hopeless and neurotic as the average human.[17] In fact there is a case for saying that most of those aliens, psionics and so on in Dick's novels are metaphors for neurosis. Contact with aliens will not clarify the sense of humanness,

---

[17] Disguised aliens: *The Game-Players of Titan*; absorbent: *Galactic Pot-Healer*; collective: *The Ganymede Takeover*; neurotic: *Galactic Pot-Healer* again. *Palmer Eldritch* presents an eponymous being that is ambiguously both human and alien, and also android (eyes, teeth and arm are manufactured); in addition this being employs a consciousness-controlling drug which halts, reverses and reruns the flow of time, and, by the end of the novel, threatens to absorb all humans into itself.

because aliens are fluctuant, fallible, and desire to merge with the human.[18]

Conversely, humans may desire to merge with a deity (as happens for instance in *Galactic Pot-Healer*) or a doll (as happens in *Palmer Eldritch*). This desire has metaphorical as well as psychological dimensions (which I discuss in Chapter 7), but it also suggests the way in which bounded consciousness is not only threatened (as happens when the deity, who is also already a robot, an alien and a human, desires to absorb humans in *Palmer Eldritch*), but is also escaped from. Yet the matter is still problematic, because humans are not bestowing soul on a doll or a deity;[19] they are seeking self in this empty or absorbent being.

Before proceeding, it is worth noting that this emphasis on shifting, merging and imperfection needs to be complemented with another emphasis. Dick's novels are full of uncannily accurate and successful simulacra[20]—simulacra that erase the things they might be said to be imitating, so that they are no longer imitations of anything, they simply are. They raise a problem of representation: representation should involve imperfection or differentiation, and this is lacking in these simulacra, though, to be sure, it will reappear when they break down, and it is to this aspect that the discussion now returns.

Robots are similarly varied, and similarly imitate or parody human needs and desires. They challenge humanness not by being stolidly or efficiently non-human, but by wanting to be human. Humans may be of a prehistoric species, or mutants, or a symbiosis of two persons, or members of various hyperintelligent castes into which humanity has evolved, or is evolving (if one can afford the operations, performed at a dubious clinic in Switzerland).[21] Or they may be psionics of one species or another, all borrowed from conventional SF, but not usually existing in such numbers, and along such a scale, from the grand to the humdrum. For instance, Dick's psionics may possess the ability to rewind time just for five minutes or so,

---

[18] This desire to merge does not take the directly sexual form that it takes in Octavia Butler's *Dawn* (1987), for instance; instead the whole fictional landscape is suffused with mergings and shiftings, and the body's passage may be into death or half-death as readily as into sexual merging. In Dick, even the most powerful and decisive aliens fail to exhibit the cool teacherly patience and the ability to heal which which the Oankali accompany their desire for 'trade' in Butler's novel.

[19] See Rilke's dazzling insights in Von Kleist, Baudelaire and Rilke 1994: 29–33.

[20] Hillel Schwartz's *The Culture of the Copy* (1996) gives an account of the involvement of modernity with copying, in myriad forms, from researching twins to camouflaging warships; he notes how often a copy that is intended to preserve individuality, such as a photograph, instead seems to threaten it.

[21] Prehistoric: *The Simulacra*, *The Crack in Space*; symbiosis: *The Crack in Space*; hyperintelligent: *Palmer Eldritch* and *Frolix 8*.

so that a broken vase never broke, a car accident never occurred; or the ability to foresee what is going to happen for the next six months, a gift which transforms politics but locks its possessor into a psychologically interesting nullity, and strains the procedures of the novel in which he figures.[22]

All this might seem zany and madcap, and it often is; if scientists do not really have dotty brainwaves, SF writers certainly do. And if you were called upon to meet a roomful of Ganymedean slime moulds, for instance, would this tend to reaffirm your liberal sense of whole and bounded self-ness—or would it confirm, in postmodernist fashion, your pleasurable bodily sense of your openness to other bodies?

That depends, no doubt, on the circumstances; we need to stir into this account of Dick's exotic cast list a description of what very often happens to his main characters, who are invariably 'human' to the point of ordinariness, and, beyond that, to impotence, failure, self-disgust and panic. There are no normal individuals, if normal means sane and stable. (There are typical individuals, but typical no longer implies normal: a basic move of the popular novel's casting is stubbornly repeated, but has been hollowed out.) Virtually anything can enter a Dick novel, though there are always typical people near its centre, but nothing can enter a Dick novel without being subject to neurosis, which is the mark of the real, as far as consciousness is concerned.

There are lots of neurotics or psychotics in Dick's novels: that is, people who are defined as autistic, schizoid and so on. The very act of classifying someone like that, as a bundle of diagnosible symptoms, fragments the human. It is as Foucault says (1978: 42–44): there is a big difference between feeling the occasional perverse or paranoid impulse, and being classified as perverse or paranoid, at the core, so to speak. One's core has centred itself on a fragment; the paradoxical result is that the onset of, for instance, a schizophrenic episode is simultaneously an extinction of self, and definitional.

With the human characters, dissolution of boundaries figures as the sense that others know you better than you do yourself: they know what you are going to say next, they have pre-scripted it, they possess your consciousness, you are living in their dreams or drug visions. You are doing this in some quite literal sense as far as the particular novel's version of the literal is concerned: in your actual, bodily behaviour, as it seems, you are as much a figment of another's drug trip as that other would be a figment of your fantasy if you lay asleep and dreamed of her.[23] Your

---

[22] The vase: *Ubik*; the accident: *Clans*; the next six months: *The World Jones Made*.

[23] Pre-scripting: the book that tells the reader what he or she is doing at the moment of reading, and will do in the future, in *Galactic Pot-Healer* and *Lies, Inc.*, and the experience of Chuck Rittersdorf, who finds himself living the TV scripts he has been writing in *Clans*; trapped inside another's drug experience: *Flow My Tears*.

consciousness has no fixed location; it is liable to wander back or forward in time, or migrate into that of another. This last happens to the participants in the 'Perky Pat' game in *Palmer Eldritch*, who, taking a certain drug, become Barbie and Ken figures, living an ideal sanitized consumer existence for short periods by entering into the Pat and Walt dolls, and living in the miniature dolls' houses which everyone owns and furnishes. Or consciousness stalls or lapses, so that you lose some crucial hours, or are trapped and frozen, moving, if at all, with glacial slowness, in some distinct time enclave, trying to crawl across a pile of logs, or trying to climb a staircase, while your body becomes heavy like a dead weight.[24] Consciousness has some of the qualities of an event that is staged (usually by hostile forces), and some of the qualities of a product that is shaped.[25]

The question 'What is to be done?' is clearly hard to address if the agent cannot contemplate a sequential future moment in which the doing can happen. Yet these novels concern ethical subjects, individuals who have to do something that will be right or wrong. It is relevant here that time is cut away from its usual flow in Dick's novels (again, in this he simply presses to extremes the contemporary SF conventions of time travel). Time may regress, rival time schemes may be inserted or may open up; or time may be closed, wholly fixed and predictable, as in the universe of the precognitive Jones in *The World Jones Made*, and the always already dreary world of the autistic child Manfred in *Martian Time-Slip*. (The postmodern element in this is the jumbling of different time schemes and enclaves in the same text; we are not dealing with the possibility that, for instance, our accepted notion of time may be invalid and another may be valid, but that several forms of time may coexist.)

The theory advanced in *Martian Time-Slip* is that autism is in fact a condition of time dislocation. Manfred Steiner, being autistic, sees time as moving faster than it does for other people. This would be fine, it would be kept under control, if the novel presented a stable sense of the objective, whereby we could define Manfred as suffering from an illusion (a 'subjective' condition). But this does not happen; there is no ruling or objective sense of time. Manfred already sees both the future decay of a certain not-yet-built apartment house, and his senile misery within it (it will become a ghastly old people's home). He has this vision while he is still a child, and while the adults in the novel are plotting, and even killing, over the tract on Mars on which the apartment house is to be built. (It is

---

[24] Pile of logs: *The Cosmic Puppets*; staircase: *Ubik* (a particularly terrifying episode in a very complex and successful novel).

[25] As Mackey remarks, in connection with 'Colony' (1953, CS1), 'Everything possesses consciousness, though it may not be like ours or share our values. There are no inanimate objects' (1988: 8).

a matter of making a big profit by staking a claim to the land before it is slated for development.) But Manfred's insight is not simply prophetic. His sense of time begins to infect those of others, it ceases to be merely a mode of seeing. Any novel that works with point of view implies different, subjective time senses, and this consideration is relevant to Dick because his narration usually shifts among three or more focal characters (see Robinson 1984: 15–16); in *Martian Time-Slip* the different time schemes interact and distort each other.[26] Even the time of the narration, though for the most part it is conventionally linear, retraces and repeats in a closed loop in certain vital episodes.

All this could be seen as a kind of defamiliarization, working by means of metaphor, reconnecting the fictions with an uncontested if painful reality. We can readily enough recall occasions (usually social occasions) when we could predict exactly what the person with whom we were trapped in a corner was going to say for the next half-hour; more seriously, we recognize that we ourselves already know our own mortality, like the unfortunate Manfred. Manfred has been granted a vision similar to that given to Shakespeare's Richard II when he returns from Ireland, though the terms in which it is expressed are those of popular SF, not those of the Elizabethan theatre. Again, several of Dick's seemingly most bizarre novels (*Now Wait for Last Year*; *Flow My Tears*) can be read as drastically defamiliarizing renditions of marriage breakdown—a familiar theme for the realist novel, and one which might well benefit from this programme of extreme estrangement. But this way of discussing Dick's novels suggests that he returns us to something comparatively stable and fixed, if unpleasant, after those startling detours through the unfamiliar, and is thus misleading. In Section 3, discussion will return to the ways in which Dick destabilizes, rather than simply defamiliarizes, the normal; the next section considers the fate of objects in his fictions, concentrating on *Ubik*, but again surveying the scope of the fiction.

2. Unstable Regime of the Fake

As was remarked above, postmodernism may be considered both a theory and an account of a historical condition, postmodernity. As the first, it is a version of poststructuralism and, like it, argues for the illusoriness of the humanist subject; as the second, it is most plausible as an interpretation of

---

[26] *Martian Time-Slip* is discussed in Chapter 9, where it is argued that in addition to this opening out of time, which is thematized in the novel, there is also a problem of signification, which gives rise to a kind of excess of meaning: Manfred symbolizes a series of incompatible things, we are invited to apply a series of different protocols of reading to him.

the consequences of a series of cultural and economic changes—changes that we can in turn see as dissolving the humanist subject, which depended on an 'objective' environment. In Dick's fiction, things either overlap with and encroach on the human, or themselves lose their identity. The result for the characters is a crisis of knowledge, and for the novels in their formal aspect a kind of entrapment in narrative momentum and the quest for explanation.

Nature is usually absent, or depleted to sterile waste, the 'kipple' or 'gubble', dust, ash, debris that constitutes what landscape there is.[27] The novels and stories take place in a technosphere rather than a biosphere, but with a twist, because technology is seldom glossy or efficient. We have both a narrowing of the scope of the natural, and an expansion of the force of the material. It is as if materiality has been drained out of the natural, concentrated in the artificial, and has then conquered other, formerly immaterial realms. By way of parody of the technologism of much fifties (and later) SF, we have, for instance, electronically transmitted prayers, or an aerosol reality-restorant, advertised, literally, in the epigraphs to the chapters of *Ubik*. These epigraphs depict 'Ubik' as both a commodity, like Harpic, and a deity. Commodities and deities both promise everything, but deliver a lot less than that, so we can see where this materialization of the spiritual is coming from, as far as satire is concerned.

Yet the material in the form of the grown, the organic, or the hand-made is depleted; ecological disaster dances macabrely with technological triumph.[28] Scientists are often insane, twisted and Germanic, with names like Bluthgeld, Lufteufel, Sepp von Einem, Gloch.[29] The material, in the form of unsensed or not hitherto sensed energies which may be channelled (usually for weapons), is rampant. Yet it is commonly the case that no one knows any longer how to repair, let alone improve, all this futurist technology.[30]

Yet this condition is not simply the expression of dystopian malaise, or of a Luddism treacherously taking up residence in popular SF, the very home of technophilia. It points to a coherent interpretation of industrialism and post-industrialism. After summarizing that interpretation, I

[27] 'Kipple': *Androids*; 'gubble': *Time-Slip* (the autistic Manfred's word for what he sees around him).

[28] The depletion both of the material and of consumption is discussed in Chapter 7, in relation to the anxiety of differentiation that Dick's novels often express.

[29] Characters in *Dr Bloodmoney*, *Deus Irae* and (the last pair) *Lies, Inc*. The breakdown of relations between minds and machines is expressed in *A Scanner Darkly*, where, in turn, the breakdown of minds is analogized as the breakdown of machines (see below, Chapter 10).

[30] Prayers: *A Maze of Death*; weapons channelling unsensed energies: *Lies, Inc.*; breakdown and ignorance: 'The Variable Man' (1953, CS1), 'The Last of the Masters' (1954, CS3), *The Penultimate Truth*.

shall consider where it gets Dick's characters. It will be found that the real problems—critical problems for us, formal problems for Dick—begin when the plight of his characters is considered. For they do have a plight, and the plight is most illuminatingly seen in human terms. The relations between postmodernism and humanism in Dick will demand a separate chapter, and will indeed occupy most of the remainder of this book.

In the modern regime of mass production, all products, being identical, are copies: fakes if you like. There is no distinction between a working model of a toaster (say) and an 'authentic' toaster. We cannot discern any original, originating toaster; the first model of a toaster off the assembly line is merely that which has a certain serial number. Since all versions of a type of toaster are identical, none has identity. When you have a given toaster in your hand (preferably in turned-off mode), you have any toaster. It is therefore possible to feel that you have no toaster; you have not a thing but an instance. Certainly, this impression depends on the situation in which you find yourself; if this situation is such that you have to interrogate things for vital meanings, their lack of thingness is bound to bother you. If you are not certain that you yourself are a person (that is, possessed of the continuity that makes for self), then the situation is worsened.

Relevant here are the ramifications of 'planned obsolescence', which preoccupied popular sociology in the fifties (for instance, Vance Packard's *The Waste Makers* [1960]). Things are produced in order to be consumed, or replaced with other things; the purpose of the cycle of production and consumption is turnover. The culture of consumer prosperity both raises the value of things, in the sense that consumption is a desirable social activity, and empties it out of them. Something is purchased with great excitement, but it is not really 'there'; the system requires that it, as it were, shimmer, fade, evaporate, as soon as economically possible after its arrival. Its arrival trembles on the brink of and is swiftly overlaid with its departure. Time for a new model or improved version; the 'old' one is suddenly looking shabby. This is what happens not only to things but to whole environments in Dick's stories: they melt, thin, dim; you find that you can put a foot through them. (Or a new item—a new suburb, say—can be inserted without anyone noticing the difference.)

In some early stories Dick suggests how the national security industry can be seen as the apotheosis of planned obsolescence: the manufacturers of fall-out shelters have but to tell you that the latest Russian innovations have outmoded your present model, and you will have to buy a new one, by the same logic as that by which you bought the old one, without ever using it, and with the whole process of consumption become completely notional.[31] In the relevant story here, 'Foster, You're Dead' (1955, CS3), the young boy who is the main character cracks under the strain. After the family's outmoded fall-out shelter has been repossessed, he takes refuge in the latest model (which his parents cannot afford) in the local shelter showroom, and refuses to be torn out of this womb, as the story makes clear it is.[32]

In this story, the split between mind and body, part of the experience of modernity, where technology replaces the body, and reason functions autonomously, dealing with people and things as data entries, or perhaps as unseen targets, has become a split between rationalization and obsession. Later in this chapter I shall discuss the narrowing of reason, the succession of confusing puzzles and desperate attempts to explain these puzzles, that shapes Dick's plots. Here we may note another form of crisis which is often undergone: feeling (emotion, affect) has become hollow, banal, without individuality, but meanwhile there comes to the surface undirected psychic material—neurosis, psychosis, violent mood swings, rejections, delusions, suspicions. (A mutation *away* from psychology would give us postmodern 'intensities', as with some aspects of both the reader's and the characters' experience in Gibson's *Neuromancer*; this is not what happens in Dick's novels.) Varieties of psychic unbalance, which involve the reduction of behaviour to symptoms, are linked to a social condition, the unreality of things in a particular regime of production and consumption.

As commentators on late capitalism have noted (see for instance Harvey 1990), the logic of selling things of built-in transience leads inevitably to the sale of transience itself, the moment, happening, or event— the television news or 'media event'. Thus the manufacture of the news, in fact of history itself, in *The Penultimate Truth*, in which most of the population remain in the underground factory-cum-shelters to which they were sent in a nuclear war. They are kept there by a small elite on the surface which devotes its time to the fabrication of newsreels and political exhortations about the by now entirely fictional conflict.[33] The elite enjoys a relatively privileged existence, supplied by the underground factories, to which it supplies only images in return. That this is the true state of affairs is discovered by one of the workers when he ventures to the surface in quest of a material object, an artificial organ for one of his comrades who is dying. By centring on an object in this way, the novel might seem to follow the traditions of popular fiction at the expense of these insights

---

[31] Other ramifications of consumption in a world in which sensuality is jeopardized are discussed below in Chapter 7.

[32] The story is given a full context in Chapter 5.

[33] For a reading of *The Penultimate Truth*'s liberal politics which is sensitive to the problem of determining truth in the circumstances of the novel, see Abrash 1995.

about simulacra, but further revelations and mysteries in turn displace the object of quest from the centre of the narrative. Again, in 'We Can Remember It For You Wholesale' (1966, CS2) the situation is that those who cannot afford expensive vacations can have memories of them implanted in their sensoria anyway, and enjoy all the glow of luxury travel on the cheap. In both cases the system, with its resemblance to postmodernity, is unstable and malfunctioning, and it is this which makes the stories happen, by supplying narrative friction. Both stories are brought to an end only by the intervention of something that at least seems to be outside the regime of artifice: in *The Penultimate Truth*, this is David Lantano, a time-travelling Native American of mysterious powers; in 'We Can Remember It For You Wholesale', it is a group of aliens and a magic wand. A formula offers itself: humanism troubled by postmodernity invokes a higher, religious reality. But in each case the end of the story is ambiguous: our formula will have to wait.[34]

It appears to many commentators that contemporary mediatized society has no 'outside': we judge TV by TV. The world of Dick's fiction is like this; there is no outside to the fake or simulacrum—but the inadequacy of the fake or simulacrum is exposed by a process of internal splitting. There is a very good example in *Lies, Inc.* What should have been a journey to another planet, to find out what is really going on there, becomes, after a series of failures and malfunctions, a journey not to an objective reality outside earth but into the psyche; the possibility that the 'inside' is a core to reality is, however, contradicted in turn, because there are other people inside the psyche, and there is also a television set, which is the channel for further intrusions either from the psyche or from primitive paraworlds existing in a quite different compartment of time.

Further, the instability of the objective in Dick's fiction finds analogy at the level of form; in particular, in the extraordinary breathlessness and haste of his plots. One effect of this haste is to reduce things to clues, to mere signifiers. The characters' desperate need to know—what is going on, what is real and what is fake, whether they are alive or dead, even— itself eviscerates their environments. Things have to be feverishly interrogated for their meaning, they cannot be enjoyed or contemplated as autonomous and self-identical. 'For a man who is starving, the human form of food does not exist', said Marx (quoted in Eagleton 1990: 202); for a person who is desperate for information and for whom all is interpretation, the objectiveness of things does not exist. They don't have 'thisness'; either they simply signify (but what do they signify?) or they fade and decay; indeed in *Ubik* they do both.

---

[34] Chapter 11 offers a more nuanced discussion.

Very many thrillers and detective stories, from Conan Doyle to Sara Paretsky, counteract this threat—that the object may be no more than a signifier—by a reassuring depiction of eating and drinking: Holmes' dark indulgence of his senses after his ascetic application of 'method', V.I. Warshawski sipping Black Label Johnny Walker in her bath, and so on. This option is not available to Dick's characters, although he very often borrows from the genre. Things are already vitiated in the world of Dick's characters; the crisis of meaning which overtakes the world and the characters in the course of the narrative pushes the condition to extremity.

Also involved is the loss of the pleasures of description, through which narrative can very often attain a freedom which is linked to the fact that the action is pausing, or finding alternative expression in the metaphorical implications of the thing described; so it is in nineteenth-century narratives, especially those outside the realist tradition, from Keats (see Bennett 1992) to Hawthorne and Poe, and such SF narratives as Clarke's *Rendezvous with Rama*, description-rich and free of narrative momentum—but many other examples from SF could be given, because richness of specification is vital to the genre. This loss of the pleasures of description in Dick can be seen as sign of a historical predicament.

The whole topic of the describing and naming of things in recent fiction constitutes a test of the hypothesis that postmodernity is less a dominant condition and more a state of crisis. This test would have to cover more than Robbe-Grillet's deliberately non-significant descriptions and Brett Easton Ellis's relentless assemblages of brand names, or the consumerism of Tanaka Yasuo's *Somehow, Crystal*.[35] What of the inexhaustible cherishing of the trivial (whether it be lint in the navel, or niceties of punctuation) in Nicolson Baker, or, in a totally different genre, the weird uses of things in Carl Hiaasen's Floridan thrillers (we may cite the weed whipper in *Skin Tight* [1989])? There is no space here to pursue the recent adventures of things and their names, since the present topic is their fate in Philip K. Dick; a fuller investigation would surely establish how unresolved the situation is. (*Ubik* begins with a rash of descriptions of the characters'—to us at least—silly and tasteless clothes. No doubt Dick wants to contradict our assumption that the future will be streamlined and efficient; but he also seems to be parodying the realist assumption that we can read from what a character wears to what he or she is like, socially and individually. Both characters and things are commonly given flippant or jokey names in Dick's SF.)

---

[35] See Norma Field's essay (1998) on *Somehow, Crystal*, which focuses on the consumerist footnotes, which make up a major part of the text. See Jameson 1970 for reflections on the modern history of the naming of everyday things, from Balzac to Raymond Chandler.

There is a scene in *Time out of Joint* which has caught the eye of several recent critics, for instance Fredric Jameson and Damien Broderick,[36] and for good reasons. In this scene (ch. 3, 35–40), the main character is at the local baths, where he is conducting an illicit affair of a tawdry kind; he goes to buy his lover an ice cream, only to have the soft drink stand shimmer, fade, and melt away, leaving behind a paper label with the words 'Soft Drink Stand' on it. We are at liberty to recall that the novel we are reading is itself just words on a page, labels from which we deduce things. Dick's prose, here and anywhere, reinforces this, being brisk, flat, efficient; things are named, schematized, not evoked in their thingness. We could even say that with Dick, style—what makes a novel characteristically Dickian—is only marked by recurring items of content and situation, though given how weird these are and how often they are repeated, that is enough.[37] It is as though his novels replicate certain of their own features, while remaining anonymous, as if manufactured, in the way they do it. It's true that there are a couple of characteristic tics of style—'chitinous', used of eyes and looks, and 'grate' used as a verb in dialogue—but these are exceptions that underline the rule that style seldom solicits our attention for itself.[38] The protocols of realism (see Brooke-Rose 1981: 87–90) are faithfully adhered to, so that the novel persists in behaving as if it were about something, refusing literariness and poetical materiality, while at the same time jeopardizing the ontological bases of realism.

Indeed, things have no thingness; in *Time out of Joint*, Ragle Gumm (for that is *his* name) is going to discover that the typically fifties small town in which he lives is a simulacrum, and in fact one set up expressly for him, though he has repressed the fact. The only element of depth in Ragle's psyche is a strange, largely aleatory skill that he happens to possess. This skill explains why the whole simulacral town was set up for him: what he thinks he is doing is guessing where the little green man will pop up next, in a silly contest in the daily paper; what he is actually doing, in the nineties (for it is actually the nineties, an interesting discovery for the fifties reader who might naturally have thought the book was set in his or her quotidian world), is guessing where missiles from the moon will hit earth. The simulacrum and the newspaper contest were fabricated to ease the

---

[36] See Jameson 1993, ch. 9 (in which, however, he argues that *Time out of Joint* is *not* a postmodern novel), Broderick 1991 and Potin 1998.

[37] This recurrence—which constitutes the Dickian megatext—is complex, and will receive further discussion in Chapter 3.

[38] The chief exception is *Ubik*, perhaps Dick's most deranged and disoriented novel, where the prose is often deliberately disjointed (e.g. 'he thrashed about noisily, making his big frame comfortable in terms of a meager chair' [ch. 1, 7]; 'he pondered, trying to envisage oldtime mail practices' [ch. 10, 125]).

strain of this. Suggestion of psychic depth (his aleatory gift) is crushed by the little green man game, which reduces the gift to banality.

True, as it is easy to observe, there *is* a reality beyond and explaining the simulacrum. In the course of the novel Ragle discovers that his environment is a fake, and escapes to the 'real' world of the nineties. Yet the reality of the nineties, when Ragle and the reader get to it, is as weird as the fakishness of the fifties (it is only grounded in itself, so so speak; see Potin 1998: 161–62), and its only depth is political—Ragle himself is depthless, though this judgment cannot be made of all Dick's protagonists.

Consumption is certainly not a possible recourse, a way of making contact with things, for Ragle Gumm, whose odd name links a bit of rubbish and a popular food item in which one engages in the process, or the imitation, of consumption without absorbing anything other than one's own saliva. When not seeking ice cream that has a purely semiotic status, he lives on warm beer and prepackaged lasagne. He doesn't actually like warm beer, in a simple sensuous way; drinking it is yet another symptom. He thinks that it nostalgically reminds him of his time in the Second World War, manning a weather recording station on a Pacific Island, but that too is a fake—a fake memory, since, as we remember, he is living in the nineties, not the fifties, and could not have taken part in the Second World War.

Dick's novels dissolve modern society into the postmodernity that, as he intuits, has already infiltrated it. All these factors and conditions constitute a critique of postmodern society as a threat to the liberal humanist individual, who depends on a sense of sequential time, on the difference between himself and others—or himself and other beings with consciousness—and on the real existence of objects. The conditions in which he finds himself have vexed or dissolved these underpinnings. The Dickian individual tends to be deranged: in a state of disaffection, panic, restlessness, helplessness. He is not liberated, as critics of liberal humanist subjectivity might have hoped, and the shell of this subjectivity often burdens him: the individual in Dick's oppressive futures often assumes guilt for a situation that is not his responsibility.

3. Consuming the Narrative

Postmodernist surveys of the contemporary condition are generally synchronic: they take a slice through all areas of life and find therein a simultaneous uniformity, if a uniformity in difference and fragmentation. Narratives are suspect, since they imply connectedness and purpose; only narratives that recount the failure of universalizing narratives are welcome. Dick's novels are aggressively plot-driven. A text by Dick is not really a picture, or an analytical diagram; it's more like a vehicle into which you step. You go on a trip. The fact that his novels are increasingly concerned with dream or drug experiences is, among other things, his recognition on the thematic level of the nature of his reader's experience. (The breakthrough novel here is *The Man in the High Castle*, which challenges its readers by setting loose within the text two other texts—the *I Ching* and *The Grasshopper Lies Heavy*—whose authority contradicts the authority of the text they are reading.[39]) The quality of the reader's engagement with pulp fiction—one doesn't read a pulp novel, one consumes or devours it—is here thematized. In the most frightening parts of *Palmer Eldritch*, and in *Flow My Tears*, the main character is a subject in the drug vision of another, a close but sinister analogue to the reader's own experience of a Dick novel.

This experience certainly has a cognitive aspect[40] which can be schematized. Firstly you discover that the world in which the story is set is different from your own in ways that make you see your own world as different from itself, that is, from what you thought it was; then you discover that the world in which the story is set is also different from itself, because it is in a state of crisis, possibly disintegration, and is split into opposing, competing units anyway. No one is any longer at home in it.

An incident in *Ubik* will suggest how this works (ch. 8, 95–100). The characters discover that there is something wrong with the coins they are using. That there should be any coins in an advanced world of the future is of course an 'anachronism' in SF terms, as the novel has already invited us to see, by way of business with coin-in-the-slot machines. Quick, see whether you have the coin with Disney on it, or the coin with Castro: and here the reader is left to guess the double difference from the present which left the world of the novel (which is set in 1992) with coins of each of these types. The characters, however, though they are so used to this Castro/Disney past that it is never explained to us, are now to be shocked in their turn, as they discover coins with Glen Runciter on them, Runciter being their deceased boss, who apparently retains the power to manifest himself in their world. The world of *Ubik* is thus different from itself, in a way that jeopardizes everyone's ideas of space and time, living and dead. Whatever existential realm Runciter occupies, the characters feel they must be occupying the opposite one; therefore, if Runciter is not dead, are the characters in the scene dead? If so, how comes it that they are dying one by one in gruesome ways? What kind of death is it that has further

---

[39] See Chapter 6, which, however, also discusses the uses of reason in the reading of this novel.

[40] Darko Suvin's writings on SF focus on the importance of this aspect of the genre.

deaths within it? And where is Runciter and where are they? An effect of cognitive expansion, itself typical of SF at its best, is pushed so far as to deconstruct the grounds of cognition itself. At the very end of the novel, Joe Chip, who took part in the scene with the coins, himself appears, or manifests himself, on the coins in Glen Runciter's pocket, and the most likely effect of this doubling and reversal is yet another unravelling of the structure of explanation which the reader has pieced together. 'This was just the beginning' runs the last sentence of the novel (ch. 17, 202): 'The Exit Door Leads In', to quote the title of one of Dick's late short stories (1979, CS5). We have not a conclusion but the sign of a closed loop or a recycling.

The overall effect of this series of transformations is funny and exhilarating as well as disruptive. The business with the coins develops into a sort of running joke, and it's clear that a subject who can be in succession a schmuck, a corpse and a virtual god, who can so lose autonomy as not to know whether he is alive or dead, yet so gain *disponibilité* as to manifest himself as if he were already legendary, is liberated as well as bewildered.

The effect of disintegration is repeated from page to page. There is a lot of plot and the plot moves quickly; situations constantly change, but each situation is critical, each encounter is a confrontation, abrupt, close to brutal. The characters burn nervous energy, passing through a series of decisions, dangers, emergencies, mistrustful alliances. The reader hurries along with them, enjoying, but distinctly harassed. Dick is plainly drawing on the form of the thriller or hardboiled detective novel, in which, for instance, the discovery or manufacture of a new corpse every couple of chapters begins to make it pointless to see the corpse in the opening chapter as the corpse that originates the narrative, or to single out any murder as the one that has to be solved. But if the content is different, the quality of the narrative form will begin to alter. There prevails a potentially hysterical, or panicky, absurdity: the problem you face at any given moment is of indisputable importance (how may the human race be saved? am I alive or dead? is the universe into which I have just been pitched actual or delusory?) yet has not presented itself in this form for long, and cannot be relied upon to continue doing so. The form is that of a game or an elaborate joke, but Dick is not Nabokov; the effect is not admiration for the author/joker's brilliant, steely control and wit, but uneasy sympathy for the characters, mixed with enjoyment of comedy.

Dick's prose is important in this. It varies in tone, from flippant to passionate, and in style, from clumsy to lyrical. The effect is often disjointed and unsettling; we don't feel that the voice of the text is steady, cool, or effortlessly competent. It is interesting that several of his most eloquent passages actually make use of quoting and crosscutting; so it is, for instance, with the passage on Arctor's final hours of coherence in *A Scanner Darkly* (ch. 13), which makes use of the dialogue of Beethoven's *Fidelio*.

Knowledge, in the form of cognitive grasp, is very important in this kind of novel, and Dick presses this also to extremes. The main character is forced to hypothesize and rehypothesize the pattern that may—must surely—be behind events. He (always he[41]) does not accumulate knowledge, building on previous hypotheses; he simply discards one theory and elaborates another. A situation of blockage develops. Contrary forces are at work, one proliferating fluidity and uncertainty, the other demanding (with something close to desperate stridency) explanation and closure. This crisis 'should not' have come about, because Dick knows very well that the pulp conventions of explanation and closure are merely formal. He conveys this to his readers by gestures of exaggeration or flippancy.[42] Nonetheless the critique, the radical destabilization of time and place, subject and object, inner and outer, dead and alive, begins to exert a pressure on the conventions that the conventions were never designed to withstand. Nor is this simply a matter of the conventions of pulp fiction narrowly considered; the amalgam of realism and fantasy on which Dick's SF is based begins to unglue. Imagination, the ability more or less playfully to invent, transfigure, escape from the vice of the single and real, is vertiginously narrowed to feverish speculation about possible plots or explanations. It threatens to become purely instrumental, while at the same time instrumental thinking is one thing that is criticized in exploitative, oppressive characters or institutions in the novel. The ordinary-guy main characters (for instance, Barney and Leo in *Palmer Eldritch*) begin to practise instrumental thinking themselves, and we begin to wonder whether our belief that they were normal and sympathetic was nothing more than an effect of identifying with them as main characters.

We begin by reading a given novel as a satirical representation of our own society; then, through a series of fantastic transformations, we are released into an alternative realm. The text is now fuelled not by exaggerated mimesis but by frantic and free interaction among its elements; but then, in a third stage (not that the three stages are neatly distinguishable in reading), action and attention are narrowed. Meaning becomes less a matter of allegory, metaphor, suggestion of relations, in all of which the

---

[41] Chapter 11 discusses *The Transmigration of Timothy Archer*, whose narrator is a woman; but that is one of Dick's late novels, meditative in form—not an instant-by-instant narrative of events but a recalling or foretelling of events.

[42] But this strain of exaggeration or flippancy repays further discussion, which it receives in Chapters 6 and 11.

novels are very fertile, and more a matter of the possible explanation, the closure.

Dick's novels begin as satirical and metaphorical, and become literal, autotelic, perhaps hypotelic. You cannot refer them back to a referent, something they have satirized or suggested by metaphors, without realizing that the referent has begun to disintegrate before your eyes. They have begun to feed on themselves, to proliferate aggressive yet unstable images that, as Baudrillard would have it, are not images *of*, do not refer to a ground. It is interesting that we find in the novels lots of powerful images both of dissolution and of claustrophobic blockage.

This juxtaposition of blockage and disintegration sums up the terror of the postmodern condition as it is created in Dick's novels of the fifties and sixties, taking control of their very forms. These remarks do not exhaust the narrative resources of these novels, and in his late novels, which are meditative and speculative, Dick contrives a new form, which treats both action and cognition quite differently. As various critics have noticed, investigation of the plight of the split subject is pressed much further in the late novels; but new problems arise, connected with Dick's religious vision, which means that in the late novels we are often asked to think, not in terms of explanation or solution (closure in that distinctly fictional form), but in terms of belief. How much does our author believe in? (Never mind what the characters or the narrator believe in, and narrators are handled sophisticatedly in these novels.) Is the author credulous to the point of unbalance? These are matters too complex to be discussed here.[43] But I don't want to conclude simply with the situation of blockage and disintegration I have just outlined. This situation is itself a compelling expression of the postmodern political unconscious. Further, in describing the way in which Dick represents postmodernity in his novels (and thence the strains which representation itself undergoes), I have been describing only part of his fictional project. As will be seen in the next chapter, he is not precisely a postmodernist even though he represents postmodernity in his novels; his fictional project is a dual one, and that in turn gives rise to problems and illuminations.

It does appear that Dick frequently organizes his fictions in such a way as to *discredit* the drive to explain that fuels them: there tends always to be something which even the last of the succession of hypothetical explanations of what has been going on will not explain. We struggle to the point where two (no more than two) incompatible explanations are possible, but then discover that there is something that each of the two fails to explain. The incident of the disappearing soft drink stand in *Time out of*

---

[43] See Chapters 11 and 12.

Joint is one example. Others are impudently placed on the last page, just when one thought one had everything tied up, as happens in *Ubik*. Analogies, either with contemporary physics or with contemporary critical theory (the notion of simultaneously using and refusing a given term, for instance), are themselves of inadequate explanatory power here. A self-delighting postmodern circularity is not available to Dick; he is more likely to think in terms of a closed loop (an important image in his bleakest novel, *A Scanner Darkly*), signifying sterile repetition.

2. Complications of Humanism and Postmodernism

Discussion in the preceding chapter turned towards the complications which result when Dick's representation of postmodernity—for this is how I have characterized the historical context of his novels—begins to destabilize not only his characters but his narratives. Postmodernism is hostile to the very notion of representation, and there is an element of fantasy in Dick: his is fiction of presentation and transformation, rather than of representation and critique. This chapter pursues these issues, directly confronting Dick's ethical humanism, an indubitable scandal and anomaly in the conditions of postmodernity, but something that is staged —and even preached—in a variety of ways in his fiction.

1. Premises and Potentials of the Genre

McHale (1992: 254) has noted a particular bias in SF, which differentiates it from most other fiction. This is that SF privileges the ontological (as also, arguably, does film: a tantalizing connection). Strange and wonderful things are invented, devised and imagined: the content of the story is strange and wonderful. This need not, however, spill over into the style and form: the manner of presentation may remain straightforward, candid, carefully explanatory. (Something like this is still true of recent cyberpunk SF, though it is denser, glitzier and faster-paced than earlier SF.[1]) It would not be correct to say that SF is a realist genre, but realism as a mode is very important to its workings. The result is that up until the late fifties SF lags behind or remains indifferent to modernist experiments with form, while genially inventing and manipulating societies, ways of life, life forms—all sorts of material possibilities. But in fact the situation has always been unstable. Because SF invents new societies and

---

[1] Csicsery-Ronay (1995) discusses the representation of works of art in William Gibson's *Count Zero*. Gibson thinks about art—its nature, the need for it, its utopian potential—by representing works of art in his novel. The move is entirely characteristic of SF, and it should make us hesitate before defining this or that representation of art or text in SF as itself metafictional. De Zwaan (1997) authoritatively compares Gibson and Kathy Acker: only the latter is postmodern*ist*.

life forms, it always leans towards the proposition that nothing is given, everything is fabricated. As H.G. Wells himself observed, to invent an interesting future device or institution is in effect to commit yourself to a radical examination of the whole society in which it is set, though at the same time you may avoid pursuing this examination to the limit.[2] For SF, whatever we can construct or imagine as human *is* human. SF gains plausibility and authority by depicting this in a straightforward realist way, but it is not certain that the constructedness of society is compatible with the assumptions behind realism. If one proceeds to build the plausibility—the realness—of an individual life or a society from 'observation' of material things, of habits, traits, customs, then one is perhaps assuming that all these things have a 'natural', positive substance, and there is an alliance between realism's reliance on the modest particular detail or feeling and humanism's valuation of the individual experience and the individual person. It need not be so, because the variety of realism called naturalism takes a determinist view of the individual; but there is a special relationship between realism and humanism.

For much of the history of SF, at least of popular American SF, the implication that nothing is given and everything is fabricated has been something between an unrealized potential and a time bomb ticking away at the heart of the genre. The shifting relations of realism and fantasy in discussions of SF will also suggest that the situation of the genre has been unstable. Sometimes, as in discussions of the importance to SF of extrapolation and of a rationally comprehensible 'novum', fantasy figures as a shadow haunting SF, a disreputable, prodigal brother who is best ignored; sometimes it is celebrated, as in discussions of the transcendence and sense of wonder to which SF can give rise—though here fantasy is assimilated to the marvellous.[3]

Further, it is plausible to explain SF as originating in an awareness of perpetual change as the engine of modern society. Even taking modernity in the most optimistic spirit, continual progress entails continual dissolution; to make new societies and even new human types is to destroy or exile or simply forget the old ones. This is the modernity of Marx and Engels' 'all that is solid melts into air' in *The Communist Manifesto*, which

---

[2] Suvin (1988: 67–69) discusses the radio talk in which Wells sketched the issues.

[3] For publishers and readers, fantasy is a particular genre that deals extensively with the marvellous; for Tzvetan Todorov, the fantastic is importantly distinct from the marvellous, because it is the name for a mode that makes its readers hesitate between magical and rational explanations; and it is often useful to speak of fantasy as the expression or fulfilment of wishes and desires. The relations of fantasy and the fantastic are complex. The semantic field is as subject to metamorphoses as are the texts that are found there, or put there.

Marshall Berman makes the title and theme of his book (1982), tracing what he calls 'the experience of modernity'.

As SF proceeds, very often, by reasoned extrapolation from the present to possible futures, and as SF reflects satirically or critically on the present, we might say that its emphasis is in fact on continuity rather than discontinuity or rupture. This bias has been productive, and has never gone unchallenged; nonetheless, from this broad point of view, the arrival of an SF writer who explores the processes of dissolution as thoroughly as does Philip K. Dick was long delayed. SF in the so-called 'Golden Age' was an uneasy hybrid: both a serious field for the exploration of, for instance, the nature of future society, and a formulaic entertainment akin, say, to the Western. (It's not that there is something wrong with entertainment, just that formula implies stability, and concern with fundamental change implies the reverse.) The logic of modernity, and of SF's self-invention as a response to modernity, demanded the appearance of a writer like Dick, but such a writer might find that the realism (and also the humanism) on which SF had based much of its extrapolation of change, and depicted its impact on plausible individuals, was breaking in his hands, as he imagined not so much specific changes as the condition of changeableness.

Philip K. Dick is a particularly challenging writer because he is *both* a humanist and a postmodernist. (Indeed it is likely that only the interesting-ness of this dual identity could excuse my persistence in employing these terms, which are themselves 'fuzzy', and are rapidly losing their edge, as their use with a variety of meanings blunts their impact.) Dick makes fictions of the disintegration of the real in contemporary society: the action of perpetual change both on what has previously existed, and on what is existing now but has no stable reality, because it is already marked by its inevitable dissolution. In this he realizes one of the implications of modernity and of SF's 'take' on modernity. He makes evident the logic of the genre itself; and some aspects of the genre make it easy for him to do this: there was always plenty of room for the improvised, the spectacular and the extreme in SF. It is the combination of spectacular transformation (as in A.E. van Vogt, and many another SF writer) and ethical seriousness that makes Dick's SF so compelling. He exacerbates modernity and drives it past its limits; in this sense his fictions anticipate our present, postmodern condition.[4] It is

---

[4] By the logic of these remarks, modernity itself is an anticipation of postmodernity. There is a point to this logic: consider that for Berman (1982), though he does not say so explicitly, the clearest examples of works that express 'the experience of modernity' are not modernist but realist—Dickens' novels for instance. Again, Anderson (1992) has argued that the condition for the great modernist art and literature of c.1900–1920 is that modernity has not fully arrived on the historical scene—when it does, we get not modernist but postmodernist art.

not merely that this kind of exaggeration or exacerbation could itself be defined as postmodernist; it is that the historical condition he sketches represents postmodernity partly because it shows modernity splitting from within.

Dick frequently dramatizes dismaying predicaments of dissolved reality and instrumental brutality. Uncertainty as to what is real and what is happening clashes with certainty that the ordinary people on whom the story focuses are being hurt, or are hurting each other, in the service of some narrow calculation. In these situations Dick appeals to kindness, fellow-feeling, readiness to sacrifice, and humility. There is a crisis of subjectivity (perceptions are at the same time totally unreliable and all-encompassing), and a crisis of the subject (people are being hurt and misused): desperate remedies are required.

Humanism is not only a recourse in crisis, however; it is also among the motives of the whole enterprise. Dick subjects SF to a complex double movement. This prevails throughout his career: there is not a humanist phase and a postmodernist phase. From the beginning of his career he depicts social structures and power structures as imagined things, and subjectivity as groundless; in dozens of early short stories the material fabric of reality dissolves, institutions and situations are manipulated by the powerful, and individuals find that they cannot know who or what they are;[5] this complex of effects is extended in the novels, and is present, if not fully developed, from the earliest of them. (Nor is it peculiar to Dick, as plenty of SF, and plenty of horror fiction twisting towards the paranoid, will illustrate from the fifties and later.[6]) But throughout his career Dick attempts to deepen the human—to affirm values such as solidarity and empathy and to endow his characters with the capacity to apprehend intense moral dilemmas, and to take responsibility. This is the sense the word 'humanist' carries in this discussion; there is at work in these texts an assumption that you can best understand ethical and political problems —problems of agency, solidarity and responsibility—by thinking in terms of being human and acting humanly.

That realism of style which has been an important constituent of SF has implied humanism all along. A sense of the real, according to realism, is built by the accumulation of small details about, very often,

---

[5] Chapter 5 discusses this aspect of the short stories, relates it to a critique of contemporary American society, and examines the recourses Dick can imagine for the individual at this point in his career. The recognition that the stories themselves are manipulations or fabrications of reality already complicates matters in these early works.

[6] In *The Closed Space* (1990), Manuel Aguirre sees these developments in horror fiction in the context of a widening development that had its beginnings in the nineteenth century. See his ch. 8, and, on Dick, p. 212.

the experiences and material conditions of ordinary people. If you bother with this painstaking process, it is likely that you will value the ordinary individual at the unheroic centre of it all. The paradox is that Philip K. Dick, whose fiction destroys the epistemological underpinnings of this ordinary person's existence, is also ambitious to extend the scope and complexity in SF of the ordinary person's experience. In his fiction, SF delivers on the potential implicit in its realism. It does this by taking on emotional depth: failure, self-betrayal, frustration, unsparing if self-destructive honesty in the characters; humour, wryness, mockery, passion in the writing. It elaborates moral dilemmas. The characters are endowed with the capacity to ruin lives, usually their own, in ways that count ethically and emotionally; to fail or even sin; to gain and lose something like grace.

The context of this move can be rapidly sketched. 'SF is a literature of ideas, not character': this has been a common defence mounted by SF fans against criticism from 'the mainstream', whether the mainstream be represented by the classic realist novel of relationships or the modernist novel of consciousness. It has always been an uneasy defence, effective more because of the prejudice which weakens the attacker than by any strength as a shield against attack, for why should literature not be concerned both with ideas and with character, supposing that these are the terms we want to use when talking about it? In the case of Dick, this defence can be scrapped. George Eliot or William Faulkner he is not, but in the context of a great deal of SF his emotional and ethical range is formidable. Further, and in a challenging way, he often *domesticates* ethical dilemmas. What had seemed to announce itself very dazzlingly and mind-bendingly as a novel concerned with, for instance, time reversal, or the political problems posed by the discovery of a para-earth inhabited by innocent natives, descendants of earlier species of hominids,[7] is also, depressingly, a novel about marital breakdown, or relations with one's boss.[8] The discovery is a shocking one. It is not merely the familiar but the banal that thereby returns as defamiliarized, with an effect of estrangement and recognition.

The two aspects of Dick's writing, the humanist and the postmodernist, are wrapped in a kind of spiral in which they mutually inspire, threaten, exacerbate and (as it were) up the ante on each other. This is what makes the anticipations of the condition of postmodernity so challenging,

---

[7] See *Counter-Clock World* (1967) and *The Crack in Space* (1966).

[8] Marital breakdown is also the concern of the series of non-SF novels that Dick wrote in the late fifties: gritty, lowdown, but also alienated and often acrid. These novels, what they say about men and women and their conflicts, and how they attempt to say it, are discussed in Chapter 4.

especially in the novels of his middle period (*Ubik, Palmer Eldritch, The Simulacra, A Maze of Death*).[9]

2. Complications of a Dual Project

Dick's fictions almost invariably involve 'little guys' as main characters, and the narrative is written from their point of view. Sometimes they intensify this feature by involving a beleaguered group of average people, as in *A Maze of Death* (1970) and *Ubik* (1969). The worlds they depict are frequently bizarre, but they are always ordinary as well. This happens partly because the inhabitants themselves naturalize as ordinary what *we* read as constructed, because it is so different from what is experienced as normal in our own lives—a classic SF effect, but in the case of Dick's fictions it is given with particular grittiness. But in addition the fictions curve back from the exotic future to what we recognize as ordinary. Details are local and circumstantial; feelings are grim but familiar—frustration and confusion, gloom and impotence; the fatigue of a hard day's work in a deadening environment, the numbness of waking in the morning in a small dull apartment;[10] being at a loss for words in the face of some ruthlessly capable person who is clearly in the wrong but knows exactly what he wants, and how to get it. There are marital problems, difficulties at work, the annoyances of commuting, troubles with the neighbours, though in every case the particular circumstances are bizarre. Material things may be exotically futurist and dazzling in their powers, but as experienced they have the rubbed, handled, slightly stale quality of the familiar, and they frequently break down, or wheeze and creak painfully. The whole ambience is surprisingly everyday—surprising, that is, in a future or alternative world that is based on drastic departures from what is familiar to us.

Yet the shifts and distortions to which these grittily humdrum milieus and familiarly ordinary people are subjected are fantastic. Space and time are themselves friable, as if the novels mimic that discrepancy, opened up by a series of modern thinkers, between the perceptible surface of the world and of the self, on the one hand, and, on the other, the invisible, atomic or unconscious or ideological substructures of the world and the self. Solid surfaces, whole environments, may crumble or melt, or reveal themselves as illusory, faked, somehow inserted into the social body like

[9] These novels were published between 1964 and 1970; after 1970 Dick's rate of production slows, and with *A Scanner Darkly* (1977) and subsequent novels he moves away from the extreme reality distortions and crowded breakneck plots of his earlier novels.

[10] But as Peter Fitting (1992a) has shown, this trope of awakening, very common in Dick, also expresses a profound alienation, a 'deconstruction of bourgeois reality'.

foreign cells; time may reverse, or splinter into parallel histories or universes, or alter or halt as a result of the perhaps unwitting ingestion of a
drug.

The narrative settles inside the successive points of view and experiences of a series of separate individuals.[11] These are ordinary people with
the glum thoughts and inarticulate frustrations that we can readily recognize. As well as being recognizably ordinary, however, the point-of-view
characters are locked in grim competition with each other, with everyone.

There is a kind of image of this shifting point of view and its implications in Dick's first novel, *Solar Lottery* (1955). A series of human operators control the actions of a 'sim' on a mission of assassination, taking each
other's place in random succession so that the sim's sudden changes of
direction are hard for their opponents to predict.[12] What might be effective in the world of *Solar Lottery* (though even there the plan fails) is disconcerting for the reader of a text by Dick, where a series of unstable,
uncertain and self-interested characters find themselves entrusted with
conveying a story whose previous course and future directions are hidden
from them—like badly briefed surgeons relieving each other at the operating table.

The conditions of the novels reflect an extreme, literal-minded liberalism: society is no more than a collection of individuals, monads, the world
no more than an accumulation of objects. (Organic nature, which might
knit things into a continuum and also take them out of human history, is
largely absent, and if there are planets, they are dead and barren, though
sometimes inhabited by aliens—who are monads just like the terrans.[13])
These competitive, monadic societies are Darwinian and Machiavellian in
their behaviours. The structures and conditions of these societies evidently
encourage the victory of the strongest, that is, of those who are most ruthless, either in interpersonal confrontations, manipulations and social
games, or in the larger contests of social groups. Machiavellianism is
equally pervasive—the use of fraud and force, especially the former, the
use of end-justifies-the-means calculation not merely to get one's way, but

[11] Dick's use of a set of point-of-view characters, sometimes as many as half a dozen, is
one thing that shapes his characteristic narrative form. This is one reason why his fiction is
much grimmer than that of, say, Ross MacDonald, who softens his depiction of a corrupt,
failed, oedipally snarled America with a reassuring narrator, Lew Archer (for instance, in *The
Barbarous Coast* [1967]). Dick's use of point of view is well discussed by Robinson (1984).

[12] The plan is explained at ch. 7, 78–80, where it is said that the sim is 'Heisenberg's
random particle' (80).

[13] There are exceptions to this observation; for instance, the aliens in *Frolix 8* (1970) and
The Ganymede Takeover (1967; written by Dick and Ray Nelson); but in Dick's fiction it is possible to be an isolated monad *and* merged with another. See Chapter 7.

to survive, and also to understand others (you know another person when you see how he or she is plotting against you).

The ordinariness of most of Dick's characters was emphasized above as a realist feature of his novels. In Dick, the ordinary is not the same as the normal, however: in fact, we are often made to realize that most of the main characters may be classified as neurotic, or even psychopathic, without ceasing to be ordinary. Qualities we loosely believe to overlap, such as ordinary, typical, normal and sane, have begun to fly asunder.[14] It appears that the social conditions which reward Darwinian and Machiavellian behaviour can reduce ordinariness to neurosis, or worse. The prevalence of paranoia as an effective and coherent way of understanding social situations is another sign of this. Individualism has apparently curved in on itself, destroying all norms, rendering the collective a conspiracy and the individual a neurotic at best.[15]

All this can be seen as a strongly satirical, socially critical aspect of the novels, yet a clearly defined humanist ethic survives—indeed, it is affirmed, often in the novels' most telling scenes. There is a lot of the teacher in Philip K. Dick: ardent, rueful, idealistic, hopeful. He passionately wants to say what he has learnt, what we need, where we have gone astray. He finds opportunities to do so, particularly in his later novels. The discourse of Ruth Rae on love and grief in *Flow My Tears* (1974) (ch. 11, 101–103) is an instance. This is a character who is at first presented satirically (the pleasure-loving Las Vegas type who has been married 21 times); the fiction then abruptly, clumsily but strikingly has her utter this humane wisdom. The meditations of Angel Archer in *The Transmigration of Timothy Archer* (1982) are another example, equally warm, and more controlled.[16] Charity and kindness, empathy and recognition of the other, willingness

---

[14] The effect is not unique to Dick: it is the sort of thing that happens to typical clerks in Gogol or Dickens; and it is a staple of crime fiction, where the killer or even psychopath is revealed in the inconspicuous ordinary citizen. An example from Dick is *Martian Time-Slip* (1964); another, this time from a non-SF novel, is what happens to Jack, Charley and Fay in *Confessions of a Crap-Artist* (1975, ch. 20, 271).

[15] Michael Melley (2000) discusses the culture of paranoia in postwar America as 'agency panic': the response of an individualism threatened by increasing collectivism is both to feel that the individual now has little power and to simplify social life as the field of a struggle between an undifferentiated collective and an individualism that is more desperately valued than ever. Starting from this point, however, we need to notice how Dick differentiates and splits open both his collectivities and his individuals. Melley is not always well equipped to do this, because of his tendency to feel that a dash of the postmodernist philosophy of the subject would have liberated us from these pains and problems.

[16] Chapter 11 offers a fuller discussion of these moral meditations as the outcome of an ethical problem that is also a narrative problem: the lack of scope for individual action in a world without grounds.

to sacrifice oneself for the other, even though the other is, as we would expect in this social Darwinist and Machiavellian society, usually unattractive and unwilling to reciprocate: this is Dick's recommendation. His novels enact the historical tragedy of liberalism, its shaping of a monadic society which makes impossible, but also makes necessary, the acting out of the most cherished individual and intersubjective values of liberalism. We will have to be kind to each other, because if we are not, we will exterminate each other, or become androids, ceasing to be personages of whom a word like 'we' can be used.

When the issue is put as starkly as this, and in a situation in which individuals seem to be constructed by their environments and conditions, it is easier to see why Dick gives his narratives over to diverse and isolated point-of-view characters, yet intervenes poignantly to teach kindness through those characters from time to time. It is also, however, hard to see whence the impulse to kindness might come *in* the individual—a question which is also faced in the late novels. It may have to come from outside, from divine direction. In the opening chapters of *The Divine Invasion* (1981), for instance, the situation of Herb and Rybys, each sealed in their 'bubbles' on a hostile planet, suggests the reduction of individualism to solipsism. The local god Yah has to intervene, compelling Herb to be kind to Rybys, who is dying of cancer. No wonder much of the narrative that follows upon Yah's forcible bringing together of Herb and Rybys concerns the problems of giving birth. The child eventually born is Emmanuel, who is God, but is for most of the novel as isolated from his playful and loving second self, Zina, as Herb was isolated from Rybys: the sense of split, and of impotence to help, is very stubborn in the novel.

In many ways Dick is a relentlessly sceptical and diagnostic writer, for whom little or nothing in existence is mysterious or essential. His sensational zaniness and his frivolity with the 'hard SF' aspects of his future worlds can distract us from this quality. It is true that he has no interest in reasoning about the means of journeying through light-years to the stars or the kind of technology that might make possible cities with billions of inhabitants. Nonetheless he still literalizes, explains, analyses and classifies in the plausible, speculative manner of much SF, although he employs psychology and theology to do so.

He classifies characters as schizophrenic or schizoid, autistic, paranoid; he speculates on or invents explanations for these conditions.[17] Nor does

---

[17] See Chapters 8 and 9. Dick often shapes his novels out of an overlaid range of alternative ways of conceiving the same thing; for instance, the child Manfred in *Martian Time-Slip* (1964) is idealized (prophet and victim), demonized (malign destroyer) and analysed (as autistic).

he see these conditions as illnesses happening to the individual, and telling only about his nature, as the psychological diagnoses might imply; it is usually society as a whole that is pathological, and very often the individual's illness consists in the fact that he takes upon himself the condition of society as a whole.[18] Dick practises a politicized psychology.

As for the other mode of reasoning and explanation mentioned above, in his earlier novels Dick invents theologies that are not merely imaginary but fake;[19] in his later novels he proliferates theodicies with apparent seriousness, but then dismantles them. He wonders whether the Incarnation, the central mystery of Christianity, was in fact a failure in its redemptive purpose, as the historical facts do indeed suggest, so that God might need to try again at another juncture in human history. (Hence Yah's intervention in the miserable, monadic lives of Herb and Rybys, which leads to the birth of Emmanuel.) He has Bishop Timothy Archer entertain the idea that perhaps the eucharist was literally a food, a mushroom, bestowing immortality; Archer dies in the quest for the mushroom, and his death would seem to make a comment on his quest—but then he manifests himself from beyond the grave, or seems to.[20]

It is clear, however, that what might have been a saving or transformative intervention in the grim human situation whose conditions I have been sketching is very often in effect sucked into it and made subject to its conditions, and, secondly, that neither the character of an individual nor the being of a deity is something mysterious and given in Dick's fictions. His personages act abruptly, impulsively, and often in contradiction of their own intentions; they sometimes lack affect, or do things without feeling consequences. They are not predictable, but they are constantly opened out for discussion and analysis. They are valuable but material— even, paradoxically, the deities among them.

Further, though Dick never retreats from his conviction that empathy is a human necessity, he treats even this with detachment. In the hypertechnological and very utilitarian societies of these novels, the

---

[18] The depiction of Ragle Gumm in *Time out of Joint* (1959) is a good example of this.

[19] The Author's Note to *A Maze of Death* (1970) explains how he worked out the religious system that prevails in the society of the novel with the help of Bishop James Pike; it is interesting that an incident in the final chapter throws into doubt our assumption that this religious system is fake even for the world of the novel, and interesting too that a later novel, *Timothy Archer*, offers a detached but sympathetic picture of the heterodox musings of a character based on Pike. (Other fake religions, positively presented, are to be found in *Solar Lottery* and *Androids*.)

[20] These examples are from *The Divine Invasion* (1981) and *Timothy Archer* (1982). The sense in which Dick means these speculations, which are offered with such enthusiasm and then put so thoroughly into doubt, will be discussed in Chapter 12, on *Valis* (1981).

category distinction between a quality (wisdom or sensitivity) and a faculty (something psionic, in the terms of the science of the SF megatext) has been eroded. This is because everything is used in much the same way in these societies. The division of labour that is behind psychic and moral categories (see Jameson 1993: 370) is different from that which prevails in our world. People with psionic powers that are amazing to us end up in mediocre, poorly paid jobs, in *Ubik* and *Clans of the Alphane Moon*. There are telepaths, who can see into one's mind or feelings; there are also ruthless people who know what one is going to say before one says it; there are deities, benign or malign or of uncertain status, who can absorb one's consciousness into theirs. All these varieties of 'bad' empathy jeopardize not only individuality but even differentiation itself,[21] but they do not finally introduce into the world of the novels a quality that transcends the prevailing laws and ways of doing business.

Again, Dick customarily defines something that is potentially valuable in terms of its recession from itself: a humorous trope, no doubt, but one with sceptical implications. Humans are defined not in absolute terms but in their differences from the mechanical, that is, the perfectly functional. The definition of a human which results from this conjunction with machines is much more oblique and ironic than Dick himself often implies. A human is one who has what a machine lacks (self-awareness, ability to change one's mind or at least feel guilt and shame; empathy) in lacking what a machine has (effectiveness, precision, self-correcting or self-repairing qualities, metallic strength). The human is found in fallibility, breakdown, and incompetence: a human is one who has the non-mechanical capacity to slip up or, to employ a usefully ambivalent phrase, break down. The implications are no less unsettling for being comical. Self-consciousness, arguably a distinctly human attribute, is associated with the capacity helplessly to watch oneself, impotent to affect one's action—as when waking out of a faint, or injured, or under a drug.

But of course *machines* often break down in Dick's fiction; when they don't break down, they tend to be valued for persistence rather than efficiency. *Dr Bloodmoney* (1965), Dick's post-nuclear novel, ends with an image of hope, a tiny homeostatic vermin-hunter going about its business: the 'natural' (in the form of doggedness, ineradicable hope and carrying on against the odds) manifest in the machine which hunts 'natural'

---

[21] Chapter 7 discusses the ambiguous treatment of deities in Dick's fiction, in relation to his critique of consumption, and his sense of the crisis of differentiation and individuation in the contemporary world.

creatures (actually mutants deformed by the bomb).[22] Deities, likewise, tend to be maimed or imperfect, or separated from themselves.

Consciousness, will, even wisdom inhere in robots or mechanical things (appliances, taxis) and at the same time the human subject seems to have less consciousness, will, even wisdom than in our contemporary world: there appears to have been a transfer and a diminution. The world is alien and over against the subject ('Les choses sont contre nous', as the Resistentialists put it[23]), yet is animate and a seeming projection of the subject, or an extension of subjectivity, which begins to seem to be every-where, and yet nowhere, or at least to be existing at a lower level. Humans feel themselves to be hampered, stupid and unfree, and other things, which have gained some consciousness, are usually simple and repetitive. My computer, for instance, has accrued some particles of humanness: it is a kind of idiot savant. Correspondingly, in working at my computer I become a little less than human, a kind of mechanism, though a faulty one that persistently (for instance) enters 'about' as 'aobut'. This is the kind of thing that Dick notices and intensifies. Something very like the condition of postmodernity is dissolving the human—and also disseminating it; yet this is the outcome of an attempt to define and even vindicate humanness.

Although the feeling tone, the ambience of familiarity and mundanity, and the point of view all remind us of the realist novel, Dick's SF is not set in Gissing's dreary London or Orwell's aspidistra'd suburbs but in an exis-tentially dissolving universe strongly suggestive of the projections of con-temporary postmodern theorists. It is an intriguing confrontation, and it bespeaks a dramatic historical conjunction. An exacerbated liberal indi-vidualism meets a wild, uninhibited posthumanism. Perhaps individual-ism has seldom in the history of modernity been so dolefully monadic as it is here, and perhaps postmodernism in contemporary society is not yet so hyperbolically or hysterically dissolvent as it is here, whatever Jean Baudrillard has proclaimed.

3. Challenges of the Critical Task

It might be the case, however, that the confrontation becomes so violent as to teleport Dick into another context altogether, the religious.

---

[22] The fight between the tiny wheeled carts which Eric Sweetscent observes near the end of *Now Wait for Last Year* (1966) (ch. 14, 221) utilizes the same trope. It is interesting that of these images of ineradicable life in a machine, one involves hunting and the other fighting. Moreover, the group of characters at the centre of *Dr Bloodmoney* are almost all equipped with prostheses; the implications of this for Dick's liberal sense of the individual are discussed by Jameson (1975a).

[23] This philosophy is outlined by Jennings (1960).

We would then be seeing the religious as the hyperhumanist, in postmodern terms, and this is one way of approaching the shift to the theological that has occupied and often troubled critics of Dick. Consideration of his late novel *Valis*, however,[24] suggests the complexities of the shift to the theological, for *Valis* is both a seriously religious novel and one in which Dick reaches a postmodernism of form and point of view. Yet even if this is so, the problem remains the same, because *Valis* is seriously concerned with the spiritual and transcendent, and yet it is also elaborately self-deconstructive as a text.[25] The fiction moves in two directions at once.

This characterization of the volatile compound that is Dick's fiction is one that will need much refinement. Dick is a sometimes recklessly experimental writer. It is his habit, and his enjoyment, to say three or four alternative things, or even several contrary things, in narrative succession and in some sort of suggestive relation in the fiction, but without making any conclusive choice between them. This might imply that his epistemology is always incipiently postmodern. Perhaps this is true. It is in the nature of the case that any formulation that implies a centre and a margin will come unstuck, and in consequence the notion that in Dick's novels one looks at postmodernity through the eyes of realism can only be provisional; but it is the best way of describing an effect of shock that is basic to his work.

Dick's fiction really is a context in which the fluidity and heterogeneity that are often idealized by contemporary thought come back to haunt aspirations to that rigour also often vaunted by contemporary thought. For this reason the project of defining what is historically interesting and humanly compelling about Dick's SF by defining it on a grid of oppositions —humanist and postmodern, realist and fantastic—has to be handled flexibly. We need a set of terms to comprehend the varying ways in which the relations of critique and fantasy, representation and transformation, dissolution and affirmation are staged, because we are dealing with a set, or a field, in which definable forces play and replay their relationships, rather than with a single entity that enigmatically shifts its shape but remains at last one thing. In Chapter 8, for instance, I vary the terms 'realistic' and 'fantastic' to 'critique' and 'fantasy'; in Chapter 9, I refine the description of Dick's humanist side by suggesting how romantic his values are. To examine the shifts and contradictions of Dick's fiction, it is necessary to utilize terms that are themselves open and shifting, not because it

---

[24] See Chapter 12.

[25] This is arguably what has happened to Derrida himself in recent years, in his very different context, but this doesn't necessarily help us to understand Dick's fiction.

is desirable to replicate Dick's shifts and contradictions, but in order to allow the historical conditions of his fiction to speak.

More particularly, criticism needs to be alert to the self-reflectiveness of Dick's fiction. Anything that can be identified as a mode by means of which the fiction is put together—fantasy (wish-fulfilment, or the fantastic), realism (plausible observation; extrapolation), political critique (satire)—is also likely to be examined and undermined as part of the fiction's content—the images, characters, institutions and behaviours in the world of the story.

3. Static and Kinetic in Dick's Political Unconscious

This chapter analyses a structure of imagery in Dick's work that is connected with movement and stasis. Building on the observations about disintegration and blockage as a condition of Dick's worlds that were offered in the first chapter, it makes use of Fredric Jameson's notion of the political unconscious, which historicizes the way in which texts are the productions of repression and contradicted desires or impulses. The literary context for Dick's work is the 'megatext' that is American SF, and this is where our discussion begins. The relation to this megatext of Dick's *oeuvre* is a skewed one, and the coherence of Dick's own *oeuvre* is sometimes hard to discern, though it is clear that his work as an ongoing enterprise and set of tropes in turn serves as a megatext within which any single work by Dick can be set. The notion of a political unconscious implies that Dick's work can be read as a response to historical conditions; but before embarking on that topic it is necessary to examine how the response to history is refracted through textuality. This precaution is only prudent, given our lack of direct access to past history[1] and given the complex, refracted and irreverent relations between a text by Dick and his *oeuvre* as a whole, and between the latter and the SF megatext. It has an additional advantage: it provides an opportunity to note the playful, freewheeling inventiveness of Dick's fiction. Given that the emphasis later in the discussion is on stagnation and blockage, this is a necessary corrective.

1. At Play in the Fields of the Megatext

It has been suggested that one characteristic of American popular culture, and one reason for its present global success, is the way in which any single work, or episode, can draw on a whole encyclopedia of immediately recognizable tropes, conventions, stereotypes and bits of common generic or cultural knowledge (see Mattelart, in Nelson and Grossberg 1988).

[1] Something that has been recognized by theorists from Jameson (1981, ch. 1) to Michael Oakeshott (1983: 27–34).

(An encyclopedia: a multiplex text to which the reader has access, consisting of bits of referential information and literary or generic lore.) This approach is particularly relevant to American SF, which may be said to draw on a shared megatext.[2]

Clearly, what is at issue is not merely a set of interrelated items of information, but a way of reading so as to mobilize the information. As Samuel Delany has pointed out, SF involves a mode of reading; the sentence 'She turned on her side' ('She turned *on* her side'), which he uses as example, would activate a range of megatextual information about androids and characters with prostheses should it occur in an SF text, just as 'What's at Stake in Vampire Films?' (Donald 1992), as title for a critical article, activates not only information about vampire lore, but also a mode of reading of critical articles which (alas) expects them to feature puns.

The genre shares an invented history and technology so ramified as almost to amount to a collective imaginary: a device or process or institution that has been introduced by a number of writers becomes the possession of all, implying a concrete history and technology, able to be referred to in any one text as casually as a writer about contemporary society might refer to ATMs or cellphones. The ideological implications of this megatext need to be explored, but it is also true that in utilizing it the genre shares in the novel's affinities to gossip, that marvellous organ of communal consent and dissent: what I can report others as claiming to be true can be true also for me, no matter how outrageous it is.[3]

So it is with Philip K. Dick. He borrows a variety of items from the SF megatext of the fifties and before: robots, psionics, telepaths, time travel, poscreds; Mars the desert planet, home of a now departed or decaying civilization; cryonic suspension during space flight; giant computers occupying whole buildings, Orwellian organizations of mind control and mass surveillance, radiation mutants, and much more. But he mixes, overlays, parodies and exaggerates. This procedure of his, however, throws doubt upon the usual contract between writer and reader, whereby the reader agrees to treat the megatext as real and thence the particular text that is drawing on it as realistic, and thence as proceeding according to the protocols of realism. The model of gossip, or of subcultural agreement among SF writers and readers, is weakened, and we have something a little closer to the avant-garde readiness to shock the reader, who is addressed across reading communities, rather than within a reading community (SF fans). A Dickian text is set at an an oblique angle to the megatext which it is

---

[2] See Brooke-Rose 1981 and Attebery 1992: 107 for discussions of this concept.

[3] The credibility of the gossip finds a new and sometimes dubious social field in the reading of tabloids—relevant to Dick's later novels, and discussed in Chapter 11 below.

drawing on, but also sending up or exaggerating.[4] The reader needs to be on guard.

The ending of *Dr Futurity* (1960) is an example (chs. 13–15). This novel utilizes the megatextual idea that one might use time travel to go back in history and correct or rearrange it; but instead of this being put into action by an individual white male, interested in his own personal history, as is often the case,[5] it is attempted by a group of Native Americans of the future, who plan to forestall and rearrange history by assassinating Western voyagers as they land on America's shores. The individualism of the trope is further disrupted: the upshot of the very complicated plot of *Dr Futurity* is that a whole series of time travellers, with different and rival agendas, arrive on the shores of California, where Francis Drake is about to land, at almost the same moment—if this hitherto innocuous temporal indicator can still be used—and may be observed shimmering in and out of existence on the ludicrously crowded scene.[6] The trope is drastically overstretched. It looks as if collective subjects cannot engage in time travel with the same relatively secure effects as the individual subjects for whom the prevailing trope was invented, and the subjects of *Dr Futurity*'s future are emphatically collective—their whole society is animated by a giant 'zygote bank' into which individuals periodically merge.

Proceeding a little further, the reader finds that the more novels by Dick she reads, the more elements are repeated: character types, institutions, items of technology, tropes, styles of name (for instance, names that make a pun in German: Bluthgeld, Lufteufel, Schoenheit von Vogelsang[7]). It is true that all idiosyncratic novelists do something like this, and it is also true that the ingredients refuse to gel into a megastory (as happens with the almost interminable trilogies and series that populate the current SF and fantasy scene).[8] Nor do they make a consistent world which the

---

[4] Stanley Cavell meditates on the sometimes uneasy relations between genre and authority: 'It is a quest for authority in one's speech in the absence of the authority of genre, of a shared present, of a grant of history' (1988: 143). This quest takes Dick well beyond whatever authority is conferred by his being a madly inventive SF writer; as will be seen in Chapter 12 below, it takes him to autobiography (Cavell's next topic), though of a very ambiguous kind.

[5] For instance in Heinlein's 'All You Zombies –' (1989 [1959]). This story uses the rules of the game of the time travel story to accomplish an astonishingly narcissistic fantasy; it's a good example of how the existence of the megatext can free a writer just as effectively as can the institutions of the avant garde (manifestos, experimentalism, little magazines and so on).

[6] 'There would be at least four other time ships. Assuming that this trip was the last' (ch. 14, 121).

[7] Characters from *Dr Bloodmoney*, *Deus Irae*, and *Ubik*, respectively.

[8] Intimately related to the importance of the megatext is that of seriality; see Eco 1990 for comments on the relation of postmodern seriality to changed attitudes to novelty and originality.

various stories might be seen to be revisiting,[9] and, further, the ease with which elements gain and regain entrance to Dick's novels should warn us to be careful about thematizing any given element in any given novel. Nonetheless the common ground between different novels is obvious and intriguing. If Dick's work is itself a megatext, how does any one fiction relate to it?

It sometimes seems that Dick writes in the way that a slapdash cook cooks, without benefit of recipe, laying out a range of favourite ingredients and combining them in improvisational fashion—throw in talking robot taxis here, next add Neanderthal hominids existing as throwbacks in the future, a peculiar mind-altering drug, maybe a time scoop, some telepathic aliens—and adjusting their metaphorical and narratorial relations as he proceeds. What (if anything) might make this dish, if not a unity, at least a coherence, with its differentiating thematic and emotional flavour, is an interesting question. If we assume that coherence is in fact aimed at, and that Dick is not simply resting content with the kind of fragmentariness and arbitrariness that we now call postmodern, then we have to agree that an author has seldom challenged himself or herself as idiosyncratically as this.[10] One would not claim that the Neanderthalers, or the time-travelling Hermann Goering, or the Theodorus Nitz bugs, or the Martian Papoolas are any of them obviously *needed* for the overall unity or thematic and affective coherence of *The Simulacra* (1964), yet there they all are.

Perhaps we should not look to define a condition that they come together to represent, but should attend rather to the process of combination. If they figure a condition, it is that of social derangement in the imagined world of the novel; there is a coherence to *The Simulacra*, but this coherence stems from a series of tropes and images of music: the eerie singing of the Neanderthalers, the jug band performance at the White House, the deranged psychokinetic pianist Richard Kongrosian: we have a coherent text, or at least intriguing signs of coherence in the text, but we do not have a coherent society.[11] This might enhance the general

---

[9] The (or rather a) megatext dictates the actual text in a significant way in the case of the 'shared world' novel, that is, a novel whose author agrees to write according to a prescribed set of rules and conditions for the given world—which very often will have been laid down by some big name in the field, such as Isaac Asimov. See the entry 'Shared World' in Clute and Nicholls' *Encyclopaedia of Science Fiction* (1993).

[10] See Huntingdon 1988 for sceptical discussion of Dick's style of composition; he sees A.E. van Vogt as precedent in SF.

[11] We can contrast these flickering and hard-to-relate images of music in *The Simulacra* with the realistic and consecutive depiction of music and musicians in *Mary and the Giant* (written c.1957, published 1987), though even in this case this element is only a counterpoint to the depiction of Mary Anne Reynolds' impulsive, unpredictable emotional life, which is the novel's main interest.

impression of realness, because our own reality is itself incoherent, or rather, our own reality might indeed constitute a totality, but to figure out how this or that weird item fits into the totality is a puzzling business; and it has been argued, in addition, that it is precisely the historical character of our world, since capitalism became a global phenomenon, that its real shape is hidden from the individual. In Dick's novels both a global picture and a comprehensive explanation of what is going on are lacking. The implied space is not, say, that of a city, whose overall structure might be revealed by the roads that traverse it (or by the railway, as in the famous passage in ch. 20 of *Dombey and Son*), but that of a cluster of autonomous cells in no clear relation to each other.

A variety of approaches to this problem offer themselves. A modicum of evaluation and Dickian canon formation is in order. *Deus Irae*, for instance (written with Roger Zelazny), is not a successful novel, and this probably has something to do with the rather desperate way in which earlier short stories are cannibalized.[12] However, though canon formation is often an illuminating game, I must confess that I am sufficiently a fan of Dick to find almost all of his novels fascinating, precisely because of this way in which certain elements recur in a range of novels. Although *Deus Irae* is a mess in the light of any criteria which I can bring to bear on it, the scene in which Lufteufel, the mad scientist become deity of the story, manifests his face as that of the god of anger in a nuclear mushroom cloud (ch. 10, 143) is a very powerful one. This deity is menacing, self-pitying, complaining, spiteful, capricious, awesome—a dramatization of Dick's fear that we get the deity we deserve, the deity that is a grotesque inflation of our vices and even pettinesses. Dick's obsession with deities as fathers, and with fathers or authority figures as deities, his meditations on nuclear apocalypse and his persistent attempt to tie it to a Germanic element in modern history and civilization,[13] and his ironic, chastened sense that if one is granted a revelation one will probably wish one had been spared the experience, all merge rather abruptly at this point in the meandering of the story.

Alternatively, critics have sought key structuring devices or patterns. One of these is the recurrent character set, analysed by Kim Stanley Robinson in his excellent book on Dick (1984), and by Fredric Jameson in his essay on *Dr Bloodmoney* (1975a). Certain figures repeatedly recombine and interact: the little guy—a minor operative or repairman, a put-upon

[12] 'The Great C' (1953, CS1), 'Planet for Transients' (1953, CS2). (*Deus Irae* was published in 1976.)

[13] Suvin (1988: 120–21) very interestingly discusses the possible significance of Dick's interest in the Germanic. See also the discussion of the Nazis in *The Man in the High Castle* (1962), below, Chapter 6.

husband; the bluff father figure or boss, merging into the gross, uninhibited figure of power; the 'dark-haired girl', perhaps kind, perhaps alluring and mysterious, merging into the predatory female, sometimes androgynous; the ambiguous saviour or devourer returning from outer space, the efficient functionary who strikes out on his own, the wise alien or robot, and so on.[14] Their differentiations and significances may be analysed to explore the dynamics of Dick's narratives (Robinson) or distributed on a Greimasian rectangle to lay bare the problems of his thinking about society (Jameson).

This discussion will take a different course, though one that draws on Jameson's theoretical work. This is the analysis of Dick's political unconscious, by way of definition of characteristic image structures, occurring across a range of novels at a level of depth and generality such that Dick was probably not aware of them, as he certainly was aware of his character sets and their role in the production of his plots. Jameson (1987) has argued that SF works its meanings not, finally, by means of narrative but by means of transformations of space.[15] What follows will look at movement through space and confinement in space in Dick, noticing a particular, recurrent blockage, and offering a historical comment on its occurrence. What we get is a broken or incomplete binary. This is a writer who thinks in binary terms (for instance, human and not-human or 'android'; male and female; fertility and sterility; powerful and powerless), but in whom binaries tend to be incomplete or to merge. The discussion outlines how this happens in the case of one historically significant binary pairing.

In Dick, movement, the ethos and narrative motivator of so much SF, is blocked. One way of defining this outcome in genre terms is to say that the protocols of SF mate with those of horror, which, as Manuel Aguirre has said (1990: 2), dwells in a 'closed space'—the labyrinth, cave, prison, tomb; the shuttered room. And this is one thing from which American SF (as distinct from the SF of Shelley or some of Wells) has tried to remain

---

[14] Some examples: the father figure: Glen Runciter, Arnie Kott, Willis Gram (in *Ubik, Time-Slip, Frolix 8*); the 'dark-haired girl' or predatory female: Donna Hawthorne, Mary Rittersdorf, Pat Conley, Charley (in *A Scanner Darkly, Clans, Ubik, Frolix 8*); the saviour or devourer: Palmer Eldritch, Morgo/Provoni (in *Palmer Eldritch, Frolix 8*). There are similar patterns in the non-SF novels, which are usually based on relations between and among two married couples; one of the women is usually strong but cold, the other gentle but distracted; one of the men is usually unstable to the point of hysteria. I discuss these novels in Chapter 4.

[15] And it is relevant to our overall theme that postmodernity is seen as having worked radical changes in the quality of urban space and in the relations of spatiality and temporality. See Soja 1988 and Jameson 1993, especially ch. 3 and the controverted but still stimulating discussion of the Portman Bonaventura Hotel in ch. 1. On spatiality in recent SF, see Palmer 1999: 83–84.

aloof—the closing of space in Dick then anticipates the ghastly conjuncture of SF and horror in the last few years, most noticeable in films, and suggestive of new reservations about technology and the body.

2. Wide Angle: Nemesis of the Kinetic

SF is a strongly kinetic form: it is very concerned with journeying, moving outwards, opening out, travelling towards or in search of wonder. Change, and even simply experience, are thereby associated with movement, in an exhilarating way.[16] This may be a matter of movement into outer space as both consummation and transcendence of Western history, especially American history: the space rocket consummates and transcends the progression from train to car to jet plane, and the problems of vast times and distances, relativistic swerves, cryonic suspension and so forth are cheerfully confronted because confidence in this linear progression is so strong; again, movement to the stars is seen as continuation of the movement of Americans to the frontier and beyond. Or journeying is imagined as part of a utopian revision of the errors and violence of Western history, as in the novels of Kim Stanley Robinson, in whom movement—hiking, mountaineering, sailing, exploring—also releases bodily energy and affirms that humans can act as the consciousness of the landscape which they traverse with such effort, alertness and enjoyment.[17]

Little of this is present in Dick's SF, and not merely because he has scant concern with space flight, and is thoroughly sceptical of the idea that colonizing other planets would be a positive thing to do. (Space colonies in Dick tend to replicate suburbia, or neglected sections of dustbowl America, when they are not concentration camps.[18]) Yet it is the megatextual point

[16] *Out of the Silent Planet* (1938) and *Perelandra* (1943), by C.S. Lewis, throw an interesting light on this matter. Both are based on journey quests of a traditional type; both concern the main character's encounter with new experience, with revelation in fact; but Lewis wants nothing to do with change as part of modernity, as he makes very clear in the third novel in the series, *That Hideous Strength* (1945). In the first novel, the main character journeys to Mars, where his quest is to unfold, by spaceship, but Lewis revises this in the second and simply has him transported by angels.

[17] See the dozens of journeys across and somehow *in* Mars in the Mars trilogy (1993–96), restorative hiking in the Sierra Nevadas in *The Gold Coast* (1988) and 'Ridge Running' (1986); softball in *Pacific Edge* (1990), but—by way of exception, for generalizations breed exceptions —the circular journey in *A Short, Sharp Shock* (1990).

[18] See for instance *Time-Slip*, *Palmer Eldritch*, 'The Unreconstructed M' (1957, CS4), 'Survey Team' (1954, CS2), and *Lies, Inc.* Or travellers may land on a previously unknown planet, barren and dull, and discover that it is a wrecked, far-future earth (*A Maze of Death*, 'The Impossible Planet'). The story on which *Palmer Eldritch* draws for its Martian colony sets the broken-down settlement in a wrecked, post-nuclear Oakland, California ('The Days of Perky Pat', 1963, CS4).

from which he begins, as can be seen from his first novel, *Solar Lottery* (1955), which concludes with an eloquent speech by a character named Preston to a group of people gathered on a new and wonderful planet, Flame Disc, which they plan to colonize:

> 'It isn't senseless drive [. . .] It isn't a brute instinct that keeps us restless and dissatisfied. I'll tell you what it is: it's the highest goal of man —the need to grow and advance . . . to find new things . . . to expand.' (ch. 17, 192)

One could not ask for a clearer vindication of the urge outwards, and in fact the society of the novel is stalled in a political and economic system that has become false, sterile and oppressive, as well as regressing to a feudal condition (the solar system is dominated by multinationals, but their power over people is based on 'oaths of fealty'). Yet in view of Dick's later fiction it is interesting that the source of this speech is a simulacrum, not the prophet and explorer Preston as his audience (devout Prestonites) had thought, but a 'withered image', endlessly repeating his encomium to expansion, unaware of the questions and replies of the audience whose arrival has triggered the speech.

As Dick sees the body as liable not only to transformation, but to invasion and occupation,[19] it is not surprising that he seldom imagines the pleasures of movement or exertion. In his fictions, stasis is imprisoning, but movement is not liberating. His novels and stories stage all the horrors of not moving, not progressing, in fact of regressing: stalemate, repetition, entrapment, stagnation, senescence, decay, collapse. Later the discussion will touch on the significance of this as a response to modernity; we have a deep structure, and a blockage, that speaks not merely of Dick's unconscious but of the unconscious of modernity. Meanwhile, the full picture needs to be detailed.[20]

There is an absence of the experience of the kinetic, either as felt or as imagined. A trip or transportation is a mere blank, unaccompanied by enjoyment of the speed and ease of movement; one simply gets in a rocket and arrives, and, arriving, faces one's dreary, emphatically ordinary

---

[19] The locus of this in *Solar Lottery* is Keith Pellig, a 'sim', that is, a simulated human, controlled by human operators who can enter into Pellig and control his actions. This process is randomized, to thwart telepaths whose function is to protect the man whom Pellig is trying to assassinate, and the operators are in turn thwarted when one of them is as it were trapped inside Pellig; he later self-destructs. Even this summary of a complicated episode (chs. 11–13) suggests how the boundaries between the Pellig thing, its operators and the telepaths are blurred, as crowds of operators and telepaths try to occupy the sim.

[20] Chapter 5 surveys the sterility of things, people and environments in Dick's short stories, and clearly this is relevant to the present topic.

problems. To put the matter another way, that which exists between destinations is not space or landscape but nullity.[21] The effect might be seen as an exacerbation of a common experience of city life: the city as scatter of locations—workplace, friends' houses, a few shops and restaurants—divided by undifferentiated·city-ness.

Alternatively, a journey is an occasion for satire of automation: talkative robot taxis that have simply replicated talkative taxi drivers, and control equally decrepit vehicles; the 'quibbles' in *The Man Who Japed* (1956) that cannot go faster than 35 mph (there is a minor traffic accident, made comical by the natives' terror of speed [ch. 23, 154]); the rickshaws in *The Man in the High Castle* (1962), hauled by sweating, straining '*chinks*' (ch. 2, 26), contrasted to the Nazis' intercontinental rockets.[22] Vehicles frequently wheeze, stutter and grind to a halt; they are given jokey names suggestive of the wonky and antiquated: quibbles, jalopies, drays.[23]

The final and most significant possibility is that movement becomes clogged nightmare and imprisonment. Movement becomes stasis. Thus the prospect of Rachmael ben Applebaum's solitary eighteen-year journey to Whale's Mouth, in a 'dray'. (His destination is called both New Colonized Land, alluding to the tradition of the frontier, and Whale's Mouth, alluding to Jonah's interrupted voyage; in the end his destination turns out not to be a place at all, but a psychic state.) The horror of confinement thus contemplated in *Lies, Inc.* becomes real in a brief scene of claustrophobia in a rocket to Venus in *The World Jones Made* (1956) (ch. 15, 134–35), and attains classic Dickian form in the plight of the main character in 'I Hope I Shall Arrive Soon' (1985 [1980, CS5]).

This character's cryonic suspension, in which he is meant to lapse away the time of his journey, has malfunctioned, so he is conscious and alert, but there is no way he can simply get up and walk about the ship—there

---

[21] One of the great evokers of sensuously rich journeys in SF is C.S. Lewis, whose character Ransom discovers in *Out of the Silent Planet* that space is not empty, but so brimming with light and life that the very term is misleading. By the time Lewis finishes off his trilogy in the earth-bound *That Hideous Strength*, however, journeys are humdrum, and about all that we can say is that cars are used by the baddies and trains by the goodies, presumably because trains are less modern than cars.

[22] DiTommaso (1999: 98 and n.18) offers an ingenious interpretation of how the characters' names in the novel relate to journeying. What one makes of this depends on what one makes of his idea that the novel is concerned with journeys towards redemption; if one doesn't find this in the novel, as I don't, then these possible meanings of the names have a mainly ironic effect.

[23] Quibbles in *The Man Who Japed* (1956), jalopies in *The Simulacra* (1964), drays in *Lies, Inc.* (1984). Drays are intergalactic rockets; in the novel they have been superseded by teleportation, which is a process rather than a mode of transportation: space is eliminated, not traversed; you undergo teleportation and find yourself at your destination.

is nowhere to walk, this is a spaceship without internal space. Instead he has to submit to the clumsy ministrations of the ship's computer, which will attempt to occupy the journey time and save his sanity. The upshot is that he spends ten years as if in a waking dream, endlessly reliving certain key episodes—failures—from his past; when he finally arrives he is not at all sure that he has actually been released from this imprisonment inside his own skull. Instead of progression—movement to a new planet and a new life—we have regression. This is not entirely horrifying in 'I Hope I Shall Arrive Soon'; there is the possibility that the repetition of the past acts as a sort of therapy. (Dick's attraction to return and recovery, to making things as they were when we were children, is discussed below.)

There is a similar turn inwards in *Lies, Inc.* Rachmael's plan to travel by dray is thwarted, and when he actually makes the trip, it takes not eighteen years but an instant, by the marvels of teleportation. It was this new device that bankrupted the family drayage line; one thing that has aroused his suspicion that something untoward is happening on Whale's Mouth, and led him to contemplate the solitary eighteen-year trip, is the fact that this form of transport—marvellous, instantaneous—only works one way. No one can teleport back from Whale's Mouth. The whole thing is an allegory for the journey to the extermination camps, which certainly can be seen as the definitive twentieth-century journey. (It is fascinating that teleportation is probably most familar to readers as the 'beam me up Scotty' effect of *Star Trek*. This is a good example of Dick's tangential relation to the megatext.) On arrival, however, Rachmael is wounded in the confused combat in progress on Whale's Mouth, and plunged at once into confinement as a 'weevil', subject to a series of nightmare visions of monsters with single eyes and devouring mouths, creatures from archaic paraworlds which, in forcing their way into Rachmael's psyche, are somehow also forcing their way into the world of Whale's Mouth.[24] His journey is into his own interior, though the boundaries between interior and exterior have been erased.

Whether we consider Rachmael's journey in relation to that of Jonah and others in the Old Testament who journey into the wilderness, or in relation that of Ishmael in *Moby Dick* (Ishmael is rescued by a ship called the *Rachel*, so the Rachmael/*Rachel*/Ishmael/Whale's Mouth connection does set up an intertext[25]), then it seems that Dick has reversed the terms

---

[24] It is this episode that Dick expands in revising *The Unteleported Man* (1966, first publication as a book) into *Lies, Inc.* (1984). The mastermind behind the frighteningly fast and insidious weapons in *Lies, Inc.*, one of which has plunged Rachmael into this state, is himself a deformed, immobile cripple, who exists in an autistically different time-world from the rest of us (ch. 11, 131).

[25] I owe this suggestion to Ryan Bishop.

of the biblical or the classic American pilgrimage.[26] There is no wilderness, no movement outside the settled community and towards the Other, but an unwitting and nightmarish curve back into the social, or the self (the two are confused because the status of Rachmael's nightmares is unclear).

We can pursue the point by looking briefly at *The Divine Invasion* (1981), which revises a biblical story in a more detailed way. This time the movement is from the wilderness back to Earth. At the opening of the story Herb and Rybys are holed up on the inhospitable planet CY30 II. They each live in sealed, homeostatic domes called 'bubbles' in neurotic, technologically mediated stagnation and isolation. Herb spends his time listening to his dream love, the pop idol Linda Fox, on the radio; he ignores the pleas for help of his neighbour Rybys, who has contracted cancer. The two isolates are forced out of their bubbles by a persistent wanderer called Elijah, who is acting in the service of the local god Yah. They become the Joseph and Mary to a new Messiah, named Emmanuel; but things go badly wrong: the child is maimed in Rybys's womb, and for most of the novel Herb is trapped in cryonic suspension following an accident, and remembers his activities as parent to the child Emmanuel on earth only as flashbacks. That is, not only does the plan to replay the story of the Incarnation break down because Emmanuel is injured and forgets who he is, but the narrative loses linear form and becomes nested in complex circles. Clearly, it is not merely the kinetic optimism of modernity that is reversed in *Lies, Inc.* and *The Divine Invasion*, but the teleology of founding American and Christian stories, stories whose reinterpreted and (to use Baudrillard's term) inverted lineaments may be seen beneath the dazzling hi-tech mechanisms of teleportation, psychotropic drugs, cryonic suspension and Artificial Intelligence systems. In these fictions, Dick draws on two megatexts, that of SF and that of Western story, including Christianity, treating the first flippantly and the second sceptically. The different elements sometimes clash: for instance, the allegory of the fate of the Jews in *Lies, Inc.* tends to get lost in the swirl of diverse narratives and images.

The same kind of shift, again dissolving conventional tropes of journey and adventure, is handled more clearly in *A Maze of Death* (1970). A group of unhappy, ordinary misfits from various planets is given a mission, sent to an uninhabited planet, Delmark-O. It seems that they have gained a concrete task and purpose in life. Not so; by a malfunction, the signal that is to tell them the nature of their mission fails to get through; the planet,

---

[26] In *Deus Irae* (Dick and Zelazny, 1976), people make journeys, called 'pilgs', into a postapocalyptic wilderness mainly populated by radiation mutations. What is being rewritten this time is probably Walter M. Miller's rewriting of the Christian history of fall and redemption in *A Canticle for Leibowitz* (1976 [1956]).

which turns out to be a far future Terra, is barren, desolate and menacing, and, what is worse, the members of the group begin to kill each other in outbreaks of abrupt rage and suspicion. As so often in Dick's novels, they rapidly become engrossed in radical questions. Who are they? What are they? Are they the subject of some sort of malign experiment? Are they perhaps criminally insane, and is this a kind of prison-asylum planet?

If this planet is a prison-asylum, the fact that it is Earth, as they discover, and that they have found themselves on Earth itself without knowledge of their purpose in life has a clear allegorical point. But at the very end of the novel matters are explained (or almost explained, for there is a final twist). The group on Delmark-O are in fact the crew of a disabled, marooned space-ship; the events on the planet, which occupied most of the novel, happened, in actuality, inside their heads, as part of a collective fantasy which they played with the aid of what we would now call a virtual reality apparatus, in order to pass the time. Their sudden violences towards each other were the emotional outbreaks of people who have to live with the awareness that they are cooped up with each other indefinitely. This revelation too can be seen allegorically: the notion is that we humans are like the crew of a marooned spaceship, passing the time in brutal fantasies until we die. We aren't going anywhere. But this implication—that the ultimate determinant is the psychic, because anything that we do or make can be allegorized as our fantasy—is not one that is general in Dick's fiction, though it is often relevant. What is common is the way a journey through objective, outer space both turns inwards to subjectivity and becomes snarled in repetition, and in fact *A Maze of Death* goes to great lengths to leave us uncertain as to whether the ultimate horizon of explanation is psychic, technological—the VR apparatus—or theological—the 'Intercessor' who, perhaps, appears at the very end (ch. 16, 185–87), and whose presence doesn't fit into the technological explanation (VR fantasy) of what has been going on.

The most thorough and intense example of the breakdown of the kinetic in Dick's work is in *Ubik* (1969). This horrifying story of dissolving realities is not easy to summarize, but here goes. After a quick and unexceptional rocket flight to the moon, the story turns inwards and becomes clogged and regressive. There is the abrupt, grotesque explosion of a bomb, and from then on everything is turned inside out like a glove.[27] In one possible explanation, the main characters are so static as to be dead, or, to be more precise, frozen in 'half-life' in a 'Moratorium';[28] in another,

[27] The image of a glove turned inside out comes from *A Scanner Darkly* (1977) (ch. 13, 212).

[28] The word conflates a variety of kinds of stasis or indifferentiation, suggesting death (mors), delay or suspension, and banal commercial locations (e.g. 'lubritorium', 'emporium').

they are struggling to determine what is happening to them and what and where they are, while common objects deliquesce and regress around them, reducing to rubbish if they are organic (cigarettes or coffee), reverting to earlier models if they are artificial (a radio, a plane). Movement through space, whether by rocket ship or up the staircase of an old hotel, is either illusory or desperately difficult.

The central episode of the novel is a struggle to get to Des Moines (chs. 10–11)—the characters think they are going to attend the funeral of the man who seemed to have died in the explosion on Luna. Here we have a group of characters who do not know that they are not alive, and who nonetheless experience the horrible deaths of some of their fellows on the way, and they are struggling to travel to a funeral; the notion has a certain macabre wit, and, as often in Dick, a quality of abyssal doubling. By this stage, all the made objects around the characters are regressing; a story that began with a quick trip to the moon continues in an antiquated biplane; the date regresses from 1992 to 1939. This journey, or antijourney, culminates in the main character's agonized attempt to climb the stairs at his hotel, his body having become an immense oppressive weight almost impossible to shift (ch. 13). From the perspective of *Ubik*, the whole tradition of SF, from Verne and Wells to Clarke, Benford and Gibson, seems to share an optimism about freedom of movement through space; the movement is now stalled, the optimism shrivelled. So much for the whole festival of expansion that is modernity in its widest signification, from Christopher Columbus to the Apollo flights,[29] which reached the moon the year *Ubik* was published.

In fact we can go further into blockage and abstraction, because this general condition has another aspect in the experience of the main

---

[29] Further consideration of the vicissitudes of the kinetic in recent SF would need to take in two novels which make a motif of car accidents, Aldiss's *Barefoot in the Head* (1969) and Ballard's *Crash* (1973). Both emphasize obsessive repetition of the crashes, and both emphasize replication—the crash as staged, filmed, imagined. Ballard also emphasizes detritus—the car reduced to shards and fragments, the human body reduced to urine, body parts, semen, mess. Formally and tonally speaking, however, both differ from Dick in offering witty, conceited, grotesque rhapsodies of violence, dazzling in their textuality. Dick is exuberantly inventive and funny in a zany way, but his language is drab, objects banalized, and sequence of events desperately important for the characters. The contrast within this general context of the end of modernity's promise and arrival of postmodernity's artifice suggests the importance in Dick of a humanist sympathy—the last thing one would find in Ballard or want in Aldiss, as regards these particular novels. (On *Crash* and postmodernism, see *Science-Fiction Studies*, 55, part 3 (1991), which prints Baudrillard's note on the novel and a series of responses, including one by Ballard, who has summarized his sense of his novel in his introduction to the 1995 Vintage edition; and Iain Sinclair's book on the novel and film of *Crash* [1999], which refers us also to various Pop Art and cinematic representations—Warhol, Losey's *Accident*—that may have influenced Ballard.)

character, Joe Chip. Though he is unwittingly enclosed in 'half-life', according to one necessary but insufficient interpretation of the novel, Joe experiences the events of the narrative as an attempt to stave off death by finding the magic restorative elixir Ubik. This death within death that repeatedly threatens him and overtakes many of the other characters takes the form of a nightmarish chill and sluggishness, followed by a withering to mere scraps, dust and hair.

In addition, however, his experience is marked by repeated sexual frustration. There is a scene early in the story where the cool and strong Pat Conley, who has just undressed to take a shower in Joe's apartment, informs him that he has sexually blackmailed her and so she is now sexually blackmailing him (but he in turn double-crosses her, literally); she works this effect by one of the time-reversals that is within her power; later, by another, she sets up a time enclave in which she actually married him (ch. 3, 27–30; ch. 5, 48–53). From this she secured a nice ring, and he, nothing. Again, after Joe and his group arrive in Zürich with, as they suppose, Glen Runciter in cool-pac, Joe misuses his authority as the new head of the Runciter organization to try to get Wendy Wright, one of his colleagues, to spend the night with him. He fails; Wendy is the first of the characters to experience a horrible shrivelled death (ch. 8, 92–94). Even when this death is plainly coming very close to Joe himself, after his horrific climb up the stairs in the Des Moines hotel, he uses his very fortunate restoration by grace of the Ubik aerosol to commence a hunt for a prostitute. This disgusts the 1939 inhabitants of Des Moines who witness it, and dismays the reader, who feels that Joe should have other aims in view at this point. He is once again saved by luck: the sexily dressed young woman he picks up is actually Ella Runciter, Glen's deceased wife, an emissary of good from another province of the half-life world, bearing more Ubik—and shortly afterwards another young woman of a similar kind is sent to help him secure more (ch. 16, 190–98).

Joe Chip's quest for sexual pleasure strikes us as grubby in the circumstances of *Ubik*, and anyway it is continually frustrated. It is as if the conflation of birth and death that is brought about by half-life, and the radical uncertainty of bodily identity (where am I? am I alive or dead?) that motivates the plot, have released some drifting sexual material into the novel's psyche. The implication seems to be that one *can* find Ubik—which is simultaneously a deity; the ultimate, shiny and wonder-working, but insubstantial, consumer product; and the promise evanescently behind every consumer product. But sexual satisfaction is not to be had. The latter is subject to the same process of blockage as movement itself. After all, in half-life Joe has no active, living and moving body; he can imagine and desire, and in a vivid way experience the onset of death and the magical recovery from this onset that Ubik can grant, but he cannot actually move or act.

This imagination of an existence wholly abstract (Ubik is the spirit of the Commodity, rather than a material thing) yet capable of the most vivid fearing and desiring, of being in the body and yet unable to live the body's life, has wider dimensions than can really be caught by the present discussion of the static and the kinetic, though it is better to see it as an extreme development along the same imaginative lines than as, for instance, an expression of personal feelings of impotence on the part of the author.

3. Imaginary Irresolutions

What is the best way to interpret this material in Philip K. Dick, of which the above is no more than a sample? It refuses to take the shape of an opposition or binary pairing. It is as if the fiction were struggling to oppose the kinetic to the static, but failing: journeys become regressions, external becomes internal. It is not merely that journeying is so important to American SF, in its adventurous, confident extraversion; it is also that journeys are close to being indispensable to any action-packed fiction such as Dick is committed to.

It is here suggested that the best interpretation is historical. What we have is a deep-seated, recurrent but historically located structure of feeling, a pole of attraction of the imagination and the fiction-making faculty: something which provides an underlying shape into which things fit for Dick. This structure is the reflection of Dick's response to his society.

In modern society, change is continual, it is the very life of society. Culture and scene are always in revision or transformation. Change is accompanied by destruction: what is established is always destroyed or, like the appliances and vehicles in *Ubik*, it is shadowed by the obsolescence that must come to it. Change strips meaning from social life and from things, yet it has no liveable contrary, there is no longer any such thing as stability, only stasis or stagnation.[30]

Dick is tempted by the notion of return to the past, or to childhood, but the attempt is usually undermined by the technology needed to

---

[30] A comprehensive discussion here would have to consider the pastoral in Dick; a rare element, because nature does not usually exist in his worlds, but present in *Deus Irae* and still more in *Dr Bloodmoney* (1965). The latter novel receives interesting discussions in Jameson 1975a, Robinson 1984 and Suvin 1976. We often meet the anti-pastoral, the neglected, unvisited stagnant rural settlement: the village in *The Cosmic Puppets*, isolated in its valley, now frozen in time; old Carquinez in the non-SF novel *The Man Whose Teeth Were All Exactly Alike* (1986; written c.1960), isolated against the sea, poverty-stricken, almost forgotten.

accomplish it: technology of replication in *We Can Build You* (1972); a kind of restoration machine or gizmo in *The Cosmic Puppets* (1957); dangerous drugs in several novels. The technology is as it were off-balance: the restoration machine in *The Cosmic Puppets*, whereby two characters do succeed in restoring a thing from a past that has been stolen from them and overlaid with a stagnant, spurious present, is really a placebo, something the characters need to convince themselves that they can restore the past; and we do not usually see a drug as a piece of technology at all, since its user cannot repair it or manipulate it, only ingest it and trust to the hidden workings of his or her own mind and body. Dick's most sustained depiction of a child, Manfred in *Martian Time-Slip*, shows us a person trapped by his monomaniac prevision of the future, and one whose malign power is to reduce others to his condition, or worse.[31] The regression that happens in *Ubik*, for instance on the journey to Des Moines, is a movement back into the past—a past which, as it happens, is brutal and racist—but a movement back into the past that has the form of a movement into the future, since it proceeds by the supersession of one machine by another model, and that by another, in the familiar modern way. Both ways of staging regression, that in which progression becomes regression, and that in which an attempted recovery of the past is undermined by technology, emphasize how the mode of modernity, which is that of progress, is the only imaginable one, and yet is such as to distort any regress or return that is attempted in its mode. The result is that modernity is twisted towards postmodernity; we have change without direction or succession, a spiral into repetition or regression, rather than a movement to something new. We seem to lose history in seriality—remaking, variation or repetition.

Does Philip K. Dick's complex dissolution of movement into stasis, regression into parody of progression, express the imaginary resolution of real contradictions, in Fredric Jameson's formula for the activity of the political unconscious? There is contradiction, and it is real in being historically based. We can speak of a contradiction between SF's confident kinetic extraversion and the unbalanced nature of change and even of time in modernity, as Dick imagines it—an imbalance exacerbated in postmodernity to such a degree that 'change' seems the wrong word for the condition. How can movement have point and purpose unless we can imagine stability? If rest (non-movement) invariably becomes stagnation and entrapment, then purposeful movement is unimaginable; if rest is unimaginable, and movement has no purpose except itself, then movement itself becomes entrapment or stagnation, and stagnation becomes

---

[31] See Chapter 9 below.

movement.[32] (For entropy is imagined as an active, encroaching force in Dick and yet entropy is also seen as the ultimate stagnation.) These propositions strain narrative logic, but then narrative logic *is* strained in Dick's novels. These novels do not abandon binary structuration in favour of free flow or of simulations without exit, as do many postmodernist thinkers, because to do that would be to lose the sense of predicament: narrative logic is strained, not dissolved or escaped.

Finally, as regards this examination of the formula for the working of the political unconscious, is the contradiction *resolved* in imaginary terms? It is given vivid form, and in terms of an imaginary, but I don't think it is resolved: the form is irresolute. Jameson's formula is already ambivalent, because 'imaginary' means both 'in the imagination' and 'illusory'; in the case of Philip K. Dick it is necessary to push this opening in the formulation a little wider, and talk of the imaginary irresolution of real contradictions.[33] 'The imaginary irresolution of real contradictions' is a good formula for the working of humour, and this is appropriate here. Further discussion of Dick's version of entropy will, however, enable us to pursue the question of the resolution or irresolution of contradictions a little further.

4. Ambiguities of Entropy

The trope of the disintegrating settlement or outpost of progress offers an interesting entrance into Dick's depiction of the rot, mess and disarray of modern life. We may see him as continuing a tradition begun with the fraudulent frontier paradise of *Martin Chuzzlewit* and the entropic, collapsing river town of *Huckleberry Finn* (ch. 21); thence, Conrad's 'An Outpost of Progress' and *Heart of Darkness*, and the degradation of Moreau's bio-technological order into savagery in *The Island of Dr Moreau*. Thus, in Dick, the desolate, defeated, decrepit planetary settlements in *Martian Time-Slip* (1964) and *Palmer Eldritch* (1965).

Dick labels this overall phenomenon entropy. Entropy is seen as a kind of ground of existence, something into which life constantly collapses back when exhausted, but also as a force always ready to infiltrate and take

---

[32] It may be that I detect this pattern and predicament all the more readily in Philip K. Dick because of my suspicion that the process, becoming and fluidity often idealized by postmodernism is sibling to the progress, 'flexibility' and 'reform' recommended by contemporary capitalism (see Palmer 1996: 115–16). It has to be added, however, that the predicament is intensified for Dick by his unease about pleasure. This latter is discussed, and historicized, in connection with food and, in passing, sex, in Chapter 7.

[33] This way of putting the matter restores to art some of the autonomy of which Jameson has deprived it, if we subscribe to Thomas Huhn's criticisms (1989).

over. In its latter avatar, it is an exception to the rule that generally prevails in Dick, that nature has no life or force of its own, having been superseded by the artificial and its panoply of manipulations and simulacra. Entropy is both a state and a process; it is what may be seen always to underlie the fabricated surface of things, and it is the force that collapses things into their own hollowness and negation, or sterile evil. Out of this paradox Dick develops an imaginary resolution of a significant kind. (The paradox is resolved if we distinguish the two by labelling one of them as indifference or nullity, but I don't think we are dealing with two things that are distinct in the fiction.)

From a historical point of view, entropy may be interpreted as the returning repressed of modernity's investment in constant change, change which devours itself and leaves modernity without a point of reference. As was remarked above, progress strips meaning from social life, in its restless and interminable onwards drive. It also generates a lot of obsolescence, waste and rubbish—thus giving dangerous assistance to the force of entropy, which is imagined to be lying in wait in any case. 'The curse of irresistible progress is irresistible regression', as Adorno and Horkheimer put it in *Dialectic of Enlightenment* (1979: 36). The only form in which an alternative to progress can present itself is entropy, which is the revenge of a repressed nature, yet also a kind of anti-nature.[34] (An exception here is *The Man in the High Castle* [1962], wherein progress, in the explicitly modern and modernist form of Edfrank's jewel, is imagined and tested; but as will be argued in Chapter 6, this novel adopts a different view of history to that which can usually be inferred from Dick's novels.)

To put the matter another way, the contradictoriness of entropy suggests that the notion of a returning repressed is itself difficult to express in the conditions of postmodernity, which jeopardize notions of depth and thence of things returning from those depths. If so, the imagery of entropy merely tightens the circle and drives us back on the situation of contradiction; but there is in Dick a kind of 'weak' entropy that can be imagined without horror, and in fact with affection. This is trash, the humble, discarded, broken-down thing or person, valued and, in many contexts, some of them surprising, made the basis of humanness.[35]

---

[34] What has all this to do with the meanings of the term in thermodynamics and in information theory? Not a great deal.

[35] An interesting parallel is to be found in the work of William Gibson, who in turn involves himself in complications analogous to those we are about to explore with Dick. In *Neuromancer* (1984) there is an exhaustion of the kinetic, whereby the reckless pace, rush and run of the early episodes in Night City (for instance, ch. 1, 7) and in cyberspace—passages in which the reader struggles to keep up with the velocity of information transmission

For instance, the eponymous Clans on the Alphane Moon, groups of the mentally sick, forgotten by an Earth that has been distracted by intergalactic warfare, have managed to make a society that is certainly not progressing, but is stable, and is clearly sane compared to that which exists on Earth.[36]

In *Androids* (1968) the notion of entropy as a dynamic force, an expanding negativity that is now taking over, is given vivid expression by John Isidore (ch. 6, 53). The implication in the context of this novel is that humans, sterile, incompetent and failing, are succumbing to entropy, the revenge of a wrecked and polluted nature, while androids, intelligent, effective and always improving, threaten to displace them. Technology, which depends on repetition and imitation, is secure against the decay which dogs human reproduction and in fighting androids, humans have recourse to technology—the VK test, other tests, the gizmos that Deckard uses in the final combat with Roy Batty and his companions. This is clearly a dangerous move: now it is technology that is entrusted with differentiating between humans and androids, so the ground of the human is more uncertain than ever. And besides, the better Deckard is at eliminating androids, the more he resembles an efficient, inhuman machine himself. It is John Isidore, the 'special', who has to assert some human value, and vital to the novel is the affinity between the retarded but conscientious Isidore and the shadowy entropy fighter Mercer, deviser of a religion of communion in humiliation, revivifier of humble creatures such as toads and donkeys (ch. 2, 23).

In *Valis* (1981), the voice of God speaks out of a collapsed beer can. It is the pot Oh Ho, with its insignificant form and silly name, which expresses divine benevolence in *Deus Irae* (1976) (ch. 3, 45–46), in contrast to the sublime, grandiose mask of the malign Carleton Lufteufel in the atomic

---

Footnote 35 *continued*

—gives way to the repetition, interruption and enclosure of the final episode in the Villa Straylight. By this point the reader knows more than the characters, if only because the Villa is filled with 'ancient' material that she or he recognizes and Case and Molly do not. This movement from Night City to Straylight is also a shift from hyper-motion to regression, incest and stagnation: the world of the Tessier-Ashpool clan. Escape comes via the release of the god in the AI machine, but this is not entirely satisfactory; a possible alternative source of value is in the trashy and bricolaged, so vividly and affectionately detailed in the novel, for instance in the Finn's den. Gibson will pursue this possible value in the AI maker of Cornell Boxes in *Count Zero* (1986), in the eponymous characters in *Count Zero* and *Mona Lisa Overdrive* (1988), and, most successfully, in the Oakland Bridge as collective, bricolaged construct in *Virtual Light* (1993) and *All Tomorrow's Parties* (1999). Very relevant to assessment of this trajectory is Istvan Csicsery-Ronay's continuing series of articles on Gibson and art (1992, 1995).

[36] See Chapter 8 below.

mushroom cloud, though Lufteufel 'himself' also exists in humble human form as a degraded old drunk named Tom who agrees to impersonate Lufteufel (ch. 17, 216–20). The paradoxical instability of entropy seems to breed further paradoxes; analogous is the way in which Mercer is both saviour and fraud.

The little guy, incompetent, social detritus—literally retarded, like John Isidore—is a common source of value and hope. The affinity with the ethos of Christianity, the valuation of the stones that the builders rejected, is clear, and is made explicit in several of the late novels. But so also, it seems to me, is the affinity with the entropic. Both the ground of hope and the horrifying revenge of disintegration begin in rubbish. It is a significant dialectic: beneath and in counter to progress is entropy, but if entropy is the return of a repressed Nature, human or even divine value is also found in rubbish. The difference between a contradiction and a paradox is not always easy to define; here Dick makes use of a paradox close to the heart of Christianity to assert a human, ethical hope. If this is felt to succeed, then we can say that he does bring about an imaginary resolution of real contradictions; but, without asking for positive role models or outcomes, which would be misguided in this case, it is significant that all these personages are marginal to the novels in which they figure.[37]

To test the matter further, it is necessary to shift ground. The rest of this book is concerned with particular novels or stories, though in most cases there is a 'wide angle' section ranging over some relevant area of Dick's output as a whole. The next two chapters consider Dick's imagination of modernity in more concrete detail than has been offered so far. The first considers the non-SF novels he wrote in the late fifties, but did not succeed in publishing at that time; the second considers his short stories, mostly written in the early fifties before he embarked on his career as a novelist. Both of these sets of fictions refer directly to the constitutive institutions of contemporary American society—the family, the suburbs, consumerism, and (in the stories) what is sometimes called the national security state. In the novels the suburbs are the scene of bitter marital dispute, and there is generational conflict as well; consumer goods, and possessions more generally considered, tend to be the source of conflict and fakery rather than of pleasure. Dick certainly pushes, or at least frays, the boundaries of the

---

[37] Jameson's formula has been criticized on the ground that it conflates art and ideology —ideology also involves the imaginary resolution of real contradictions. He escapes from this danger by going further into it: if art is ideological, ideology is utopian, and so therefore is art. Formulations as sweeping as these are not easy to test, but, on the evidence of what we have discovered here in Philip K. Dick, Jameson's formulations do pass. A utopian glimpse comes when the ideology of change and the consequent fear of stagnation are pressed to extremities: out of the entropic, if in a 'weak' form, hope peeps.

realist novel, attempting to find symbolic structures for his bleak view of contemporary life, but he is not entirely successful. The effect is that the characters are imprisoned with a narrow range of things and possibilities, and turn grimly on each other. In the stories, which almost always involve abrupt and radical shifts in reality, Dick does test the possibilities of local and specific resistance to oppression and rationalization—the family, the child, the ordinary individual who balks. The results, again, are not encouraging; more interesting is a recourse to the value of the imagination which, after all, is what powers the stories themselves. Fantasy itself is seen to be subject to the forces that structure and deform society as a whole, but society is seen as the product of organized forces of fantasy. In Chapter 11 I try a different tactic, again ranging over the scope of Dick's novels, but this time isolating characteristic kinds of event in Dick's fiction, and testing how one particular kind of event, the gesture that expresses empathy or solidarity, fares in his narratives. Important in this discussion is *The Transmigration of Timothy Archer* (published after Dick's death in 1982); here Dick in many ways returns to the non-SF novel he had attempted in the fifties, and in a more relaxed spirit, as may easily be seen if we compare the depiction of Angel Archer, the narrator of this novel, to the depiction of any of the female characters in the earlier novels.

Part II

4. Mired in the Sex War: Dick's Realist Novels of the Fifties

In the years from about 1955 to 1960 Philip K. Dick wrote a series of novels that are framed in a style of grim, everyday realism. They are not SF. All concern small-town or suburban life in the forties or fifties; all centre on conflict between the sexes, and the most powerful (*The Man Whose Teeth Were All Exactly Alike*, *Puttering About in a Small Land*, and *Confessions of a Crap Artist*) concern bitter marital conflict.[1] All struggle to attain metaphorical resonance and, simply, narrative excitement, though all are telling, shocking and observant in many passages. None was published at the time—*Confessions of a Crap Artist*, probably the best, and certainly the one that approaches Dick's SF in its offbeat humour, appeared in 1975, the rest after Dick's death. They have not received much discussion and it is not hard to see why. A story by John Cheever, a play such as *Who's Afraid of Virginia Woolf?*, a film such as *The Graduate* compensates the reader for its unsparing depiction of the emptiness and desolation of family life in the contemporary suburbs with some exuberance of language or elegance of form. Noir films and novels from the forties and fifties are at least vividly dark, and tightly plotted. 'Adult' films of the fifties, similarly interested in sexual issues, offer melodramatic confrontations and resolutions.[2]

---

[1] These are not Dick's only 'realist', as distinct from SF, novels. Others include the very early *Gather Yourselves Together* (written c.1948 and published 2000), which Jake Jakaitis has interestingly discussed in relation to *The Man in the High Castle* (conference paper, publication forthcoming), and the late *Transmigration of Timothy Archer* (published 1982). The late fifties novels do share themes, concerns and formal qualities and are therefore worth discussing as a group. The distance between them and *Timothy Archer* may be measured by the fact that the main character in the latter is a much-divorced bishop, and the narrator is the most sympathetic, and warmly rendered, woman in Dick's fiction.

[2] See the excellent discussion by Klinger (1994). Klinger points out that the fifties 'saw an explosion of discussions and representations of explicit sexuality that made sex an aggressively integral part of public life' (141). Dick rather conscientiously works through the issues —abortion, contraception, adultery, alcoholism, hints of paedophilia, problems with restless youth, problems with race—but he struggles with narrative form. As we will see, he tries to make bitter, unresolved narratives of domestic conflict cohere by means of networks of offbeat symbolism.

There are pleasures for the reader of Dick's fifties realism, but not of this liberating order. As for those who enjoy Dick's SF, remembering the amazing inventions, wholesale transformations and menacing exercises of power over reality that are on offer, they may be struck by a glum remark of Leo Runcible: 'When you live small you think small' (*Teeth*, ch. 10, 130). These are novels of frustrated repetition rather than transformation. They offer acrid observations, not startling vistas. (The question of whether these novels do incorporate at least glimpses of larger vistas will be taken up later, in discussions of *Confessions* and *Teeth*.) These novels resemble boxing matches—the characters batter away at each other in a confined space, take a breather, do it again, until we begin to fear brain damage. The fighters are flailing painfully; no one dances like a butterfly and stings like a bee in this contest.

These novels seize on a basic tension in realism, that between metaphor and metonymy, and twist it till it breaks, so that the everyday observation with which realism works becomes observation of empty or abstract objects, neither resonantly meaningful as metaphors nor cohering into useful semiotic systems. This frequently makes the novels telling as critiques of fifties society, and it is notable that they are often directly concerned with sexual sterility (childlessness, fear of impotence, fear of deformity) and that they often feature disputes about unexciting bits of sexual technology (Tampax, diaphragms[3]). But Dick is using a mode of writing that depends on things having a certain meaningfulness and also solidity as things, while suggesting that in this society things lose meaningfulness and thingness: the result is that these novels tend to undermine themselves in critiquing a set of social circumstances that they stubbornly refuse to stand outside of, or transcend.

Yet this conclusion takes us too far, too quickly. For a student of Dick's *oeuvre*, these are fascinating works. Their formal features need a more careful discussion, and so do their historical implications. Both topics come to centre on their depiction of marital conflict.

1. Wide Angle: The Fifties and the Scene of Sexual Contest

Dick's realist novels offer an unsparing dissection—dessication might be a better word—of the failure of the fifties promise of consumer comfort, security, and stability, based on the nuclear family in the suburbs. (A

---

[3] Tampax: *Confessions*, ch. 3; diaphragms: *The Broken Bubble*, ch. 10, 110; ch. 15, 163–64; *Puttering About*, ch. 14, 174; *Teeth*, ch. 12, 165; *Confessions*, ch. 11, 144. Perhaps Dick would have engaged in some pruning of these passages if the novels had been accepted for publication at the time.

promise at the time, a myth in retrospect.) If you are a man, you are supposed to work hard, accumulate consumer goods, and retreat to enjoy
them in the haven of your own home, with your wife and kids. It doesn't
happen here. The job is boring or worrying, home life the scene of frustration and conflict, possessions the counters and props in this scene of
frustration and conflict—not things you enjoy but things you make use
of in the struggle. Private life offers no alternative to the calculation that
may be necessary in one's business. The life of emotions and affections,
which private life is supposed to encourage, is dangerous, destructive and,
above all, confused. Property is no consolation; the house, the car, the
drink in the evening, all these become sources of insecurity or means
towards trickery and calculation in conflicts with spouses or neighbours.

This depiction of the fifties is related to shifts in class and status from
the forties to the fifties—from Roosevelt to Eisenhower, to put it in shorthand. The shifts are carefully delineated in *Puttering About*, where the
young couple Virginia and Roger first move to Los Angeles to profit from
the wartime industrial boom, working in aircraft factories, tired, restless,
doing well as workers;[4] then Roger sets up as a small businessman, and
we witness quarrels over their child's private school, and an affair between
Roger and another parent at the school: middle-class problems. And the
dissection of the failures of the fifties' promise is accompanied by perceptions of the revolt to come in the sixties, among the young, among
women. The coming revolt of the young is rather indefinite in the depiction of Art and Rachael in *The Broken Bubble* (which is in general less
certain about historical setting than the other novels in the series), but is
much more coherent in the sustained, patient tracing of the moods,
demands, rejections of Mary Anne Reynolds in *Mary and the Giant*. Mary
is a kind of James Dean without the swagger, the good lines, and the male
freedom—Dick approaches the revolt of the young from a characteristically idiosyncratic and demythologizing angle. The coming revolt of
women is an element in all the depiction of sexual conflict which is central
to these novels, but most notable in the power of strong, destructive

---

[4] Ch. 7, 82–86. For instance: '[They] lay on the couch or washed a few things, or sat round
discussing what to do with their money, which opportunity to take advantage of. They had
earned their money. The servicemen had begun to return; they had little or no money and
many of them wanted to go to school on the GI Bill, or they wanted their old jobs back—
saved for them by law—or they spent their time with their wives and children, glad to be
able to do that and nothing else. For the warplant workers, something more was required,
something more tangible. They had got used to having something in their hands, some real
object' (ch. 7, 85–86). A.D. Harvey concisely evokes the effect of the wartime boom in
California: 'opportunism, moral disorientation, disillusion and boundless appetite' (1994:
565; he is drawing on the film noir of the period).

women such as Sherry Dombrosio in *Teeth*, and Fay Hume in *Confessions*. (In a more extended discussion of *Teeth*, below, I shall examine how the theme of race is in tension with the depiction of marital and neighbourly conflict that centres on the reactions of insecure men to strong women.)

Dick is good at catching historical changes in class and status because he is completely serious and unsnobbish about the jobs people do (selling real estate, designing packaging, selling used cars[5]); he is good at catching the stirrings of revolt because he has such a feel for inchoate frustration, the way resentment precedes revolt, the way people do what their moods prompt, even though they cannot give a rational account of why they are doing it.

There is clearly something intensely at stake for Dick in his depiction of the conflicts of men and women. We shall observe this in the SF short stories and again in the SF novels; there is hardly any work by Dick that does not in some way express the anxiety that women are adept, competent, ruthless, unnurturing and threatening, while men are fumbling, inept and resentful. But in the novels under discussion the sense that women are cold yet wayward, while men are the prisoners of their emotions and resentments, receives a very thorough dramatization. These novels are really realism filtered through melodrama, with its raw emotions, appetite for confrontation and intensity, and heart-on-sleeve directness, and it is in the confrontations between husbands and wives that the melodrama is richest.[6] We have the hysteria of melodrama, the way repressed or simply thwarted desire is expressed by and on the body, but not its clear-cut division into good and evil, villains and victims.[7]

Other kinds of women, who figure in the SF novels—the mysterious dark-haired girl, or the vulnerable kindly type—hardly figure at all in these novels. Nor do avuncular powerful males like Glen Runciter in *Ubik*. These Dickian types are all, so to speak, ordered out of the ring in the realist novels to clear space for the important contestants. Dick uses a

[5] For instance, Nat's Auto Sales in *The Broken Bubble*, ch. 5, 50–52. Vonnegut (2000: 47–48) and Pynchon (1979: 7–8) will give brilliant, funny impressions of selling used cars; the passage in Dick is not funny or brilliant, but is quite without patronage—there is no sense that writing about this profession is 'sensitive' for a novelist.

[6] One point of reference here is noir fiction. The episode in *The Broken Bubble* in which the outwardly mature and sensible, though unhappy, Pat runs away with the rough young workman Art, and they hole up in a motel, is very like noir, though there is no dramatic heist involved, and the outcome is not violent or doomed. The salient point about noir is that it is startlingly hospitable to grim, doomed pictures of the lives of ordinary people, as Geoffrey O'Brien (1981) has pointed out, and see also Pratt (2001).

[7] On melodrama and hysteria, see Brooks 1976. Relevantly hysterical episodes in the novels under discussion include that of Pat's afternoon painting, issuing in a suicide attempt (*The Broken Bubble*, ch. 18, 203–206; ch. 19, 220–23) and the astonishing party at Carleton Tweany's place (*Mary and the Giant*, ch. 9).

particular kind of scene, a long, wrangling, unstable, inconclusive but hurtful confrontation between (usually) husband and wife, to express his sense of what is happening between men and women—a sense which is, for him, somewhere between an analysis and an anxiety.

His customary procedure is to take a point-of-view character through all the stages of a bitter mood—denial and fairness; self-recrimination, anger, and lashing out; scenarios of different kinds, and responses to those scenarios; mental reservations and concessions—and to have them act on the last of the impulses, without rational relation to or much in the way of memory of all the others. This sense of drifting frailty and instability is acutely caught, and all the characters suffer from it. Then they do something violent (in word or deed) to the other person and that, though unintended, false or thoroughly out of proportion to most of their previous thoughts and impulses, is what crudely attaches them to reality (that is, they transfer the mood to another, the one on the end of their blow or gesture). Meanwhile we infer that the other character, the one who is not the point-of-view character, is passing through the same cycle. All these impulses are uncentred, unstable, and, even in the women with their cool rationality, unsuccessfully articulated. There is always a supplement of gesture—a blow, a touch, eyes averted. We see a good or intelligent impulse rise for a moment, and then be lost, replaced by the mean, bigoted, rationalizing, violent. For example: Leo reports Walt for driving under the influence, causing him to lose his job, which is in effect taken over by his wife. Walt rapes Sherry, and for calculated motives: he reckons that if Sherry becomes pregnant she won't be able to keep the job in which she has displaced him; later, when she does become pregnant, she determines to thwart him by having an abortion, and he succeeds in thwarting that too (*Teeth*, ch. 6, 55; ch. 12, 165; ch. 16, 212–19).

In all this there is no person in the sense of individual connected inner life; continuity of personality is a kind of persisting framework of neurotic or at least shifting, inconsistent and unstable habits, a rough cycle of emotional shifts one might recognize in a given individual. It may be that neither males nor females, though they seem so strongly marked when in these situations of accusation and demand, violence and betrayal, would be anything continuous or coherent were it not for the conflict with the other. There is a hint that to get at another person, to hurt or bewilder them by something one does or says, is to secure recognition from them: you hurt, therefore I am. In these ways, the liberal humanist character is even more bleakly threatened than it is in Dick's SF, and the effect is unaccompanied by a postmodern ontological excitement. Reality—things, houses, cars, neighbourhoods—remains stolidly in place, but dead, seldom warmed by human investments in it.

We have the male as hysteric, as 'feminized', his desires and resentments overbearing his ability to think and argue, so that his resort to violence is itself a sign of defeat. The scene in which Walt rapes his wife begins as an argument over an overdrawn cheque account. It is Walt who registers the strain on his body:

> His hands danced in the air and he clasped them together. They at once separated; he could not keep them clasped. His toes, in his shoes, writhed. His tongue crawled. As if, he thought, my body is breaking up. (ch. 12, 159)

It is Sherry who remains calm and outwardly rational:

> 'There's no use trying to reason with you,' she said. 'You're too emotionally disturbed. When you get this way you're like some sort of animal.' (160)

The woman's power is clear, and sometimes attractive in a tough kind of way (this is true of both Sherry and Fay), but she has nothing much to exert it on, or for. Hence the violence that boils around Fay in *Confessions of a Crap Artist*—a sign of her power, but futile. Sherry is not so lucky; her husband's hysterical weeping clears up, and he engages in a calculated rape.

Of course this, grim as it is, is not the whole picture. A realist novel can be a stream of distinct observations as well as embodying a governing thesis or obsession. There are unpressured passages in which we see men and women inquisitively exploring what it is that the other sex does, their secret business so to speak: Jim Briskin goes shopping with the teenage mother-to-be Rachael (*The Broken Bubble*, ch. 19, 212–13); Sherry Dombrosio visits her husband Walt at his workplace, pokes around, asks questions, then accompanies him and his boss to a baseball game, which is described with an anthropologist's eye, a set of rituals to be recorded rather than explained (*Teeth*, ch. 8, 100–106). Then again, there is a sensitive passage in *Teeth* (ch. 7, 79–80) on how married couples know each other's bodies—a passage that could never occur in the SF works. But the evening at the baseball ends in a fight between the two men, a fight somehow, the novel feels, provoked by the woman's presence; and Walt's sensitive response to his wife's body simply hardens his determination to keep her in her place.

2. *Confessions of a Crap Artist*: Fay Hume in History

The main characters in *Confessions of a Crap Artist* are Jack Isidore, his sister Fay, her husband Charley Hume, and her lover Nat Anteil. Jack is the 'crap artist' of the title, and is the narrator in that his point-of-view chapters are in the first person and he begins and ends the novel with more general meditations on his life and where he has got in it. Further, the story begins when Fay and Charley take him up to live with them in Marin County, and ends when he leaves again, after Charley's suicide and Fay's remarriage, to a young neighbour whom she has seduced. It is Fay, however, who is the challenging character.

Most of the story takes place in the Humes' house, which is important to the whole fiction. *Confessions of a Crap Artist* is a story about people's relations to things: Jack's collections (rocks, milk bottle caps, bizarre 'scientific' facts, cuttings—all an ironic comment on his pretension to be an impartial narrator); Charley's handyman activities, his yard, his property; and, above all, Fay's house, big, expensive, definitely her house rather than Charley's, and a curiously abstract, willed possession at that, because she is certainly not interested in housework or otherwise living in the house.

What is the effect of Jack's presence in the novel?[8] These realist novels, so relentlessly tied to ordinary settings, narrow possibilities and perspectives, are shadowed by a transcendence occasionally glimpsed but always denied. By 'transcendence', here, is meant a larger vista or value than might be open to the point-of-view characters, and also the kind of larger structure of meaning that might be created for the reader by the symbolic connections of elements of the novel—what Yeats called 'emotion of multitude' (see Donoghue 2001: 42). It is the kind of thing that comes about ontologically in Dick's SF—some reality inversion or metamorphosis of perception, or, more likely, a whole set of them, which can be set in relation to the desperate strivings and calculations of the characters whose point of view carries the narration. In the SF, the conjunction of ontological vastness and individual confinement—not just in space but in emotions, relationships, personality—often produces glimpses of terror or insight for the characters, and moments of generosity or mutual kindness. The little guy on whom so much centres is in a big, unpredictable world. What is more, there is a dialectic: the ordinary can be released from its confinement, but, conversely, an ordinariness can be discovered in, for instance, a creature from the intersystem void—and the effect of this is consoling.

Dick continually seeks for equivalents in the realist novels to this opening out in his SF novels. He explores sexuality as granting release

---

[8] Paul Williams in his introduction (12–13) quotes an enthusiastic letter from Dick on Jack as a misunderstood centre of goodness and even saintliness. I doubt that this is accurate, though it would certainly fit Jack's distant cousin J.R. Isidore of *Androids*.

from the narrowness of personality and personal conflict (*Mary and the Giant*, ch. 15, 146–51; *Puttering About*, ch. 17), but sex is very often associated with violence in these novels, which involve several scenes of marital abuse, and several episodes tangling with paedophilia. And sex is almost always associated with the struggle for power between men and women. *Mary and the Giant*, a novel which tends to veer between patient rendition of the main character's changing moods, and scenes of hysterical violence, suggests how music might expand the world for musician and listener, and assembles a varied cast to explore this (a record shop owner, a black pianist, a white folk singer). The result is simply to suggest, however, that we are better people when we play music than after we stop and before we start.

More complex is the possible effect of the strange occurrences and odd things that Dick periodically introduces into these novels; for instance, the Horch (a radio-controlled car) and the bubble of Thisbe Holt (a container for voyeurism at an optometrists' convention) in *The Broken Bubble*. Since there are a variety of episodes involving driving and used car lots in the novel, and the notion of a broken bubble can apply to the relationships the novel examines, the reader is encouraged to read these weird inventions as symbolic, and to be led by them to a sense that the novel is larger as a meaning than the sum of its rather miserable parts (quarrels about diaphragms, for instance). This does not really work in *The Broken Bubble*, although, as we shall see, the subplot involving Neanderthal skulls in *Teeth* is a more complex case.

So is that of Jack Isidore in *Confessions of a Crap Artist*. He collects odd things, he is an odd person. His oddities might well demystify the pieces of property that others live by and fight over in the novel, and his narration, coming as it does from one who is in effect alien in that he lacks sexual feelings, might give us distance from the conflict of Charley and Fay. And to some degree this is what happens. We do suspend judgment on Fay, who can thence become the most compelling of Dick's cold, destructive females, because it is so clear that Jack is not qualified to understand her. The emotional centre of the novel is Fay, her strength, selfishness and vitality, and the presence of Jack does allow for a kind of space around her, so that she becomes something more than a symptom of Dick's anxieties about strong women. She becomes a potential rather than, or as well as, a repetition or mechanism.

As a narrator, Jack has his uses, then, though he doesn't really suggest an alternative to the narrowness of the suburban struggle, but simply an alternative narrowness. As an actor in the story, however, he too is destructive. His blandness, expressed by his pompous autodidact's language ('respiring'; 'empirical verification') is funny, but it is also slightly misleading. We tend to see him as a kooky figure of fun, suggesting an innocent nostalgia for the days when boys read *Thrilling Wonder Stories* and believed in the imprisoned ships in the Sargasso Sea, and in another world inside the earth. (Jack is haughtily superior to his workmates, who merely believe in UFOs and people from outer space.) But during his time at the Humes', his habits come close to corrupting him. This is funny when he blandly reports to Charley that Fay is having an affair, and then, when he gets no response, rewrites it in the style of a bodice-ripping romance. But it is less funny when he allows the group of end-of-the-universe people he is associating with to read his story, and thence let the whole community know about it. It is only in his meditation in the last few pages of the novel that he arrives at that awareness of his own capacity to do wrong, which after all is rather the beginning of life as a moral agent than some admirable achievement.

What is it, then, that Jack both distracts us from and reduces to such glassy blandness that it can be contemplated? It is the Humes' marriage, and in particular the character of Fay.

Fay has a good, sardonic speech in which she notes, 'This is the country. This isn't the city' (ch. 4, 56) and the isolated landscape of Marin County/Point Reyes Station is well depicted, but the combination of affluence, monotony and female isolation is very suburban. Fay is a strong, educated woman,[9] quite unwilling to absorb herself in housework and motherhood. She always gets others to make the breakfast and do the washing up, and is vivid, as well as brutal, on what is unattractive about children:

> A child is a filthy amoral animal, without instincts of sense,[10] that fouls its own nest if given a chance. Offhand I can't think of any redeeming features in a child, except that as long as it is small it can be kicked around. (ch. 4, 54)

Fay uses others; she gets what she wants. She never gives up when she sees her way to this: she gets others to do what she doesn't like doing herself. She gets Jack or Nat to do the dishes even though she thinks men

[9] Wives are usually better educated and of a slightly higher social class than husbands in these novels. This is true of Virginia in *Puttering About* (Roger's business is financed by Virginia's mother) and Sherry in *Teeth*, as well as Fay. Biographically this relates to Dick's marriage to Anne at this time, but its effect in the novels is to suggest a potential in the women, something different from their coldness, rationality and waywardness. The men seldom possess any knowledge that is not useful and practical, but the women do. The men who are exceptions to this rule, Jim Briskin in *Puttering About* (whose ex-wife is a painter) and Joe Schelling in *Mary and the Giant*, are not involved in such bitter conflicts with women.

[10] The text should probably read 'instincts or sense'.

should not do such demeaning things. It is quite possible that she has married Charley (a rough, uneducated man, always talking about how much things cost, but successful in business) in order to obtain the big, burdensome house they live in, which, as Charley feels, is totally her house nonetheless. Having got the house, and a family, she begins to reject Charley and turn to Nat, a more sensitive and better-educated person, though he would not have been capable of earning enough to set up that household. So she is not very nice at all. Yet we can see—at least, we can easily see now, since *The Feminine Mystique*—how her role has trapped an aggressive and vital person in a situation too small for her.

Fay is restless, impatient, coarse, callous, reckless. Everyone, including herself at times, defines her as selfish and manipulative. This is a classic case of the political being the personal, in that she and others ascribe to her character what can be seen as her response to a whole social and cultural predicament. But of course it really *is* her character, she takes responsibility for it as her self, as one must in bourgeois, or any, society, and the novel adapts its narration, in particular of her emotional violence to others and their physical violence to her, in order to accommodate both that and the wider sociocultural, historical determinations.

One interesting thing about the Humes' way of life is that Dick does not take the material comfort (the big house, the property, the space filled with pets and rooms and appliances) for granted. For both Charley and Fay all this is the result of work and willpower, not something that just comes if one is a middle-class person in this time and place. Dick assumes that people need food, shelter, and space, and grab as much of it as they can; this is a kind of survival instinct (a matter to be explored, with dubious results, in the metaphorical structure of *Teeth*). He sees it as part of Fay's strength, as well as selfishness, that she follows this drive. What is fascinating, however, is that Fay has a much more *abstract* relation to her house than either Jack (who loves the housework and the kids) or Charley (who has made the property his own by working on the duck pond and chicken run and so forth). The house is reified for Fay, and this, combined with that fierce drive for survival and shelter, is also a reflection of her historical homelessness, her being a misfit.

Fay is Dick's best account of something that obsessed him, the aggressive, capable woman for whom nurturing has no attraction. She doesn't like children or the conventional aspects of being a wife and mother; nor has she the least interest in comforting and cosseting men. She is a keen gardener, a potter, and an idiosyncratic dresser, and that's about it, as far as conventional femininity is concerned.

But she demands a man; as Nat perceives, with a certain awe as well as horror, she has started an affair with him because Charley is in hospital after a heart attack (which she may well have goaded him into). And she says that the man of the house must be an authority figure, must give the order and rule the house. And she demands the house. She is masterful in getting a man to be her master: not a stable position. She berates Nat for doing the dishes, which a man should not do, though she has made him feel he should do the dishes (ch. 13, 166–69). Yet her changeableness and inconsistency, refinement and coarseness, aggression and compunction is just what fascinates Nat, through whom we see her most impersonally.

The cultural history of the fifties emphasizes propaganda about roles and ideals of femininity; this hardly seems to have affected Fay, or indeed the males in the novel. Fay understands her world in terms of the *male* role and ideal, as if nothing else counted, though her whole personality is making her undermine it. This is not only because she has a strong sense of power; it is also because she realizes that male and female stereotypes are not symmetrical and equal: the statement, 'the man is the breadwinner' has a lot more importance than the statement 'the female is the homemaker', which simply occupies the space left over after the statement about males has been made.

This depiction of Fay as trapped and inconsistent, yet as powerful and effective—indeed, at times, sinister—is the achievement of the book. (The episode in which she gets Charley to bring home a cat that he had befriended at work, then gets rid of it, as if disposing of a rival, is an example of the latter, and is the sort of thing that motivates his plans to kill her [ch. 5, 64–68].) There is a telling scene near the beginning (ch. 3) when Charley, having bought her a packet of Tampax with furious resistance because she won't buy them for herself, hits her for making him buy them, all the while noticing striking things about her—not merely how strongly and decisively she moves, but that there is no one like her for receiving a gift. The scene gives full expression to Dick's misgivings about strong, aggressive women who have no interest in nurturance, and his sense that society in some way encourages this (everything is focused on the woman, she controls the house, it is she whom the advertisers sell to [ch. 11, 139]). Yet it suggests the ways in which this is a historical situation, not just some betrayal or aberration. Fay is so strongly realized in her mannerisms, violent moods, opinions, tricks of speech (Jack notices how Nat picks some of them up after he becomes her lover), that the men's analyses of her selfishness and manipulativeness, which the novel makes very plausible, have a context to be a part of. And both men, Nat and Charley, understand and admire as well as fearing and (in Charley's case) detesting her.

How do the men cope with Fay? Her brother Jack is at his weakest on this point. But then, siblings are like that, and, besides, he is himself thoroughly domesticated: he enjoys cooking breakfast and playing with the kids; he actually lives in the house that she wilfully owns. He is her counterpart, a sign of the arbitrariness of sex roles that is everywhere implied in the novel. The other two are more complex.

Charley is on the verge of violent revolt against Fay from the early scene in which he hits her in the chest for having made him buy her Tampax, and she thinks of leaving him, then does not. Dick's control of the scene's various strands is important for the development of the novel: how Charley should not have done it (quite clear to him); how he couldn't help doing it; how, of course, he got into the situation because he let her make him do this trivial but enraging chore.

But this is not going to be a story about wife abuse. Much of the middle part of the novel is concerned with Fay's toughness and manipulativeness, and with the men's bitter analyses of it, accompanied by grudging admiration. It is not so likely that she is happy with her own power and effectiveness: she is lumbered with her weird brother Jack in the house; Nat as lover and replacement for Charley is a wimp; her feelings about her life in Marin County are mixed; but her point-of-view chapters only give us glimpses of this.

Charley has a heart attack while playing badminton; the episode (ch. 8, 96–99) vividly gives us Charley's sense, which is probably the novel's, that Fay's sheer energy and lack of empathy (she has no interest in people who can't look after themselves) has helped bring this about. While he is in hospital she has an affair with Nat, perhaps choosing him as replacement for Charley, as she and Nat are aware. Charley festers, several times proclaiming very emphatically his intention to kill her when he recovers and goes home. He is so blunt and hysterical that neither we nor the characters believe him, but, sure enough, on the way home he buys a gun and commences to put his plan into effect. He is weak, not yet recovered, and this gives everything a horrible glaze of confusion and infirmity. He clumsily but stubbornly slaughters all the animals (the horse, the sheep, the ducks, the dog); but when Fay arrives home he hasn't the strength left to kill her—he has mislaid the gun, she easily eludes him, and he kills himself instead, feeling in the instant of his death that Fay probably wanted to bring about this result anyway. It is a powerful bit of American Gothic; he even stumbles around after her with a pitchfork. Although the sympathy is with Charley, there is something very poignant about how Fay eludes Charley: at this point, she is not just the woman who had him conned and outwitted all along; she is the living, lithe and full of energy, eluding the dying. So, although the novel would like to share his paranoia about her, it cannot.

To appreciate Fay's aliveness we have to take a step beyond the paranoia about cold women that understandably oppresses Charley. In appreciating it we are in effect recognizing that her coldness and selfishness are not some perversely natural traits (as if to say, this is what women are now like), but historical products. This is what her confined situation has made of her strength and intelligence, though of course that is no consolation either for Charley or for Fay. The strongest and most complex side of the novel is, thus, a thoughtfulness about personality and history in the case of Fay. For all the text's manoeuvres with Jack, this achievement does not take us beyond realism, and there is no reason why it should. The novel observes Fay, her context, personality, actions, effects; the process is compelling because in it Dick is plainly dealing with his own feelings about women, but tough observation is what we get. *The Man Whose Teeth Were All Exactly Alike* is more ambitious, and attempts to devise a symbolic structure for its observations.

3. *The Man Whose Teeth Were All Exactly Alike*: Modern Marriage and Deformed Violence

The most vivid and upsetting scenes in *The Man Whose Teeth Were All Exactly Alike* again depict violent, unsparing, ravelled marital conflict. The plot of the novel, however, concerns a feud between the two couples whose fights with each other are given such sustained attention. This feud is connected with race, and because it involves a hoax Neanderthal skull, it sets going a series of ambiguous racial metaphors. How do the different elements of the novel interrelate? It is almost as though the feud, and the metaphorical structure, centred on race and the fake skull, are linked attempts to escape from that obsessive attention to the battle of the sexes that is so marked in this as in other novels of the series—an attempt to broaden out, to provide a context for the sexual conflict in matters of race, and also class[11] and property. If so, the attempt is not entirely successful, because the scenes between the Dombrosios, in particular, have a dismaying nastiness that nothing else in the novel quite equals. The possibilities are nonetheless very interesting. There is a clash between categories: on the one hand, that of individuality, basis of Dick's humanist values, and on the other hand, race, class, and gender, the factors according to which,

[11] There is an interesting meditation on class by Janet Runcible at ch. 9, 117–19. Not an organized thinker, Janet in fact segues into thoughts on gender roles (Sherry Dombrosio should not work; the Dombrosios are 'Communists'); she relates class and teeth in a way that is not as inconsequential as it looks, given the novel's later interest in fused teeth: 'They have their teeth straightened and worked on as little children. You can tell what sort of background a person has by his teeth, she realized' (118).

in postmodern materialism, all social life is shaped. Yet the novel spirals out of its specific history and social setting; by the end, the ruling metaphor is one of all humans (Neanderthalers, Indians, local pioneers, contemporary characters) as the creatures of deformed but primitive drives.

The feud will concern neighbours in the rather rundown district of Carquinez, north of San Francisco: Walt and Sherry Dombrosio, Leo and Janet Runcible. Walt works in San Francisco for a company that designs packaging; Sherry is of a higher social class than he, and a calmer temperament. She is somewhat like Fay Hume—cold, intelligent, wayward, teasing. She is not satisfied as a housewife, wants a job, and he is threatened by this. Leo, who is Jewish, is a pushy restless realtor, a newcomer to the district, aggressive and full of plans; Janet is depressive, absent-minded, alcoholic.[12] The feud, which is precipitated by an incident involving race and racial prejudice, is unnecessary. The two men are in many ways alike, and the conditions in which all four of them live are very similar; but this means that they produce very similar behaviour patterns —resentment, insecurity, mean lashing out. The conflict grates along for a while as a humdrum neighbourly quarrel, then shifts into an elaborate plot involving the discovery of a hoax Neanderthal skull, and in turn the discovery of the basis of the fake on another kind of deformed skull, which reflects on the more immediate past of settlement in the district, and perhaps threatens its future.

The emptiness of private life in the suburbs, the violence of marital relations: these we meet frequently in this series of novels. As readers, we may well hope that the narrative will grant us some escape from this repetition of neurotic conflict; anything would serve—a murder, the arrival of a handsome stranger, an alien invasion.

The first stages are not promising. After Walt and Leo have quarrelled, Leo reports Walt for drunken driving. Walt loses his licence; Sherry has to drive him to work, which is humiliating for the husband. Then he loses his job and, what is more, Sherry, a competent person, replaces him in it. Walt's revenge on Sherry, by which he regains his masculine self-respect and reimprisons her in the home, and in fact in maternity, is the ugliest episode in the novel; meanwhile, his revenge on Leo ushers in some wider perspectives, and can be connected to the clash between the two men that started the whole imbroglio.

Walt plants a fake Neanderthal skull, on the model of Piltdown Man, in

---

[12] It was remarked above that Dick narrows the range of his female characters in these novels. Janet might be seen as an exception, as one of the soft, vulnerable women whom we meet in the SF novels, like Joan Trieste and Annette Golding in *Clans*; but in fact she is a passive-aggressive person whose manner is confused but whose actions are almost always destructive.

some diggings on Leo's place. He has the skill to do this because of his work in packaging, a form of fakery (ch. 2, 18: Walt and a colleague play at drinking from fake beer cans, and so on). Leo is taken in, hopeful that the discovery will bring him fame and the district publicity and settlers—good for a realtor. But the fake is not a very good one. The experts show easily enough why it is inauthentic, then discover where it came from (the old graveyard for original European settlers to the district), and why the skulls were deformed, the basis in turn for Walt's amateur prehistoricizing. It was something in the water, especially near the old lime kilns. Here many of the 'chuppers' worked (they were early settlers, mostly of Italian descent); thence their overgrown jaws and fused teeth. The experts even find evidence for this, in photos kept by the poverty-stricken remnants still living in the broken-down coastal settlement at old Carquinez. We have a relatively impersonal investigation of clues and places, as in a detective story, punctuated by Leo's bigoted outbursts against the old settlers and their descendants, but then leading to his energetic response (buying up the water company so as to give the community better water and enable future development, which he hopes to finance). This plot, spun out of the feud between Leo and Walt, does provide some clarifying onward momentum and an alternative—at least for the reader—to the ravelled emotional entrapment of the marital scenes. It also serves as a metaphor.

The novel is quite strongly conscious of matters of class, gender and race.[13] It is more explicitly conscious of these possible determinants than were most realist novels of the late fifties (novels concerned with the gritty tensions and everyday details of suburban or small-town life). Perhaps this stems from Dick's background as an SF writer, in that an SF writer has to think of the basic categories of his or her imaginary society and, having formulated them in some more or less schematic way, see what follows from them in the way of social and material detail. Early in the novel, Walt invites Charley Halpin home for the evening. Charley, who repairs Walt's car, is a black man. Meanwhile, Leo is also entertaining that evening—in his case, a rich young couple. He hopes to sell them a house and later to make the man a business partner. Leo's guests see the black man at the neighbours, and suspect the district is not the kind of place they want to settle in. Leo, who is Jewish, responds furiously, and they leave in a huff; but though he would appear to have done well in all this, Leo is in fact disturbed by a variety of emotions, notably his lingering disgust at and

---

[13] There is an important African-American character in *Eye in the Sky* (1957), and Native Americans figure in *Dr Futurity* (1960), as well as in *The Penultimate Truth* (1964). But only in *Teeth*, *The Man in the High Castle* and *Lies, Inc.* is the treatment of race and racial violence central to the structure of the novel.

anger with his wife, who was as usual drunk and distrait when he arrived home, and probably also his anger with himself. (He was planning to sell to his prospective partner at a very low rate, thus bilking the owner of the house who had employed him as realtor, as his wife points out with the sudden violence—'You wicked shit' [ch. 3, 35]—characteristic of emotional life in the novel.) What Leo does next, thus churned, is to ring Walt and abuse him for having lost him a client. (Janet, ineptly trying to be a loyal wife, later follows up by abusing Walt's wife Sherry.) So these two men, bigoted and sexist and unstable in so many ways, but on this evening both honourably enlightened about race, have contrived to get into a quarrel about their behaviour nonetheless. Thence the incident of the drunken driving, Walt's conflict with Sherry, the fake skull planted by Walt, Leo's humiliation when the imposture is revealed.

The upshot mixes up Neanderthalers, early settlers (the deformed 'chuppers' whose descendants survive in old Carquinez) and Native Americans. It is as if all these had come together in the rubbish heaps that people are constantly finding in the district, blended in the mess, the seepage and leakage, that is the district's unreliable water system (highlighted in the first chapter of the novel). The skulls are found with the Indian arrowheads and other artifacts that people are constantly uncovering. The experts say that Neanderthalers probably lived on after modern humans appeared and were even, it may be, enslaved by them or interbred with them (ch. 13, 174).[14] The speculation is made into a metaphor by the fact that, to fabricate his fakes, Walt robbed the old graveyard of skulls that already had Neanderthaloid heavy jaws and fused teeth, though these came from contaminated water rather than from Neanderthal ancestry.

The fake Neanderthal plot has been discussed as a kind of relief from the strains of the depictions of marital conflict in modern Carquinez. The reader can take refuge in historical and scientific detective work. It's the kind of thing that might have enthralled Jack Isidore. But this response is inadequate. There has to be some stronger connection between all this material to do with deformed skulls, stretching back through history to prehistory, and, notably, what Walt is doing to Sherry. He rapes her, making sure that neither of them uses contraception. Then when she finds she is pregnant he thwarts her desire to have an abortion. He threatens to disclose her plan to the police. He will make sure that, becoming a mother, she will have to give up the job she has (in his view) taken from him. He even threatens to sell the car so as to tie her—or both of them—permanently to

---

[14] Dick returns to this idea in *The Simulacra* (1964), in which a group of Neanderthalers is found to be living, and waiting, in the woods of Oregon.

the house.[15] But what if the child of these ruthless manoeuvres turns out to be deformed? The fear is irrational (the bad water that deformed the 'chuppers' is not affecting the inhabitants in general), but it issues in a kind of dream sequence, at the very end of the novel, in which Walt imagines taking their son, not only deformed but retarded, to a 'special' school (ch. 18, 243–49).

The plot concerned with a fake deformity and the discovery of this underlying 'modern' deformity is thereby reconnected with the novel's sense of the neurotic emotional instability of ordinary life. The implication is that the behaviour of the contemporary husbands and wives expresses something different from the strains of life in the fifties or (to quote Janet Runciter), how 'the whole structure of family life has broken down, since World War Two' (ch. 9, 119).

The novel's modern humans, Walt, Leo, Janet and Sherry, are Neanderthalers, in the rough but illuminating sense that they are the prey of primitive uncontrollable emotions, impulses, and violences. The point is no doubt unfair to any actual 'primitives', Neanderthalers, Native Americans, or the simple rustics of old Carquinez; nonetheless it says something brutal but definite about the primitiveness of these realtors and designers of packaging and their wives. Modern humans are unstable, frail, destructive and underhand.

This move back into the archaic is not uncommon in SF, including Dick's SF: examples include the tendency to image races or nations by way of extraterrestrial species, and classes by way of biologically differentiated castes, and the tendency to draw on Earth's imperial or feudal pasts to depict authoritarian or aggressive far future or alien societies, as in Frank Herbert's *Dune* (1965), for instance. Inventing new ways of looking at social difference, power and so forth is what SF is committed to, even if some of these inventions are contentious and others are mere repetitions; the move into the archaic in *Teeth*, whose setting is the known society of contemporary America, has different implications. Like others in the series, the novel keeps banging up against the grim limitations of contemporary life as Dick imagines them: the breakdown of the relations of men and women, the sterility of private life, the abstraction of objects. The implication of *Confessions of a Crap Artist*, as we saw, is that personality— Fay Hume's destructive but compelling personality—is a product of history, and is natural neither to Fay as an individual nor to women in

---

[15] In all this Dick makes skilful use of the car as weapon and pawn in the marital struggle. Also relevant, rather embarrassingly so, is Walt's dream about buying a car—a pink Willys.

'Pink. I wonder why pink.'

'Like a pink jellybean,' he said. (ch. 8, 97)

general. Circumstances in *Teeth* are more complex, because the violence is nastier and the main characters are more intensely intertwined. Dick does invent a set of images that suggests an 'emotion of multitude', a resonating meaning that conforms to the general notion of transcendence that was advanced earlier in the discussion, and this is a feat, given that no free-wheeling transformations and revelations are possible in the world of *Teeth*. But since the images imply that humans are primitive, the move is out of history, out of the world of 1950s America to which this series of novels responds so observantly and toughly.

5. The Short Stories: Philip K. Dick and the Nuclear Family

Fantasy as a genre and the fantastic as a mode have attracted much recent attention. This attention is an episode in the politics of a literary criticism become intensely alert to the menace of ideological complicity that waits on every literary form and critical practice. Liberal humanist criticism is seen as having privileged 'classic realism' and as having practised a mimetic criticism. As the fiction of, for instance, George Eliot both reflects reality and reflects on it discursively, so liberal humanist criticism of Eliot's novels both mirrors the texts, rehearsing themes and moral implications without attempting theoretical distance, and engages in sympathetic dialogue with their moral concerns and lessons (see Eagleton 1983, ch. 1). More recent criticism, on the other hand, privileges the fantastic, which is seen to subvert the ideology behind classic realism, not at the level of theme and social comment, but at the level of form—a ruptured syntax of plot, dismembered characters, a refusal of explanation or closure.[1] There is a sharper split, likewise, between literary text and critical text; the latter does not mirror or attempt to serve the former. The critical text privileges both the subversive irrationality of the fantastic text and its own discursive rigour and theoretical acumen.

Science fiction, as an impure form, often fantastic, but often spelling things out explicitly, presents an interesting challenge here, especially in Dick's case. It might be said that by its adherence to extrapolation and explanation SF ensures that fantasy will always be under final (ideological) control, but the case is more open than that. Dick is a writer who stands at a tangent to the SF of his own time.[2] He mixes parable and fantasy with licentious impurity, and some of the problems and rewards of this emerge strikingly from a study of his short stories, which were mostly written in the period 1952–55,[3] often at the rate of several a week.

---

[1] See Jackson 1981 and Aichele 1997. Aichele opposes 'modern' (realist) and 'postmodern' (destructive of orders of reference and meaning); for him the chosen form of the postmodern is fantasy.

[2] See Chapter 3 above.

[3] Levack (1988: 142–45) prints a chronology, by which one may gauge Dick's rate of production; he was especially prolific in 1954 and 1955.

The directness of these stories might surprise readers of novels such as *Ubik, The Man in the High Castle,* and *A Scanner Darkly*; they are often parables or polemics and their moral/political point is clear, yet, like the later novels, they very often dissolve the texture of reality, hollowing out nightmare worlds into which the 'real' world may be sucked in a few moments, jeopardizing the epistemological confidence that would seem necessary for political judgments and moral actions. At these moments, we are not dealing simply with the marvellous (that which we accept as characteristic of a given fictional world that is different from our own world), but with the fantastic, as defined by Todorov: we don't know what kind of world we are in or which rules to apply. The world-transforming and world-dissolving imagination is at large in problematic ways in these stories. The result is, however, less a dialectical interplay between the demands of urgent political commitment and the energies of radical critique of the grounds of reality, than a fascinating instability and uncertainty.

It is not merely a question of the fantastic as a literary category; it is a question of fantasizing, of imagining, as an activity which is literalized and examined in many of the stories.[4] Dick desires to ground value in the imagination, but is alive to the way in which imagination may serve the powerful and destructive. The opposition between a linear, rationalizing attitude and a free, fantasizing attitude only exists in a particular subset of his stories and is subverted elsewhere (because rationalizing is seen as a cover for destructive or oppressive fantasizing).[5] He desires to ground value in the private life, seat of nurture, affection, creativity, but sees the private life as vitiated by the outside world, or poisoned by women's withdrawal from nurture and creation. The criticism of society that is expressed is friendly to a socialist or feminist reading, suggesting the deformation involved in capitalist social relations and the power of patriarchy, but the values are liberal (affirming the individual's capacity to repair destruction, or to refuse cooperation, to 'balk' as Dick put it[6]). These stresses, between collective diagnosis and individual values, and between valuing the imagination in (some) individuals and seeing it as behind the shaping of social reality as a

---

[4] This is the case with many of the great works of the fantastic and the uncanny, for instance, E.T.A. Hoffmann's 'The Sandman' (1816). The pursuit of refined and exact theoretical accounts of the fantastic and the uncanny has not always acknowledged this aspect of many of the works it takes as examples.

[5] Dick's dealings with what might be called romantic humanism, a belief in the affirmative powers of the individual imagination or prophetic vision, are always complex. The topic is pursued below in Chapters 8 and 9.

[6] Dick in a 1977 interview, reprinted in *The Philip K. Dick Society Newsletter*, 6 (April 1985): 2.

whole, need not yet surface in the writing, because in the short stories Dick can still rely on the trick ending, the final reversal or revelation, characteristic of popular magazine fiction, and because short stories can easily be noncommittal as to whether a character is individual or typical.

The historical context has been sympathetically examined in Barbara Ehrenreich's *The Hearts of Men* (1983): the multiple, unexpected forms taken by the withdrawal of men from the values supposed to underpin capitalist, patriarchal society, a movement of withdrawal under way before the spectacular upheavals of the sixties. But in many of his fictions this context is refracted through Dick's often painful and hostile feelings about women. The origins of these feelings are no doubt to be found in the author's life; two recent biographies (Sutin 1989; Rickman 1989)[7] have begun to bring this tangled story into the light, from the death of his twin sister when he was an infant, to his bittersweet relations with his mother and his wives and women friends. This discussion will, however, focus on other stories, the ones that Dick shaped by using a very inventive imagination; partly, at least, with the effect of illuminating the condition of his own society. When all the psychoanalysis of the life, and of the stories in relation to the life, has been done, insofar as biographers and critics are competent to do it, we still need to understand how this writer shaped (or misshaped) his fictions so as to reimagine the life of his society.

1. Humanness and Fantasy

Two of Dick's stories about typical families will set a framework for the discussion. In the first, 'Human Is' (1955, CS2), a woman is married to the very embodiment of impersonality, bloodless rationality and careerism. The couple are childless. Lester Herrick is repelled by children, finds eating tiresome, is quite humourless. Presumably he is about as much fun in bed as a computer would be. The reader who could warm to this person, or mistake what he stands for, has not been born. As the story unfolds, however, he returns from an expedition to another planet, quite

---

[7] It seems to me that Rickman's biographical interpretations and psychoanalytical speculations highlight how difficult it is to interpret the stories by the life: we are left wondering how one whose life was apparently so painful and bizarre could have written stories which express insight into general social conditions. Either the whole society was to some degree unbalanced—which is distinctly plausible—or Dick's particular history is of less importance to understanding his works than Rickman assumes. (Rickman himself bridges the gap between the mess of the life and the perceptiveness of the stories by heartfelt but unhelpful invocation of Dick's prophetic genius.) Very relevant to the issues raised by Dick's case, however, is Louis Sass's discussion (1992) of the affinities between madness and modernism.

transformed; he is now tolerant and considerate, loves cooking and kids; his speech has changed, taking on a touch of archaic formality which lends it an odd charm, and (as his wife remarks) he now uses metaphors, which he formerly despised as inexact.

The husband's body has been taken over by an alien, a member of an ancient race desperate to escape its dying planet. What should be done about the alien possession, reminiscent of many a paranoid story of the fifties—including some by Dick? In learning the answer to this question we learn more about the society which produced the husband in his former manifestation. The alien must be eliminated: of this the authorities have no doubt. A swift 'vibro ray' to the head will do the job. But before they can act, a legalistic condition must be fulfilled: the wife must witness that this is not her true husband. Fortunately, the alien has merely stored the rest of the husband's personality, so that when the intruder is killed, the husband can be reinserted and the former marriage can resume. (The conditions of the universe in which personalities can be removed and sub-stituted would seem to make it implausible that the aliens would store what they removed and would allow it to be replaced—but who are we to judge this other race in our ruthless terms?) In the climactic gesture of the story, the wife refuses to bear witness. The authorities are powerless, and she and her kindly alien, with their newly adopted child, will live happily ever after.

The story is a parable; humanness is something learnt, or lost, not innate, and the individual can make a difference, for instance by refusing to co-operate with the authorities. But it has elements of fantasy: the world can be abruptly transformed, and the transformation can be literal, not simply metaphorical. 'Lester Herrick came back from Rexor IV a dif-ferent man': this is not to be read as mere phrase, or buried metaphor. And the new, alien but human Lester Herrick learnt his humanity from books: 'The Rexorians have only vague knowledge of human beings . . . The Rexorian idea of Terra is based on centuries old Terran literature. Romantic novels from our past.' The arrival of a new Lester as if by magic suggests wish-fulfilment, but his niceness is the product of *his own* fantasy, that humans are as they are depicted in books—a fantasy that reflects on this story. Nonetheless the new Lester embodies Dick's 'credo' about humanness. 'For me, *Human Is* is my credo. May it be yours.'[8]

Dick was just as emphatic about a later story, 'The Pre-Persons' (1974, CS5), which is equally direct in its morality, and which outraged many readers. To those who were outraged, who included Joanna Russ and Ursula Le Guin, he replied defiantly, in the words of Luther, 'Hier steh' ich;

---

[8] See the story notes contributed by Dick to *The Best of Philip K. Dick* (1977).

ich kann nichts anders.'[9] Because the story is, for better or worse, offensive, whereas 'Human Is' is unlikely to annoy anyone, it is worth discussing its morality and its fantasy, though this entails briefly digressing from our nominated period (the early fifties).[10]

Like 'Human Is', 'The Pre-Persons' is set in an outwardly typical American family and concerns what it is to be a person. In fact it is a ferocious attack on abortion and on women. In the society of the story, a child is not legally a person until the age of twelve, and if a pre-person fails certain tests or is unwanted by his or her parents, then 'abortion' can take place before this coming of age—abortion by vacuum pump, on the model of foetus abortion, in case anyone were in danger of missing the polemical point. This horrible state of affairs exists because women (feminists) wanted it; men have proved powerless in the face of women's withdrawal from nurture and kindliness.

This time the gesture[11] on which the story hinges is the decision of the father of a boy slated for abortion to climb into the truck collecting children for elimination. He offers *himself* for abortion, on the grounds that he cannot pass the tests and is therefore not a person. This action dismays the functionaries who routinely carry out abortions (who are analogized with the functionaries who exterminated the Jews), and with this glimmer of hope the story ends—prospects bleak (Dick redrafted the ending to make it bleaker), moral imperatives brutally clear.

The question of wish-fulfilment presents itself differently this time. If we ask how such a horrible institution as the abortion of twelve-year-olds came about in the world of the story, then we can give two different explanations. One, from the text, is that it came about because women wanted it. The second, from conjecture, is that it came about because Dick wanted it; that is, he wanted to give literal, aggressive expression to his conviction that when a foetus is aborted a person is killed, so he made those to be aborted in the story undeniable, twelve-year-old persons; he harboured many hostile and troubled feelings about women, so he ascribed the institution to women. It is not necessary that polemic be subtle or civil; polemic

[9] See the story notes contributed by Dick to *The Golden Man* (1980); 'An Open Letter to Joanna Russ', *Vertex*, October 1974; and the letters to Joanna Russ and Mike Bailey in *The Selected Letters of Philip K. Dick 1974* (1991: 243, 258–59, 269).

[10] Abortion is, however, treated in the non-SF novel *Teeth* (discussed in the previous chapter). Sherry is in conflict with her husband Walt; she has in effect taken over his job; he rapes her, she attempts to procure an abortion—so that she can keep her/his job, it may be —and he prevents this; as the novel ends they are awaiting the birth of the child which might possibly (for reasons unconnected with their actions) be deformed. A complex matter, rather brutally handled by Dick.

[11] The place of gestures (incidents involving impulsive kindness or commitment) in Dick's later novels is examined in Chapter 11 below.

may gain its power from repudiation of subtlety and civility as no more than the masks that hypocrisy wears; we cannot, then, object to the story's polemic style. But SF gives its author very great scope for such wholesale and abrupt rearrangements of contemporary consensual reality, and if we disagree that the movement to allow abortion stems from women's withdrawal from nurture and kindliness, then this scope begins to seem a loaded matter, one whose ramifications are worth examining. Even the humane Ursula Le Guin begins *Always Coming Home* (1988 [1985]) by abolishing most of humanity, a frightening way to open space for an utopian, unaggressive community based on dance and handicraft, as she knows, since in *The Lathe of Heaven* (1973 [1971]) she had set up a world in which a character solves the population problem by an act of effective imagination, by which most people are obliterated. (*The Lathe of Heaven* concerns a man whose dreams come true, literally; he and his dreams fall into the hands of a destructive psychiatrist/social engineer.) This does not mean that *Always Coming Home* has the same qualities as 'The Pre-Persons', but it does remind us that in SF the author reimagines worlds, and also shows us other people—perhaps perniciously—reimagining worlds.

2. Wide Angle: Sterility of the Society of Production

This reflection opens the way for a re-examination of Dick's earlier stories. We may begin to see how Dick construed abortion as poisoning the springs of creativity, always threatened by the conditions of modern society, and often flowing with an intoxicating liquid anyway—and this fear becomes especially urgent when we consider that the social setting of 'The Pre-Persons' is the nuclear family, itself a threatened and precarious source of value in Dick's eyes. Dick's social thinking was bound up with thinking about fantasy and other modes of creativity, and how precarious or dangerous fantasy can be. (Here 'fantasy' refers not to the genre, or to the mode—the fantastic—but to an orientation or an exertion of desire in the subject.)

There is a difference between telling stories and, for instance, making up scenarios of future wars in the course of developing weapons—but there is also a similarity. There is an important difference between fiction and myth, if, as Kermode suggests (1967: 38–39) a myth is the kind of thing you try to enact in the world, as the Nazis did with their anti-semitic myth—but there is also a similarity. Dick's stories reflect on these dangerously blurred boundaries. Imagination may make new versions of the world, and worlds are remade, unmade, infiltrated and subverted every couple of pages in Dick's fiction, but this is seldom a game, exhilarating as it is for the reader to catalogue the dazzling reality inversions of a story such as 'We Can Remember It For You Wholesale' (1966, CS2). There is always a value at stake and, at the same time, imagination is repeatedly the threat to that value, for it is the imagination of the evil or sterile that produces the world that cries out for remaking.[12]

It is remarkable how often sterility is a threat or a condition in Dick's stories. This is something that was touched on in discussion of the pervasiveness of stasis in his fiction, and it is most obvious with those stories, common in his output of the early fifties, which treat war and power. These are strongly anti-militarist and anti-capitalist stories. The setting is almost invariably a sterile wasteland, composed of slag, ash, trash, rust, the pulped, undifferentiated residue of a civilization which has destroyed itself and now nourishes nothing. Here all that survive are a few soldiers, tough but radically unsure of what is going on or whom they really ought to be fighting ('Second Variety',1953, CS2);[13] or robots, supposedly doing the fighting on behalf of a humanity forced underground by radioactivity and the destructiveness of interminable technowar ('The Defenders', 1953, CS1); or a giant gun, still relentlessly defending a civilization that no longer exists ('The Gun',1952, CS1). In these stories, the real enemy is hypertrophied technology and the attitudes that give it power. The earth's natural resources have been destroyed or depleted, while technology not merely survives this process, but waxes more dominant. Thus we have societies that can produce self-reproducing robots, or androids outwardly indistinguishable from people, or (to draw examples now from the later novels) weapons that have a 'tropism' for human brain waves, or robot taxis that have a tropism for a customer, while the surviving humans have to make do with ersatz coffee, revolting synthetic pap for food, tacky clothes. In the later novels in which this vision of a technologically advanced, materially destitute society finds more detailed expression, it is often the case that most people are sterile, or that the elite is sterile (*The Penultimate Truth*, 1964), or the handful of humans left alive are mostly sterile so that the prospect of a baby is a matter of luck and an occasion for celebration (*The Game-Players of Titan*, 1963).

It tends to be the sterility of men that is more emphasized. Thus in *Androids* Rick Deckard checks his lead codpiece (for protection against radioactivity) before venturing from his apartment to hunt androids, which society *can* reproduce with dazzling efficiency (ch. 1, 10). Indeed,

---

[12] See Mackey 1988: 14: the 'real' world is actually the product of the mind that has the strongest idea.

[13] They find themselves fighting androids frighteningly indistinguishable from, significantly, young women and little children. The space between the public world of warfare, occupied by males and machines, and the private domestic world in which we expect to find women and children, is obliterated—a topic that this chapter revisits below.

to return to the short stories, in 'The Last of the Masters' (1954, CS3) the focus is on the sterility of a robot with a male name, Bors. In the future sketched by this story, advanced technology has been wiped out by an anarchist revolt everywhere except in a secluded valley where a super-robot organizes and maintains a replica of the old civilization. The humans he rules are totally dependent on him, rusting and out of sorts as he is, and when he ceases to function his achievement will perish with him. (He is destroyed at the end of the story.) It is not clear why he does not replicate himself, or educate his human servants: it is simply a given that he is sterile. The old, technologically advanced, highly organized civilization is a civilization of production, but now under Bors it can do no more than maintain itself.

The stories repeatedly present a society in which everything delicate, artistic and domestic has disappeared, in which problems, replicating like mutants (or literally as mutants, as in 'The Golden Man', 1954, CS3) are met with violence, in which society is organized in a state of war tension and war urgency. Given this, it is interesting that Dick never suggests at this stage of his career that the 'feminine' side of life offers some sort of recourse. The reasons for this will be considered when the stories with a domestic setting are discussed; meanwhile it is worth noting what sort of recourse is sometimes suggested in stories dealing with hypertechnology, or, more generally, with production.

In 'The Variable Man' (1953, CS1) 22nd-century society is dependent on a set of vast computers (called SRB machines) incessantly calculating the odds of victory in a war against an alien planet which blocks Earth's expansion into outer space. The humans who rule (we meet two main characters, one evil, one less evil) have evidently lost their capacity to invent and develop technology; we see this from the evil character's rigid faith in the SRB machines and his recourse to mega-violence (pulverizing a whole mountain range to eliminate one man), and from the less evil one's erection of a paranoid proliferation of weapon systems to protect himself from the first, his rival. He is directing work on a 'faster than light' bomb for use against the aliens, but this cannot actually be completed because no one can understand the wiring. Nevertheless the computers indicate that earth now has the edge over the aliens, because of the nearly complete FTL bomb.

The situation is thrown open by the arrival of the 'variable man' (so called because he throws calculation of the odds into disarray, he is the unpredicted variable), a handyman inadvertently time-scooped from the early twentieth century in the haste of war preparation. This man is a natural fixer; he fixes a child's toy, by instinct, though quite ignorant of its electronics, and is then used to complete the weapon's wiring. He does this just before the evil figure, having failed several times to eliminate him, eliminates the less evil figure's laboratory complex in a big, hyper-technological battle. These episodes of destruction certainly make the point about the mindless crudity of violence fuelled by overdeveloped technology; meanwhile, the variable man has rewired the missile so that it may carry a human rather than a bomb, thereby transforming the whole situation. Earth will no longer need to fight the aliens to reach outer space. (The parable is what is important here—there is no particular attempt to invent plausible technical details.)

In considering Dick's short stories, we could speak both of an anxious questioning of the human basis or centre for society, and of an exuberant breaking open of the category of the human. According to the latter possibility, it might seem woefully dull to speak merely of men, women and children as human when there can be robots, mutants, androids, aliens, elves, speaking taxis, intelligent dogs, grimly astute spiders, a male animate shoe seeking out, animating and reproducing with a female shoe, a set of small creatures who incarnate Bach's Goldberg Variations, and so on.[14] It is true that all these life forms are anthropomorphic, but also true that it is this that enables them to replace or compete with the 'conventional' humans in some way or other. And they all seem to have the capacity for moral agency and the making of life choices. But it is the way of questioning and, if possible, reaffirmation that is taken, not that of playful celebration. 'The Variable Man' reaffirms the single human centre, the ordinary American (from 1910, the age of Edison) who can fix things in a time in which technology has become destructive and out of human control.

'The Variable Man' is one of several stories in which technology is rehabilitated from within, by the rediscovery of the virtues of tinkering (as in 'The Turning Wheel',1954, CS3), or of the value of making rather than replicating, as in 'Pay for the Printer' (1956, CS3). 'Pay for the Printer' is another story[15] treating the dependence of consumers on processes of production of which they have lost control through ignorance. In this case the humans peevishly depend on benevolent aliens called Biltongs, who can replicate ('print') but cannot make, and who have now become exhausted and sterile, worn out by what were originally efforts to save humanity from the consequences of nuclear holocaust. (The Biltongs

[14] Elves: 'The King of the Elves' (1953, CS1); taxis: 'We Can Remember It For You Wholesale' (1966, CS4), *The Game-Players of Titan* (1963) and *The Unteleported Man* (1966, later published as *Lies, Inc.*); dogs: 'Roog' (1953, CS1) and 'Adjustment Team' (1954, CS2); spiders: 'Expendable' (1953, CS1); shoes: 'The Short Happy Life of the Brown Oxford' (1954, CS1); Bach: 'The Preserving Machine' (1953, CS1).

[15] See also 'Autofac' (1955, CS4), discussed in Chapter 9, and later in this chapter.

were first drawn to earth by the flashes of the holocaust, visible from outer space, and then set themselves, with kindly intent, to preserve the natives' way of life by 'printing' their artifacts.)

At the end of the story, one of the human characters makes a crude, amateurish cup, without recourse to a Biltong, and this is a sign that civilization can remake itself, the hard way. Technology is reconnected to 'hands-on' labour, and to craft, as distinct from science, in that repairing or making of this sort is a matter of trial and error and 'feel', not abstract reason and standardized process.

The existential significance of repairing seems to be that it implies a dedication to maintaining the 'individual' industrial product, and breaks the circle of endless replication of exactly similar, standardized products. In Dick's imagination products of this sort (that is, of the assembly-line industrialism which is most appropriately worked by robots, standardized machines making standardized machines, as is often the case in SF stories) do not really exist, because they lack individuality, since each can merge in or be replaced by a designedly identical item. That is, his objection is not merely on social grounds, the point that this process disempowers consumers, and even technocrats, by making them dependent on a process of which they have become entirely ignorant, or which has become homeostatic. It is also on existential grounds: this process violates some fundamental law which any reproduction ought to follow, whether it be of people, or androids, or goods. Production and procreation ought to follow the same laws, at least in this respect; a humanist idealism, extended in fact beyond humans, beyond animals or works of art, to demand individuality even for manufactured things, comes into collision with the material conditions of modernity.[16] A thing can't be a real thing unless it is in some sense an individual thing. And thus the repairman or maker who restores thingness to industrialism is himself an individual, a variable man who disrupts abstract calculation, a quirky ordinary guy who refuses to go along with rationalizing power. (He also tends to be a figure from the past, suggesting that the 'hands-on' worker or artisan is now outmoded. This is something that is pursued in grim, passionate detail in Dick's late novel, *A Scanner Darkly*, in the context of a postmodern erasure of differentiation.)

It is interesting to compare Dick's thinking here to that pursued in Octavia Butler's *Dawn* (1987). In *Dawn* the human survivors of massive

---

[16] Dick is here strengthening what Slusser (1992) has called 'the Frankenstein barrier', which SF has erected because of its fear of the consequences of tampering with nature. Since he is concerned with the making of things as well as humans or sentient beings, his position is, however, interestingly radical and sweeping.

planet-wide destruction are rescued, re-educated and (eventually) re-bred by the alien Oankali, whose civilization, ethically challenging and probably superior to that of humans, is centered on biomodification of the most intimate and indeed erotic kind, and allows absolutely no place for technology, so that tables, beds, bowls and so forth are all grown, all organic. There exists almost nothing in Oankali civilization that is made and is therefore a dead, manipulable or instrumental thing. To this critique of technology Butler joins an imagination of the possibility that humans might need to abandon their humanity by interbreeding with the Oankali and becoming part of a new race.[17] Dick, writing in the fifties, still imagines the possibility of a humanly affirmative making, an individual person creating or fixing an individual thing, but he tends to set the matter in a nostalgic frame: more a memory than an agenda.

3. Fragility of the Nuclear Family

Individualism, the basis of liberalism, is thus offered as the only hope in several of these grim, post-apocalypse stories, and not only by the decisive actions of some lone hero, but also by the stories' implications about the existential bases of thingness. The short stories whose setting is closer to home are, however, even less confident. The domestic is the scene of consumption rather than production, separated from the centres of power and decision. In this setting, the existential meagreness of everyday things is approached differently. In the stories whose setting is a war-wrecked earth or a sterile, hypertechnological future, the main characters can hardly not know that their surroundings are appalling and they are powerless. In the domestic or small-town stories the main characters are specified as cursorily as their homes, towns and jobs, and that is a sign that they are not sufficiently differentiated from them to be able to know them.

In 'Breakfast at Twilight' (1954, CS2), a typical family (husband just about to set out for the office, kids just about to set out for school, wife ready for a day in the kitchen and living room), gathered round the breakfast table in small-town America, is abruptly precipitated forward in time. The McLeans discover ash and radiation filling the familiar streets: their town has almost been obliterated by bombardment (not surprising, as the bombardment is so severe as to have opened the space-time crack through which they have tumbled). Their society has been transformed: all is organized for the war effort, children separated from parents, wives from husbands; books burnt, edible food scarce, people's minds narrowed and

---

[17] See White (1993) on XENOGENESIS, of which *Dawn* is a part, in the context of a postmodern imagination of 'the post-human body becoming'.

nerves stretched by war tension. The success of the story is the meeting of the family from contemporary America and the soldiers and official from the near future, from whom they learn what life is like now—for the time is only seven years hence.[18]

Although the two societies are totally different, they are close and connected, so the reality of each is jeopardized. Each society seems so all-encompassing to its denizens as to be 'normal', and both parties are right, since peaceful domestic life is—must be—normal, yet bureaucracy and war have to be recognized as contemporary normality. Both are wrong, too: the contemporary suburban life is narrow and illusory (power is elsewhere), the future life is straitened, lived in a mist of uncertainty. (In this context, as so often in Dick, the question of what is real cannot be distinguished from the question of what is good, since terms such as 'normal' or 'natural' encompass both.[19])

The story gives imaginary shape to the contradiction that we find ourselves living—and does little to resolve that contradiction (along the lines of Althusser and Jameson's formula). Mary, Tim and their kids make their escape back to their own time by utilizing the same time-warp that flung them out of it, but they cannot warn their neighbours what awaits them in a mere seven years. Tim fumbles over the words, no longer certain what is real. A neighbour suggests that the wreckage of their house (caused by the future bombardment) must be due to the explosion of their furnace, and they can only agree.

Very many of Dick's short stories demonstrate the instability of their deliberately unremarkable settings. Stories of this type begin with a standardized version of the small town and small family which is supposed to be the Rockwellian repository of stable American values—values antedating standardization and deriving their authority from that fact. There is the husband, there the wife; here is the city hall, here the gas station. Being SF, this is literature of ideas and extrapolations rather than literature of highly individualized characters, after all; individuality of character is a mere convenience, signified by giving the main character a distinct name, though in thousands of SF stories he is the same undifferentiated person (young, white, middle-class male of average opinions). But in the Philip K. Dick stories of this type everything dissolves around the main character almost as soon as it is sketched in. Because everything is typical, standardized and immediately specified, it hardly exists. It may be dissolved,

---

[18] The headnote to the original magazine publication makes an interesting mistake here, announcing that the interval is a hundred years; this is what it 'ought' to be, since the change is so great (*Amazing Stories*, July 1954).

[19] I owe this point to my student Gerard Wood.

invaded, subtly infiltrated and modified, pitched forward or regressed in time, discovered to be a fabrication. It is monotonous, uniform, transient and precarious. The moment of dissolution is often described, always horrifying (even when, as in 'Adjustment Team', the purpose behind it is benign—indeed, in that case, divine); it is almost always seen in the same way, as a matter of melting, thinning, wavering, so that the substance of things and even people loses body and you can see through, poke a hand through, sink into it. This is the realm of the 'metamorphosis' that Rosemary Jackson sees as a key and subversive element in the fantastic. It is uncanny: the homely becomes unhomely.[20] No doubt the catch is that the homely never was homely: as far as the stories are concerned, there never was a distinct, autonomous private life, lived from out of its own centre—lived from a production that was independent of what prevails in the wider society (procreation of babies rather than production of commodities, to put what is missing in shorthand formula).

This lack of the domestic and private is common in Dick's fiction: it is noticeable because his novels and stories so often begin from a family, a 'conapt', a bed in which the main character has been sleeping and is now awakening (see Fitting 1992b), but establish at once that this family, home and bed do not occupy a private space. They are pre-occupied by technology; they are shaped by competition, usually between husband and wife (the marital wrangle which begins *Androids*, and which concerns the role of the Penfield Mood Organ, sums it up neatly, as well as being funny), but reflecting the behaviours of the wider society. Sleep itself is not one's own. *Lies, Inc.* begins with a dream which seems personal to the dreamer in classic Freudian fashion, because it is about his father ('Abba'), but which is a technological intrusion into his psyche, a broadcast he was not supposed to receive.

All this is not solely true of Dick's short stories; it is worth bearing it in mind when the works of the sixties and later are considered. The later works involve a sustained attempt to imagine some other space of the private. The means used is very often drugs, and here Dick borrows directly from the counter-culture of the sixties—but with the effect of redoubling that lack which he had already imagined, because the drug trip is a trip into a more hectically dissolving version of the public space which already oppresses you if you leave your conapt. Fredric Jameson compares the fifties and sixties in the context of the history of the postmodern:

---

[20] See Freud's 'The "Uncanny"' (1985 [1919]), and numerous commentaries on this essay, for instance that by Jackson (1981: 63–72), and the essays collected in *Para.doxa*, 3, 3–4 (1997), *The Return of the Uncanny*.

Thus the economic preparation of postmodernism or late capitalism began in the 1950s, after the wartime shortages of consumer goods and spare parts had been made up, and new products and new technologies (not least those of the media) could be pioneered. On the other hand, the psychic *habitus* of the new age demands the absolute break, strengthened by a generational rupture, achieved more properly in the 1960s. (1993: xx)

In Dick, however, we see that an enthusiastic embracing of at least some aspects of the new *habitus* only reaffirms what he had already conveyed: the sixties are even more emphatically homeless than the fifties. But there is more to be said of small-town life in Dick's short stories of the fifties.[21]

The setting of 'The Hanging Stranger' (1953, CS3) is a small town with typical buildings and stores, tired hurrying commuters. The main character, accidentally late for work, discovers a corpse hanging from the lamppost in the town park, and then discovers that no one among his fellow townsfolk will acknowledge that it is there. He learns that this is because his fellow townsfolk are now possessed by, or have become, insectoid aliens—he sees the creatures descending in 'a cone of gloom', 'a prism of black' over City Hall before merging with the citizens. Yet as he looks again, the people are the same: 'Dulled, tired faces. People going home from work. Quite ordinary faces.' The rest of the story concerns how he makes it home, attempts to tell his family but has to kill one of his children when he realizes it is an alien, escapes to a nearby town, tells his story to the local police—and is then led out to hang from the lamppost of that town's park, to serve in his turn as a lure to expose anyone who (like himself at the beginning of the story) has accidentally been missed in the alien takeover.

When the main character discovers that his fellow citizens are indifferent to the hanging stranger, he discovers that those who had seemed as typical as himself are insect aliens, 'Pseudo men. Imitation men', so that the typical reveals its meaning as hollow. People are interchangeable and therefore prone to follow group feeling, because they are without stable standards independent of the group ('There must be a good reason, or it [the corpse] wouldn't be there'). So far we connect the parable to social injustice—witch hunts or lynchings. The injustice cannot be redressed because no one will admit it has happened. But the broader implication of

---

[21] Chapter 7 returns to the relations of the fifties and the sixties. The focus will be on Dick's imagination of consumption, and it will again be seen that he elides the differences between the two periods; just as he cannot imagine a real private space in the fifties, so he cannot imagine the sixties as a decade of consumer abundance.

the story is that we are ready to be taken over, or have already been taken over. The process itself has no intrinsic interest (the depiction of the aliens is unremarkable horror stuff) because it is merely the consequence of our readiness to be taken over. And it is appropriate to the story's pessimism that it has a circular form, and the individual through whom we saw everything is eliminated at the end, becoming another hanging stranger. The main character was merely part of the aliens' operating procedure, and merely helped Dick to tell the story; his resistance to what happened to the rest of the community offers no hope. In the final paragraph another man who had been overlooked is lured out to identify himself by his horror at the main character's corpse, to which everyone else is again indifferent.

Dick's sense of the precariousness of typical American life is free-floating; the important thing is that the precariousness itself be demonstrated, that we see how open to takeover, infiltration, dissolution or 'adjustment' this life is, and that it is drably typical, as in other SF stories and films of the fifties: there is no special place or agent of horror such as the House of Usher or Count Dracula. 'The Commuter' (1953, CS2) treats the main character's discovery that a suburb, complete with its own railway station, neat tree-lined streets, drug-store where the local teenagers hang out, and so on, has been inserted into his city without anyone's awareness. The means by which he stumbles across this is vividly depicted (a typical peevish nondescript clerk tries to buy a ticket to a station that does not exist, and the main character is alerted by this incident); so are the consequences (when he returns from his visit to the inserted suburb he observes buildings on his own street which he is not sure existed before, when he gets upstairs he finds a wife and baby where formerly there was a girlfriend); but the 'explanation' is a mere gesture (something to do with a rejected plan for a new housing development which has evidently gone ahead anyway) and there is nothing uncanny about the suburb itself. The instability and thus permeability of ordinary 'reality' is the point, not the explanation the story offers.[22] The explanation is as unexceptional, both in genre terms and in terms of the given society, as was the process needing explanation.

There is no equivalent in the suburban or domestic stories to the repairman or craftsman who sometimes offered hope in the stories dealing with hypertechnology. The main character usually has an undefined job as a

---

[22] Other SF stories of the 1950s also treat the possibility that an alien existence can be inserted into quotidian American reality, for instance Frederik Pohl's 'The Tunnel Under the World' (1954), A.J. Deutsch's 'A Subway Named Möbius' (1950), and Jack Finney's 'The Body-Snatchers' (1955); but in these cases a serious, and often an ingenious, explanation is offered.

functionary in an office or store, and all he does in his story is discover and perhaps himself fall victim to the reality change. If anyone achieves something more hopeful it is, as we shall see, neither a man nor a woman but a child.[23]

So it is in 'The Father-Thing' (1954, CS3), an aliens-are-amongst-us horror story whose setting is domestic. A young boy, Charlie, discovers that he has two fathers, the ordinary decent human one and a horrible alien one, denoted by chitinous hard eyes and the clear intention of getting the child into the garage and devouring him, so that he may be replaced by a 'Charlie-Thing' of approximately the form and morals of a large maggot. (This is what has happened to Charlie's 'natural' father, whom the alien is imitating, so that the first impression was that Charlie's father was having a bad day, not 'being himself' very well.) Charlie arrests the process of infiltration in an interesting way: he calls upon two of his peers, one the local bully and tough guy, Tony Peretti, the other Bobby Daniels, 'the little coloured kid' who is 'good at finding'. Together they locate the aliens, and destroy them with several gallons of kerosene.[24]

'The Father-Thing' hovers between metaphorical and literal; early in the story Charles is worried because his father is out in the garage 'talking to himself', and so he doesn't know which one to tell to come to supper. There are literally two fathers out there. By the time Charlie and his peers kill the monstrous grub, the 'real' father is gone forever (just as the 'real' Lester is gone in 'Human Is'); however, insofar as the monstrous grub is a metaphor for the way one's father can sometimes seem, frizzling him with kerosene is not a proper solution. It is true that if we choose to read it as a revenge fantasy, stemming from Dick's feelings about his own father, then this issue does not arise, since revenge must simply have its course; but the success of the story is in its depiction of young Charlie as an ethically responsible person, and in this respect 'The Father-Thing' mixes the fantastic and the ethically discursive. In fantasies, characters tend to be

[23] In Dick's novels, the main character is very commonly married, but the marriage is invariably embittered and usually childless. A very interesting exception, *Martian Time-Slip*, is discussed in Chapters 8 and 9 below; a group of late novels, *The Divine Invasion*, *Valis* and *Radio Free Albemuth*, also involves children, but in the first two of these the children, Emmanuel, Zina and Sophie, are gods, albeit amnesiac or impaired—and in *Martian Time-Slip* Manfred is autistic. The child is potential saviour or seer, and in this the novels are like the stories; but he or she is outsider, decentring notions of the human. The opening episode of *Frolix 8* is closer to the short stories: a father tries, and fails, to protect his son from a bureaucratic and heartless society that will consign the child to the social dustbin on the basis of a faked test result.

[24] The version of the story published in French in 1956 adds a final sentence to the effect that elsewhere another beast is crawling into a refuse dump to await its opportunity: the story is thus made circular, like 'The Hanging Stranger' (Levack 1988: 95).

driven, by the author's desires and their own, rather than being agents; by asking 'What is to be done, what recourse is possible?' Dick is not only looking for ways to bring his stories to a close, but also challenging the process of fantasy.

'The Father-Thing' and 'Human Is' could be seen as counterparts, one treating an evil substitution, the other a benign one. Dick often works in this way; for instance 'The Defenders' and *The Penultimate Truth* (1964) offer contrary versions of the situation in which the bulk of humanity is driven underground while others pretend that war still rages on the surface, though peace has long since resumed. In one case the pretence is benign, in the other it is malign. This could be described as 'dialectical'[25] thinking, but there is no synthesis, nor a negation of the negation. The fantasy could go either way, and this suggests both that fantasy is free, and that actuality is frighteningly exposed to manipulation, because, in the long run, actuality is produced by fantasy (and the political question is, whose fantasy?).

In 'Authority and the Family' (1972), Max Horkheimer argues that the family tends to replicate the structure of authority that prevails in society as a whole, and to serve as society's way of imposing its norms on the growing individual (who, for instance, interprets the father's power and money as reality, as how things are, and begins to learn to accept broader social arrangements as reality in the same way). But he also suggests that the family can sometimes protect its members or serve as a source of solidarity against the rest of the world. It doesn't necessarily operate as does the rest of society—by competition, by the notion that you are to be valued by the amount of money, power and success you have—but may try to live by love and co-operation. More recent accounts of society and the family suggest that the division between the public, individualist, competitive male world and the private, co-operative female world of the home places impossible burdens on the latter, and on men and women, who are forced into rigidly demarcated roles.[26]

Many of Dick's stories ask whether the family works to protect its members from the harsh inhuman pressures of the rest of society, or to impose on them the values which rationalize those pressures ('rationalize'

---

[25] This is Patricia Warrick's overall interpretation of Dick's fiction (1987).

[26] See Coontz 1992: 52–65. As we saw in the previous chapter, Dick's non-SF novels, written in the late fifties, offer a similarly grim interpretation of the plight of husbands and wives, the wives trapped in the home, the husbands unsatisfied by their jobs, the wives tending towards coldness and calculation and the husbands towards hysteria. Dick's interpretation has behind it some thinking about changes in social conditions and gender relations, as can be seen most clearly from *Puttering About in a Small Land* (1987, written c.1959), which takes Roger and Virginia from the war years to the early fifties.

in the psychological and the Weberian sense). This is why the stories often focus on fathers' relationships with their sons. A militarist, aggressive society cannot reproduce itself unless the males who are to do the competing and fighting learn the appropriate values from their fathers. 'The Father-Thing' is one of a series of stories exploring whether children will be destroyed by their parents, or their parents' values, or will be able to save themselves (or, in the case of 'Project Earth' [1953, CS2], the human race itself); others include 'The Cookie Lady' (1953, CS2), 'Tony and the Beetles' (1953, CS3), 'Jon's World' (1954, CS2), 'A World of Talent' (1954, CS3), 'Foster, You're Dead' (1955, CS3), and 'The Pre-Persons' (1974, CS5).

'Tony and the Beetles' and 'Martians Come in Clouds' (1954, CS2) both begin with angry scenes between hard-boiled fathers and their young sons who, they fear, may be too soft; both culminate in the destruction of innocent non-humans. In the first, the father worries that Tony enjoys playing with the 'beetles', as they are chauvinistically called (their correct designation is 'Pas-udeti'), offspring of an alien race which Terrans have subjugated in the interests of trading dominance. When Tony persists nonetheless and visits the alien city as usual, accompanied by his robot servant, he finds that his beetle playmates have themselves become chauvinist and aggressive, encouraged by recent news of a victory over the Terrans. The upshot is not that Tony changes also (he is simply left bewildered); it is that the other life-form present, the robot servant, is cruelly dismembered by the aliens.

'Martians Come in Clouds' begins with the father worrying whether his son could cope were he to encounter a 'buggie'. Strange, apparently sentient but passive aliens have started floating to earth from outer space, and of course they must be exterminated as quickly as they are detected. The child does meet one, at dusk in a suburban street; the shapeless thing is helplessly caught in a tree. As he stands there, uncertainly, it communicates to him, in a very intimate way, telepathically. It tells him where it has come from and what it wants: it has drifted from Mars, from its ancient, played-out civilization on an arid planet, and it wishes to make a home for its race over the oceans of the wet, abundant earth. It is quite harmless. The child finally tears himself away and alerts the authorities; the buggie is burned where it hangs in the tree, and the boy becomes a hero. His father can boast about him at work.[27]

---

[27] The aliens, who drift to earth and wait passively where they have fallen, contrast strongly with the aggressive, purposeful humans in the story. This contrast is developed in *The World Jones Made* (1956): we have the 'drifters', alien entities who, when they randomly arrive on earth, are incinerated by mobs incited by the dictator Jones. Jones himself is locked into linear purposiveness, because of his power to predict the future—a sterile power, which renders him grim and miserable. The contrast between the drifters and the self-pre-empted

In these stories, then, fathers subject sons to brutal values, but the victim of the violence is some even more vulnerable third party. Perhaps the presence of the third party, and also the neutral ground on which the story takes place (the planet to which Terran–Pas-udeti war has not yet come; the tree) stands for the slim hope of a better outcome; certainly, as we shall see with 'Foster, You're Dead', space is handled in a significant way in these stories. What is suggested, however, is not merely that the family is often used to inculcate violence, but that the process is precarious. What if there is no alien, or no robot, on which to project the violence simmering between father and son, and yet needing to be inculcated?

In several other stories what is tested is the other possibility that Horkheimer mentions, that the family will serve to protect its members against the values of the wider society, rather than impose them. 'Sales Pitch' (1954, CS3) concerns a husband coming home from a hard day at the office, and a hard commute (since people now commute to outer space) to face a robot, which gains entry in the foot-in-the-door manner of salesmen, and is programmed to do all manner of jobs—and to persist in demonstrating and otherwise selling itself until it is purchased. The robot, 'almost seven feet high. Massive. Solid', makes mayhem, ripping things apart to show how it can repair them, blasting a tunnel into the ground in case of H-bomb attack, spraying, disinfecting, doing the husband's taxes, sharpening his pencils, rewiring, remodelling.[28] The story, like the robot, is monomanically unsparing, careless of civility. The focus is on the intrusion and moronic coercion involved in advertising—the appliance not only sells itself, but announces that is designed to replace wife and husband, in the home, the car and the office. The exasperated husband eventually flees beyond even the commuter belt, strains his rocket past its limits, and crashes into a star, still accompanied by the robot. These stories make a connection between the militarized, that is, aggressive or destructive side of society, and the consumerist side, which is often seen as merely bland and seductive.[29] If

Footnote 27 *continued*

Jones is varied in the final scenes on Venus, where the junction of a drifter and another piece of flotsam called a 'wad' reveals that the drifters were actually intergalactic spores, relying on chance to bring about a conjunction with their complement and give birth to a complete organism. Here the contrast is between the drifters and the humans who witness their life-cycle, the inhabitants of 'the Refuge', Terrans laboriously mutated to adapt to life on Venus.

[28] Dick believed for a period in the mid-seventies that he was actually taken over by a personage from another time; this personage organized his life (even got him to file for income tax), in similar fashion, if benignly. This is a bizarre instance of the Dickian 'dialectic'.

[29] Thomas Hine (1986: 123–37) notes the illuminating conjunction in fifties society between the promise of a pushbutton house, thronged with labour-saving gadgets, and the threat of a pushbutton holocaust—as easy to bring about as the operation of that marvellous washing-machine.

the home is the seat of human, kindly practices, since it is where children are commonly brought up and people commonly make love, then the world of the market is literally breaking down the walls.

In 'Nanny' (1955, CS1) robot child carers become more and more formidable fighting machines, engaging each other in desperate combat in the parks whither they take their human charges; the process is designed to blackmail concerned parents into buying ever more expensive models to replace those rendered vulnerably obsolete. It is a trifle difficult to find a parallel to this Dickian extrapolation in the actual history of child care; better to turn the story around and see it as allegorizing the arms race, that is, making the brutal futility of the arms race evident by placing it in the family, remembering that the protection of our children is among the rationalizations offered for the whole vast structure.

The story that expresses this most successfully is 'Foster, You're Dead' (1955, CS3).[30] In the world of this story, national defence has been privatized, and devolved to the local community: it is agreed that each family should buy its own shelter, and each town finance its own self-defence screen.[31] The main character's father has refused to buy a shelter. Since the shelters are never used, they are never tested, nor do they wear out; their 'defects', supposed to be due to advances in Soviet technology which render them insecure, are simply proclaimed by the manufacturers as they introduce more expensive models.

Bob Foster is right, and he serves as Dick's mouthpiece in this, but his insight is irrelevant in the face of his wife's irritation and his son Mike's misery. (So is the fact that Foster, a maker of old-fashioned wooden furniture, is short of money.) The child is harassed at school, where fall-out drill dominates the curriculum, and in his free hours he haunts the local shelter showroom, with its brash, genial salesmen on the model of car dealers. Bob Foster gives in; he buys his family the most expensive and elaborate shelter on the market, thereby rejoining society. Mike, pathetically, takes the shelter as womb: 'a little self-contained cosmos . . . faintly warm, completely friendly, like a living container'.

[30] When this was published in Russian (*Ogonek*, April 1958), 'the author's complimentary copy was destroyed by the U.S. Post Office as Communist propaganda' (Levack 1988: 96; but Rickman [1989: 266] doubts this anecdote).

[31] Hine's discussion (1986) of the contemporary preoccupation with fall-out shelters is very illuminating. He suggests that speculation about the moral issues (would the householder be obliged to shoot a neighbour who tried to force his way in, having improvidently failed to build his own shelter?) had a chastening effect: people did not like what the speculation was telling them about the relations of private and public morality. (The period here is the early sixties, later than Dick's story.) On the Eisenhower administration's policy on fall-out shelters, see Winkler 1993: 120 (the date is 1958, somewhat after the publication of 'Foster, You're Dead').

'Foster, You're Dead' gains a dimension from its focus on the child rather than the father or husband (as in 'Sales Pitch' and 'Nanny'); here the child is wholly a victim. The story expresses the harm done to the child by society's double insistence that there is some fearful threat and that there is a sure refuge from that threat. The threat of the bomb (and thence of social humiliation and ostracism if one's family opts out of bomb culture) comes to stand for all the threats the larger social world presents to a child, and the womb-shelter offers itself as solution. But when the model Foster has bought is supposedly outmoded by the latest Soviet advance, and payments fall behind, the shelter is repossessed and the child is plunged into complete regressive neurosis. In the last scene he is torn, hunched and foetal, from the display shelter in the showroom where he has taken refuge.

The implication of the story is again that consumerism (the notion that every activity is the province of selling) has the effect of displacing alternative power centres and centres of emotional stability. The fall-out shelter replaces not only home, but mother (womb, source of nurture and reassurance) and father (source of authority and reassurance, as Mike Foster's father had tried to be) for the child. 'There is no such thing as privacy . . . there are no private lives', as Dick said in 1974 (P. Williams 1986: 157). Now there is no third party to suffer; the child is the one to suffer, and his suffering goes beyond physical damage. 'Foster, You're Dead' expresses the failure of the family to sustain the positive role Horkheimer envisages for it. Fathers cannot resist the pressures of the wider society, and, for Dick, it is fathers who count. In 'The Pre-Persons' the only way in which the father can express what he knows to be right and try to help his child is by joining the children; an appropriately non-violent, Gandhian gesture, whatever we think of the imagined circumstances in which it is made, but almost as close to futility as the actions of Mike Foster's father.

Dick's short stories mix bizarre fantasy and direct social criticism; they hybridize the literary form in which reality is amenable to the author's imaginative play, and the literary form which is expected to reflect existing social conditions and may not only comment on them but prescribe solutions. In defending humanist and romantic values—freedom, imagination, the hope that the child or 'little guy' can make a difference—Dick repeatedly sets his stories in the family, and then suggests that both the family and the small-town or suburban setting which is supposed to centre on the family are vulnerable and unstable, no source of reliable value.[32]

---

[32] The suburban way of life was the subject of fierce controversy in the fifties and sixties. In his emphasis on routine and emptiness Dick might seem to join with the 'cosmopolitan'

In stories such as 'Breakfast at Twilight' and 'The Hanging Stranger', what is truly chilling is not that the ordinary human person and environment can be manipulated into inhumanity or into naturalizing evil conditions as normal, but that the ordinary human person and environment is not substantially 'there' to be manipulated. And it is true that this throws into question the notion of representation, on which the realist story depends, since representation assumes 'thereness'.

4. The Duplicity of Fantasy

But is not the imagination itself a locus of value? Surely we can find value in the author's free creation of his story, if it is not to be found in the characters or their actions. This is that zany or wonderfully surprising quality that draws many readers to Dick. In fact, stories such as 'Sales Pitch' and 'Foster, You're Dead' renounce fantasy, however we define it. The refusal to be other than bluntly explicit is part of the literary effect. Further, the stories repeatedly curl back on their own shaping spirit. They are self-involved and self-critical.

Two contrary stories will enable us to examine the duplicity of fantasy in Philip. K. Dick. In 'Small Town' (1954, CS2), a bitter, unsuccessful 'little guy' pours all his spirit into the modelling of a miniature of his town in his basement, but as he does so he crosses the line between imitation and creation. He begins to modify and 'improve' his model of the town. This development in the story is not yet fantasy, because the assumptions that shape his alterations are those of society in general, but the story metamorphoses into fantasy when the new model becomes the 'actual' town, which then entraps the story's other characters (his wife and her lover). In 'Exhibit Piece' (1954, CS3), which is set in the future, the man responsible for curating a museum exhibit on the typical suburban family of the Eisenhower era devotes himself so fervently to his task that he starts to act as a person from the fifties, wearing wide ties, adopting the appropriate slang. Then, when he steps into the exhibit, it becomes real—indeed, an instance of the hyperreal, that which is seemingly more real than the real. This simulacrum seems to offer him a comfortable home and friendly family, all a distinct improvement on the drab totalitarian conditions of his present.

Footnote 32 *continued*
critics of the suburbs, as Gans calls them (1967), but his suggestion that this emptiness and routine is part of what makes the suburbs vulnerable in the wider, nuclear world is unusual, and characteristic of him in its combination of empathy and allegorical scope; it aligns him neither with the critics (for instance, Richard Sennett [1970]), nor the defenders (for instance, Herbert J. Gans [1967]).

The story gives us what 'mainstream' fiction is often shy about: a sense that escape can be good. Let the reality principle go hang. But take 'Small Town' and 'Exhibit Piece' together as variations on an idea, and we have not a dialectic or a resolved contradiction, but an instability. In 'Small Town' the wife's lover analyses the main character's inability to face reality and his regression to model-building easily enough in pop-Freudian terms. Then, when he sees what is going to happen, he suggests that the two of them simply let him regress into his model world—it will leave them free for their affair. He offers no realistic standpoint outside the fantastic terms of the story, so it is poetic justice that he and the wife, as well as the model-builder, are absorbed into the model-become-town at the end. At the end of 'Exhibit Piece' the main character's unpleasant colleagues, from whom he has so gratifyingly escaped, manage to put a fifties newspaper across the gap he slipped through; it announces the discovery of a cobalt bomb, and thus explains how the comparatively pleasant fifties gave way to the grim future of the story's present, bending time in a non-linear and fantastic way in the process. It all depends on who is doing the imagining, the main character with his wide ties and naïve tricks of idiom, or those who came up with the cobalt bomb.

Where does the author stand? In stories such as 'Sales Pitch', he stands angrily outside the fiction, which he wields as a weapon, refusing the role of ingeniously extrapolating SF author; in stories such as 'Small Town', he stands inside the fiction, since it is easy to see how his imagining is subject to the same traps as that of the characters. A sign of this is that it is easy to read 'Small Town' or, for instance, 'Pay for the Printer', as allegories of authorship (the author as creator of miniature worlds, or of 'prints').[33]

The question is one of politics (who has the power to impose their fantasy as reality?), but Dick tends to treat it on the level of individual morality. Rather surprisingly for one who imagines wholesale transformations and subversions of reality, he suggests that the moral thing for the individual to do is to concentrate on the specific, the local and present. We cannot know or control the whole, the whole is itself a fantasy, the more dangerous in that those who have dreamed it up, the powerful, do not acknowledge that it is a fantasy; we can only make sure that the next small step we take is a moral one. Emphasis is now on the gesture, the single action which may possibly be clever and moral enough for its insertion into the whole situation to (as it were) catch the situation off guard and make a difference. In the novels the gesture is often one of empathy

---

[33] See Jameson 1987: 56, though he is referring to the SF's text's inclusion of images of reading, rather than of writing. Other relevant works by Dick are 'Stability' (c.1947, CS1), 'Prominent Author' (1954, CS2), and *Radio Free Albemuth* (1985).

which, by affirming human solidarity, takes a small step towards the social, and away from the isolation in which characters live as monads, to use one of Dick's terms.[34]

The problem Dick faced in writing his short stories was that of reconciling existential openness, or relativity, with political or ethical closure. In the first case, all is fantasy, not merely the shape of the story but the shape of the society the story treats, which is not offered to us as 'reality' within the story; in the second case, the story is a parable treating what has been done to us and what we should do, or value, in recourse. This problem is not solved in the stories; their pattern, if we try to trace it across a set of realizations, is that of an instability not subject to dialectical analysis.

[34] See Chapter 11.

6. *The Man in the High Castle*: The Reasonableness and Madness of History

The Man in the High Castle (1962) is Dick's most popular novel, and one of his best. Along with *Time out of Joint* (1959), this novel examines the split between the scene of ordinary life and the scene of power politics that is often featured in the short stories, though in this case it is not the suburbs and the national security state that are in troubled relation, but two kinds of experience of history.[1] As in the stories and in *Time out of Joint*, *The Man in the High Castle* simultaneously engages with the possibility that the ordinary person can make a difference, and questions what it is that he might make a difference to—questions the boundaries of the material and the textual. Humanism and postmodernism are, again, enhanced and in conflict.

The novel's extrapolation of an alternative history in which Germany and Japan are imagined to have won the Second World War and occupied most of the United States is detailed, specific and stimulating. By contrasting the details of our own world, of *The Man in the High Castle*, and of *The Grasshopper Lies Heavy* (the novel of alternative history that figures in the story), the reader can take part in an intelligent game of 'what if?'. At the same time the action of the novel arouses strong sympathy, because it climaxes in an incident in which the Japanese official Tagomi, the most convincingly virtuous person in Dick's novels, saves the life of another sympathetic character, the Jewish-American Frank Frink. All this might mean that *The Man in the High Castle* is a successful humanist novel, and, if so, this would be significant. Many of Dick's statements in interviews and occasional pieces (see for instance Williams 1986: 64) suggest that it is the capacity for empathy that makes us human, a vital matter when the whole project of the novels can be seen as the defining of what true humanness is—an interpretation which the author encouraged and which critics have

[1] It is useful to differentiate these two novels both from the early experiments in reality-bending that preceded them (such as *Eye in the Sky*, 1957), and those that followed in the sixties and seventies, such as *Ubik* (1969). The moment of *Time Out of Joint* and *The Man in the High Castle* is one in which the lines to suburban realism—to call it that—are open, and Paul Williams is right to suggest (1986: 85–95) that in these novels Dick is utilizing what he learnt in the late fifties when he wrote the series of quite idiosyncratically realist novels discussed in Chapter 4, before returning to SF—to call it that.

taken up. Dick's own writing often exemplifies this capacity for empathy —in this instance, in its intelligent understanding of mean and unpleasant characters such as Robert Childan and Joe Cinnadella. Here in *The Man in the High Castle* the narrative dramatizes the value of fellow feeling—and it does this without exaggerating its efficacy in the grim, impersonal or absurd macrocontext of history. When Tagomi saves Frink, he 'balks': the little guy is refusing to go along with the routinized, mechanical processes of power, and this 'balking' is exactly the action on which Dick pins ethical hope.[2] It may be that the convincingness of these moments of hope is connected to the novel's thoroughness and seriousness as alternative history. The relevant issue here is the connection of ethical humanism to the procedures and assumptions of the realist novel: careful detailing of circumstance to create a lifelike effect, the interpersonal dealings of typical-seeming characters—all this working to carry the burden of an interpretation of history and of the condition and prospects of society. In fact, for reasons that will become clear, this discussion will concentrate on the treatment of history in *The Man in the High Castle* and on the problems the novel encounters in relating the local and the global.

Emphasis on humanism and realism might, however, seem misplaced. What of the novel's complex suggestions of the subjectivity or contingency of the given—not merely of the world as an individual perceives it but also of 'public' history? These suggestions are offered at several interconnected levels of the novel. We have the presence of the *I Ching*, with its Taoist sense of 'the moment' in history; we have the novel's treatment of fake and authentic objects and people. (This is varied: Tagomi's pistol, the jewel that Ed and Frank make; characters who are not what they seem: Joe Cinnadella, Baynes, others at various times; the Japanese culture of appearance, formality and composure, but also the deceit and Machiavellian calculation into which people are forced in the course of the story.) We have the presence in the text of two other texts, both of which enforce the arbitrariness of the given, and thence of the text we are reading, and of the reality that we live in and, if we are a touch old-fashioned, accept as given: the *I Ching* and *The Grasshopper Lies Heavy*. All this might seem to undermine and deconstruct that sense of the solidity in history of the 'real' on which the humanist novel relies, and to assimilate *The Man in the High Castle* to later novels such as *Ubik* or *The Simulacra*.[3]

[2] Dick in a 1977 interview, reprinted in *The Philip K. Dick Society Newsletter*, 6 (April 1985): 2.

[3] *Virtual History* (Ferguson [ed.] 1998) is an interesting acknowledgment on the part of professional historians of the value of speculating about alternatives. Niall Ferguson's introduction is, however, anxious to delimit the borders between history and fiction. It is not only the issues raised by alternative histories that he fends off, but also the issues raised by the historical novel more generally considered (*The Man in the High Castle* is dismissed on p. 441, n. 8).

Yet it is the contention of this chapter that *The Man in the High Castle* does provide us with a good opportunity for assessing Dick's humanism. It takes soberly the processes of extrapolation by which its 'novum' is built up; it sets its social psychology in history. By the time of novels such as *Ubik*, *Palmer Eldritch* and, in a different way, *Valis* (1981), Dick carries his sense of ontological and epistemological instability so far as to imagine the condition that we now call postmodern: dominance of the simulacral and eclipse of the natural; blurred boundaries, reality dissolves or nestings, time regressions or unhingings, ravelled failure of the rational (incidents and outcomes that simply cannot be explained in terms of linear, cause-and-effect logic). Yet Dick's ethical and political urgency and even anguish remains important in the later novels: solidarity and kindness still need to be justified and acted on, even in conditions that undermine what makes them conceivable. The outcome is at times an electrifying tension, and at times, simply, a lack of fit between ethical humanism and freewheeling postmodernism.

If it is true that the element of humanism in *The Man in the High Castle* depends on its engagement with history, then that engagement cannot be straightforward. History in the second half of the twentieth century is complex and daunting. It is open to reasoned analysis, it is the product of instrumental rationalization, and it is seemingly irrational or insane. The question of what it is that a novel attempts to engage with when it engages with history does not permit of a simple answer. In what follows it is argued that *The Man in the High Castle* reaches the limits of extrapolated recreation of history, and that it does this in the course of its engagement with the dreadful, undifferentiating aspects of twentieth-century history,[4] the way events are often so vast in scale and so indiscriminate in effects that anyone who contemplates them is afflicted with a kind of vertigo. The novel's moments of fellow feeling are explicitly connected to an ethic of the local and humble, which is Dick's recognition of the interdependence of realism and humanism, but they are narrated in the course of a series of attempts to sublimate the dreadfulness of twentieth-century history. It

---

[4] DiTommaso (1999) makes an analogous division of the world of the novel, into 'sensible' and 'intelligible', but offers a very different interpretation, whereby the sensible world is found to be wholly unreliable, and each of the main characters receives an 'Inner Truth' as an in-breaking of the intelligible, to redemptive effect. This interpretation commits DiTommaso to a certain confidence that the novel believes there is a truth, and to a systematic account of how all the main characters are in some way redeemed—even Childan, even Juliana. As will be seen in what follows, my reading sees the notion of redemption as very difficult to apply in any thoroughgoing way to a whole range of characters. In this I follow Rieder (1992), who gives us the best guide to the complex and unresolved relations between (as he terms them) the ethical and the metaphysical.

is uncertain how successful these attempts are, and how successful we could ask them to be, but the subjectivist aspects of the novel, such as the implications of the *I Ching* and of *The Grasshopper Lies Heavy*, should be seen in relation to these attempts.

1. Wide Angle: The Loss of History

It is useful to define *The Man in the High Castle*'s dealings with history against what is characteristic of the rest of Dick's novels. This section discusses the separation from the past that obtains in these other novels; the stagnation and 'shallowness' of the institutions or system that have replaced what existed in the past; and the frivolity with which material and social conditions are detailed. These generalizations are very broad; novels such as *Time out of Joint*,[5] *Dr Bloodmoney* and *The Penultimate Truth*, which are exceptions in various ways, are temporarily set aside.

Most of Philip K. Dick's novels begin with the characters separated from their past history by a disastrous break or a process of decline and disintegration. The social narrative is in ruins. There is neither shared past, nor shared project. There was a 'World War Terminus', or social and ecological collapse.[6] The result is that the past from before the break is now irrelevant and barely remembered. It is sketchily narrated, or simply alluded to. If we have decline or devolution rather than disaster or collapse in a given novel, it is not directly regarded, nor made the thematic centre of the novel (see, for instance, the continuing suppression of the remnant radicals and students in *Flow My Tears*, which is alluded to but not directly presented). Or the break may be spatial rather than temporal: the distance between earth and its colony in *Martian Time-Slip*,[7] or, in a different sense, the paraworlds which relativize the history of 'the' world in such novels as *Now Wait for Last Year* and *The Crack in Space* (both 1966). In short, the explosion of heterogeneity—spatial, temporal or even genetic (mutations and new humanoid types)—shreds history to pieces. Material, concrete passages of history (war or political breakdown), and passages across space (from Earth to a colony planet), and ruptures or openings in the fabric of

---

[5] See Jameson's discussion (1993, ch. 9), which takes *Time out of Joint* as an example of precisely that sense of history as coherent and consecutive which I see as dissolved in most of Philip K. Dick and which he finds lacking in the postmodern films he goes on to discuss.

[6] 'World War Terminus' occurs in *Androids*; and see *The Game-Players of Titan* (1963) and *The Simulacra* (1964). (But it is true that a 'Third World Insanity' is contemplated in *The Man in the High Castle*, ch. 15, 244.) For ecological collapse see, for instance, the overheating of the planet in *Palmer Eldritch*.

[7] See Jack Bohlen's meditation on how hard it is to convey Earth's traditions to young Martians, ch. 5, 74–76.

space-time[8] all have a strikingly similar effect. It becomes impossible to establish cause and effect and the sense of human beings as experiencing movement through social time as a collective. History is junked.

Peter Osborne (1992) has argued that modernity involves a change in the quality of temporality itself; for instance, modernity involves the entrance of the concept of 'history' rather than the history *of* this or that. (But if we ask 'Entrance into what?' then 'Entrance into history' is the answer we cannot help giving, being modern ourselves, and this usage is followed here.) If so, then in many of Dick's novels, this change is so sweeping and exacerbated that *time* is fissioned: it can reverse or regress, cells or autonomous compartments can open within it, its 'binding' can be loosed, it can be wholly subjectivized.[9] The quality of temporality is postmodern rather than modern. Yet the possible significance of the change is still historical; it is not, for example, an instance of some transhistorical perspectivity such as we might associate with Nietszche. (An objection here is that most varieties of postmodernism ambivalently proclaim both a view of the present historical moment and a revelation about the arbitrariness of 'scene' through history, and there is an analogous ambivalence in Dick's own sense of the subjectivity of reality. It is not clear whether it has become thus or was always thus.)

Very often, especially in the earlier novels, the disaster or collapse leads to the rule of an authority, a 'Unity', which may be based on an all-encompassing ideology or simply on a method.[10] As Dick's career proceeds from the fifties to the sixties, this authority is depicted as less political (that is, less a matter of government, police and so forth) and more diffuse. The authority that was constructed after the historical break has stagnated and

[8] The operation of the 'Hobart Effect' which reverses time in *Counter-Clock World* (1967), the discovery of a parallel earth in *The Crack in Space* (1966).

[9] Something similar happens in a more recent novel, and one that begins as 'hard' SF, Greg Bear's *Eon* (1985). At first an alien object is to be explored spatially, as in Clarke's *Rendezvous with Rama* (1973), and, if not understood, at least mapped with the mind. But in *Eon* the object proves to be so complicated and multi-compartmented that this empirical procedure breaks down; at the same time the narrative, involving an extension of the conflict between the US and the Soviet Union, also loses coherence; the dimensions of the asteroid turn out to be unimaginably great, the contemporary humans are involved in the history of a far future humanity itself divided into factions and engaged in a millennial struggle with unseen 'jats', alternative worlds open up, and the main character at length finds herself in a revised version of Cleopatra's Egypt. What is perhaps meant to be read as transcendence is a lot easier to read as a postmodern loss of history, which is consumed by proliferating versions of space-time. ('Time-binding' is loosened in *Flow My Tears*, 1974.)

[10] It is in *Vulcan's Hammer* (1960, based on a short story of 1956) that the ruling authority is called 'Unity'; Morec in *The Man Who Japed* (1956) is an example of an explicit ruling ideology in an early novel; and Hoff's Relativism in *The World Jones Made* (1956), and empathy tests and colonization in *Androids* (1968) are examples of methods of social regulation.

become degraded, it is now no more than a set of formalized, unexamined assumptions. In fact social and political interactions are literally governed by rules of a game in *The Game-Players of Titan*, though there is frequent cheating and bluffing; legalism is often important, and there are often quasi-trials or legalistic confrontations, invariably hollow and absurd in the context of the prevailing unscrupulousness and violence.[11] At the same time society begins to be seen as the arena for drives and energies that are primarily psychic. This is the case, for instance, in *The Simulacra*, where the populace's belief in the ruler, the 'First Lady', is depicted as a kind of collective neurosis.

The society of the novel has no shared narrative that it is pursuing: rulers are not precisely extending their power, ruled are not precisely revolting. Resistance or revolt is often an element, but seldom provides strong narrative drive. Nor does the narrative follow a form which is common in detective and thriller novels of the sort that Dick borrows from in other ways, whereby a crime that seems to originate in the present of the novel is actually found to have originated in the concealed past, which can thereby be recovered, so that solution of the crime is recovery of the history of the society, or community.[12] What is remarkable in most of Dick's novels, by contrast, is the *irrelevance* of the past.

What follows from this is that the past, horrible as it is if it involves something like 'World War Terminus', is so to speak 'shallow'; and so, very often, are the other kinds of founding division in the novel, those which do not involve a division between past and present but one among different castes or even human species into which the novel's society is divided (as in *Solar Lottery*, *The Simulacra*, *Frolix 8*, and, peripherally, *Androids* and *Palmer Eldritch*). Whatever the suggestiveness of this kind of thing as metaphor for the classes and races into which our society is divided, it supplies none of the narrative momentum, none of the motivation for the various conflicts that occupy the story. There are incidental insights, but otherwise we tend to forget whether a certain character is a 'Norm' or a 'Bee' or a 'Gee' or whatever, for instance in the cases of Willis Gram in *Frolix 8* and

---

[11] See for instance Deckard's legalism in *Androids* (ch. 4, 39; ch. 12, 110; ch. 14, 165); the trials in *Solar Lottery*, ch. 16, and *Vulcan's Hammer*, ch. 11.

[12] '[A] *national* crime, an ancient fact successfully repressed, a past injustice whose contamination threads its way into the present' (Ross 1992: 61). James Ellroy's *LA Confidential* (1990), classifiable as a postmodern thriller in all sorts of ways, is nonetheless an excellent example. Equally relevant is Robert Harris's *Fatherland* (1992), the best since *The Man in the High Castle* of the novels based on the premise that Germany won the war. In *Fatherland*, the present-day crimes that motivate the main character's investigation lead him to uncover the dreadful, founding crime of the whole state (the extermination of the Jews) and thence force him to confront the horror of history itself.

John Isidore in *Androids*. (We forget that Gram is a telepath and a member of a supposedly superior caste, we forget that Isidore is a 'special' and supposedly retarded.) Similarly the Hobart Effect in *Counter-Clock World* (1967), the most drastic break between past and present that can be imagined, is shallow in that once the narrative gets under way the novel has other things on its mind.[13] The story is not motivated by this premise or circumstance, determinative as one might have thought it to be, since it makes everything go backwards in time.

Paradoxically, it is possible to read the dazzling reality inversions and dissolves in several of these novels as means to a familar end, and one that is usually pursued by the realist novel: the depiction of marital breakdown and its accompanying emotional turmoil. It turns out that life is still the same in this weirdly conditioned society—even when the Hobart Effect prevails, so that the dead are exhumed to life, food is vomited rather than ingested, and so on (and the political circumstances are also very complicated). The story still focuses on whether the main character should leave his wife. So it is also in *Counter-Clock World*.[14]

This sketch is to some degree arbitrary: it depicts absences or a lack of depth, and hesitates over what might fill these gaps. Perhaps an unfettered libido; in a situation where the historical has been eclipsed and the political has stagnated, the social collapses into the psychic. That is how one puts the matter from the perspective of *The Man in the High Castle*. From the perspective of postmodernism, the blurring of boundaries is the content of these novels of the fifties and, still more, the sixties, and that condition, after all, *is* history now: a paradoxical historical condition which is founded on an end of historicity, but which exerts its own imperatives nonetheless.

One further point about the novels of the sixties concerns the quality of the extrapolation, or rather lack of it, that might be seen as shaping

[13] Compare Martin Amis's *Time's Arrow* (1991). In this novel, however, the condition is not general but is confined to one man's experience; it is related to a specific history, the extermination of the Jews, in a way that is very relevant to what I discuss in relation to *The Man in the High Castle* later in this chapter. It could be argued that the time reversal that afflicts Tod Friendly/Odilo Unverdorben in this novel is ambivalently both the nausea in the face of history that afflicts Tagomi in our novel, and the means of a utopian redeeming of history.

[14] This matter of marital breakdown is largely extratextual in *The Man in the High Castle*. It remains on the fringe of the text. The novel was originally dedicated to Dick's wife of the time ('To my wife Anne without whose silence this book would never have been written'); but later editions replace this with a dedication to Dick's last wife, Tessa, and his son Christopher. Anne Dick has published her own account of the marriage (1995). The novel does end with the hope that Frank Frink and his ex-wife Juliana will get back together. As we saw in Chapter 4, wrenching marital conflict was thoroughly explored in the novels Dick wrote in the late fifties, but did not succeed in publishing at that point.

these novels. There is often in Dick's novels a frivolity, an angry or irreverent refusal to be serious and detailed in the specification of things, devices, vehicles, appliances, proper names, and frequently institutions and classes as well. The material features and the political and social outlines of the future world, which we expect to shape the narrative, are introduced in a flippant fashion. People drive in jalopies or quibbles, they exchange bits of extraterrestrial truffle for currency, the aliens they deal with are called papoolas, or Ganymedean slime moulds, they are kept under surveillance by juveniles or occifers, they are vexed by coin-in-the-slot appliances and even coin-in-the-slot doors. *Coins*, rather than any kind of readily extrapolated futurist electronic banking; and, regarding doors, what about the sentence 'The door dilated' of hallowed SF tradition? Surely a door could be got to dilate even in *Ubik*'s dystopian future? But in *Ubik* the door remains stubbornly shut both to Joe Chip and to SF tradition, and that happens because Joe cannot find a coin to open it.[15]

In order to move to an imagination of the basic ground, or rather groundlessness, of our present condition, these novels sweep with an angry flippancy past all sorts of material details and specifics. Thus the chirping and clutter of papoolas and quibbles in the opening pages, before the narrative reveals its frightening depths and instabilities, out of which will emerge a more abstract, but also a more pressing and frightening, image of the contemporary condition. Evidently, were these novels to take extrapolation seriously, they would have to take seriously that narrative coherence and existential stability which is precisely what they will proceed to doubt, harass and undermine.

2. Local History

The Man in the High Castle is very different. It is quite true that the characters in this novel, as in many others by Dick, live in the aftermath of a disaster that makes a violent historical break: the defeat of America and Britain; the Nazis' use of the atom bomb, the extermination not only of the Jews but of the Africans as well. But they still live in a history, and one that is continuous both with this disaster and with what existed before it, on the other side of the break. Jews are still being killed (it is in this context that Tagomi saves Frink); Africans are again being enslaved (ch. 1, 24: the situation gives rise to sociocultural anxiety in a character going about his ordinary business, and this is typical of the novel).

---

[15] There are 'entrance-sphincters' in *Solar Lottery* (1955; see e.g. ch. 15, 156), but that isn't quite what we want. On SF tradition, see for instance Delany 1976, and Suvin 1988: 63–64 (discussing Delany's characterization of SF).

The Nazis plan to use the bomb again, this time in a surprise attack on their allies, the Japanese; the plan is code-named 'Operation Dandelion'. The Japanese are depicted in the novel as decisively more civilized, and as capable of history in the sense that, though their culture is traditional, it is changing in response to their occupation of the West Coast of America.[16] Among the Japanese characters, there is a carefully specified difference between the Kasouras, who are young, and the elderly Tagomi, though both generations are evidently able to respond sympathetically to American culture. The Kasouras are named Betty and Paul; Tagomi is Nobusuke, though he is usually the more formal 'Mr Tagomi'. In contrast, the Nazis go on doing more of the same: more annihilation, more feats of technology and organization of a sterile, reflex kind, notably the conquest of space. Further, once they learn about the surprise attack the Nazis are planning, the Japanese, who have the capacity to change, are asked to choose to fold themselves back into the nullity of history. This is because the German Chancellor Bormann is dying, and Heydrich, one possible successor whom the Japanese might support, is opposed to Operation Dandelion—though by every other rational, Taoist and simply human criterion he is the nastiest of the lot.

It was suggested above that there is also continuity with the history on the further side of the gap torn by the Axis victory. But whereas the latter is cataclysmic, and somehow abstract and undifferentiated, at least as concerns the Nazis, the former lives on as, literally, a collection, of small, loveable, familiar things. The vast energy and productive force of America under Roosevelt (that which won the war in our history) is forgotten, or never came about. Instead we have short-order cooks, Mickey Mouse watches, bottle tops and baseball cards. This sounds (and is) sentimental, but it is also the locus of a fascinating cultural evolution in the novel's present—history as deep, mundane structures, not *histoire évènementielle*, which is strikingly immature and pathological in the case of the Nazis.

Helga Nowotny (1994) provides a useful context for this conflict

---

[16] Suvin (1988: 115) feels that this depiction of the Japanese is too kind, given their behaviour as conquerors in Asia and the Pacific in the period up to 1945. He is probably right; what has happened is that Dick has, as it were, shifted the Japanese from one historical plane, in which barbarity dominates, to another, more local and with more potential for positive action. The problem of the lack of fit between the two planes in the novel will be discussed later. (It is also true that if one shifts the terms, one can see the Japanese as wise aliens, resembling for instance the wise aliens in Le Guin's *The Lathe of Heaven*; but this is more in the nature of a strobic flash than a clear light in which one would contemplate them in a sustained way.) Dick's wry, appreciative depiction of the Japanese aesthetic of the industrial object influenced later SF: Mr Ito in Norman Spinrad's 'A Thing of Beauty' (first published 1972), and the student Yamazaki from whom we learn of the 'Thomasson' in Gibson's *Virtual Light* (1993).

between the global and local. Using an analogy with time in the theory of relativity, she talks of the discovery of 'proper time' (*Eigenzeit*) — time for and of the individual life. The contemporary problem, she says, is one of aligning proper time with public time, especially in a situation of radical change in which the future is first deprived of promise (decline of the notion of progress) and then replaced by an 'extended present', a mutation in the history of the future with which SF has been dealing since Dick.

We can see this 'proper time' in *The Man in the High Castle* not only in the subjective enclosure of the characters, but in the impulse to collect, to make a past, a temporal continuity, out of mass-produced things (for example, bottle caps). The crucial episode in which this proper time is confronted with, and shattered by, public time (itself not only destructive but secretive, conspiratorial) is that in which Tagomi has to use his revolver (collected and played with in proper time) to kill the German assassination team. To trace how the novel arrives at this moment, and where it goes from there, however, it is necessary to look more carefully at its dealings not so much with different temporalities as with different histories and cultures. We begin with the cultural evolution brought about by the Japanese occupiers.

They collect the trivial kitsch artifacts of America's past and, unwittingly, of its present too, since the colonized Americans dedicate themselves to fabricating simulacra of these relics and collectables, which Japanese collectors then buy. The term 'colonized' can be used, because the Americans are in the position of colonized peoples manufacturing native art works for the tourist trade. The ironies slice in almost every direction. The Japanese are indeed the superior race, not merely more powerful but genuinely more cultured (they appreciate jazz, Nathanael West and Jean Harlow, though the natives, now self-hating and confused, can no longer do so [ch. 7. 109–13]), but they are also easy to fool. The Americans are the humble natives, stagnating in their traditional crafts instead of taking part in the modern world, but their fate has not the pathos of, say, West Africans turning out fetishes and images of deities for the tourists, since their sacred objects, now faked, are relics of Buffalo Bill and Disney. These artifacts have more of a camp numen.[17]

The matter is more complex still, for we are dealing not just with artifacts and with satirical observations on their manufacture and exchange, but with an ongoing history of culture and of intimate feelings, some acrid, some hopeful. But before discussing this, it is important to take account of

---

[17] 'Kitsch' is no doubt the better word for what we usually encounter in *The Man in the High Castle*. Andrew Ross distinguishes usefully among schlock, kitsch and camp in the context of the sixties (1989: see 145).

the alternative accounts of history in the relevant texts (*The Man in the High Castle* and *The Grasshopper Lies Heavy*). These too are based on distinct, rationalizable details. If you actually know something about, for instance, cybernetics or the potential of lasers, then it is better to put your knowledge aside, in reading the novels that were discussed in the first part of the chapter. Such knowledge will not help you to appreciate the fiction. But if you know, for instance, that the British might easily have been led into the battle of El Alamein by the mediocre General Gott instead of Montgomery, or that several of the soon-to-be-decisive American aircraft carriers might easily have been anchored near the doomed battleships in Pearl Harbor, then your appreciation of *The Man in the High Castle* and *The Grasshopper Lies Heavy* is enhanced (ch. 5, 67; ch. 6, 80).[18]

What both passages offer is history as contingency, the accretion of discrete chances, outcomes, opportunities (the fate of a general, the movement of a couple of ships). This has defects, because it could well be argued that history stems from the vast, frequently indifferent operation of impersonal forces that in the long run, or in the mass, iron out local contingencies such as who was in charge at Alamein. This is precisely the shadowy, abstract threat that the Germans present to the Japanese and the Americans in the novel: impersonal force figuring only as remorseless annihilation, so the novel itself implies that the history that works in terms of the operation of impersonal forces is evil.[19] The novel sets out to bring history as the contingent accumulation of details into relation with history as the grim sweep of impersonal forces, and it turns out that this relation is unstable and hard to categorize.

The Man in the High Castle links the social forces at work in the novel's present (the collecting of quaint American artifacts, the cultural interrelations of collectors and forgers) with possible understandings of history as accessible to reason. *The Grasshopper Lies Heavy*, a novel of alternative history in which the Germans and Japanese were defeated, does not in fact give our 'real' history. No one would be sadistic enough to *imagine* our

---

[18] Both theological and postmodernist interpretations are in danger of underestimating this simple aspect of the novel and of neglecting what it might mean. This neglect need not follow from a theological approach; there is plenty of warrant in Christianity (though hardly in its Gnostic variants?) for a patient respect for the humble and everyday. Rieder (1992: 226) offers a careful account of the place of the novel's realism in its procedures.

[19] How does a novel, which works by means of characters or at least personages, express the possibility that agency belongs to systems rather than to individuals? Dick tends to seek imaginative resolution of the problem by a kind of hypertrophy or overload of individuals and individual characterizations—lots of emphatically characterized personages engaged in confusing self-serving conflict. *The Man in the High Castle* varies this by differentiating its world into global and local levels—which gives rise to new problems.

history as alternative to that which prevails (the history detailed by *The Man in the High Castle*); instead Hawthorne Abendsen, the author of the novel, has, for instance, imagined that the Germans were defeated by the Americans and the British. The British capture of Berlin is graphically narrated (ch. 8, 124–25—the point of view is that of a German character in *The Grasshopper Lies Heavy*). The Russians are of little account in *The Grasshopper Lies Heavy*; but the misgivings that the Japanese in *The Man in the High Castle* feel about allying with the Germans (and thence with the worst element among the Germans, as the plot unfolds) may be analogous to those that may be felt about the Anglo-American alliance with the Russians in our history. Then again, just as *The Grasshopper Lies Heavy* improves history, so that its readers in our novel see it as a 'fantasy' or a 'utopia' (ch. 6, 83; ch. 10, 158), so also does *The Man in the High Castle*. In our history, the Americans (that is, for many readers, 'we') dropped the atom bomb on the Japanese, even though we may feel that the Nazis were so evil that they 'should' have been the ones to use the bomb, as they plan to do in *The Man in the High Castle*. As it is with the relations of colonizers and colonized, so it is more generally: the novel's serious play with details enables a complex reflection on history.[20] The general effect is to suggest, as we read, that we have to take responsibility for the whole of history, since we recognize ourselves now in the Americans, now in the Japanese, now in the wish-fulfilments of *The Man in the High Castle*, now in those of *The Grasshopper Lies Heavy*.

Further, it is from local detail that an ongoing history is imagined. What happens is that Frank Frink and his buddy Ed defy and depart from the degraded colonial economy. They stop faking native collectors' items for the Japanese. They set out to make new things, authentic things. They use modern tools to handcraft abstract pieces of jewellery. That which is abstract does not imitate; under the Nazis what is called 'modern' art is representational, that is, it imitates things rather than making meanings (ch. 3, 39). Edfrank's work is a breakthrough to the modern—and also an escape from the modern, at least as we know it.

Modern industrialism is in fact the field of imitation and replication, a

---

[20] In her (1995) essay on *The Man in the High Castle* as illustration of postcolonial theory (Fanon and Said), Cassie Carter reads the novel as a fierce deconstruction of 'Americanism', which is seen as largely and perhaps constitutively violent and fascist. Carter does not, however, consider the possibility that people, for instance the Kasouras or the American users of the *I Ching*, might assimilate or learn from other cultures, sometimes in a context of colonialism, sometimes in a broader context. Nor does it seem accurate to see the Japanese, either in our history or in the novel, as wholly the products of colonialism or of a process of mimicry, though this is certainly how the (unreliable) Childan sees them in several vivid passages.

matter that figures very largely in many of Dick's other novels, which critique this culture of replication. Yet, as regards the history he is visualizing, Dick imagines a form of making that *is* modern, not only because Edfrank's jewels are abstract, and the process of their making is industrial as well as manual,[21] but also, in the context of the novel, exactly because it breaks with imitation and replication. This is a utopian conception in that it goes one better than what prevails in actuality.

Then one of Edfrank's jewels migrates from the context of its making. It passes into social life, moving from Edfrank, to Robert Childan, to Paul Kasoura, and eventually to Tagomi; it is intimately connected with the crucial incident whereby Tagomi saves Frink from the Nazis, because just as Tagomi saves Frink without having met him, so the jewel changes Tagomi's life in a fundamental way, without his ever knowing that Frink made it.[22] Contemplation of the jewel saves him from the despairing remorse brought on by his killing of the Nazi agents who are sent to kill himself, Baynes and Tedeki,[23] but it also precipitates him briefly into another time, which we recognize as our time, in an unlovely form. It is significant that this passage of social life involves the Americans and the Japanese in a complicated coming together, crossed by mistakes and mutual ignorances, but hopeful. Outside this pattern of exchange and potential change, however, are the Nazis, the masters of the grand, impersonal, annihilating forces of history.

In one of the novel's early scenes, we meet the aged Wyndam-Matson, manufacturer of fake collectors' items for the colonial market. Though he deceives the Japanese, he is a classic collaborator in his attitudes. He accepts their mastery as historically inevitable: 'I know the Japanese fairly well, and it was their destiny to assume dominance in the Pacific' (ch. 5, 68). He has naturalized that which is not given and determined at all, as *we* cannot but know. Ironically, Wyndam-Matson himself proceeds to discourse on fakes: here is the cigarette lighter that was in Roosevelt's pocket when he was assassinated, nicked by the bullet: but how do we know it is authentic, a genuine relic? One can show a certificate of authenticity, but

---

[21] There is a detailed account of the up-to-date tools they use in ch. 9, 131.

[22] The Germans have discovered that Frank is Jewish; to deport him to his death they need the co-operation of the Japanese, who are the occupying power. This is refused by Tagomi. Frank was reported by Childan, whom he had deceived in the course of a con trick whose purpose was obtaining money to set up the jewellery business, yet it is Childan who gets possession of one of the jewels and, recovering cultural pride as an American, thrusts it on Tagomi.

[23] Baynes (Wegener) is the German agent who brings the Japanese news of Nazi plans to use the atom bomb against them; Tedeki is the representative of the Imperial General Staff come to San Francisco to meet Baynes; Tagomi, merely a trade official, provides cover for the meeting.

of course this too could easily be a forgery. Wyndam-Matson's collabora-
tionism is thus cynical, because he is aware of the gratuitousness of things
('the word "fake" meant nothing really, since the word "authentic" meant
nothing really' [ch. 5, 64]). How could things be arbitrary and history be
inevitable?

When Edfrank wants to threaten Wyndam-Matson's business, Frank
visits the store of Robert Childan, an antique dealer, disguised as the agent
of a (fictional) Japanese admiral, and pretends to discover that the 1860 Colt
.44 on offer is a forgery. He exposes fakery by further fakery. At one point
he even begins to write a (fake) cheque (ch. 4, 54–57).[24] Later his partner
Ed, sweaty and nervous in the role of salesman, visits Childan with a sample
of the newly made, authentic jewels. Childan, skilful at exploiting this kind
of naïve blue-collar tradesman, takes the jewels on consignment, intending
to steal them, paying Ed nothing, running no risk (ch. 9, 146).

Wyndam-Matson can afford to be complacent, but those with less
power, such as Childan and Frank, are more vulnerable. The moment of
social life that concentrates the vulnerability that these people experience
is that of selling: anxiety to please, to guess the very desires and snobberies
of the customer. Ed, so strong when it comes to leaving Wyndam-Matson
and setting up the jewellery business, is at his worst when selling the jewels
to Childan, and Childan gets very tangled in his dealings with his cultured
Japanese customers, Betty and Paul Kasoura. This is history in mundane
detail: the compromises and power relationships involved in salesmanship.

Dick historicizes this relationship through his depiction of Childan.
Mean, restless, self-despising, miserable, prejudiced, resenting and
envying the Japanese, imitating them and hating himself for imitating
them, Childan is a telling portrait of *ressentiment*. He is an unpleasant soul,
but the novel shows that he is trapped and pressured by history, not by
innate meanness of character. Childan admires, or he makes himself
admire, the Germans, but this enthusiasm simply seems gross and tasteless to the cultured Kasouras. At one point he defends the Axis victory, for
racist reasons, though he is aware that it was a victory over his own
people, while the Kasouras calmly dispute his interpretation of history
(ch. 7, 111). The Kasouras themselves have learnt to appreciate American
culture—not only steaks, but photos of Jean Harlow, jazz ('authentic
American folk jazz', for the Kasouras; 'Negro music', for Childan [ch. 7,
109]), and the novels of Nathanael West—which, as it happens, are full
of people like Robert Childan. Nor is this simply a matter of colonialist con-
noisseurship: Paul Kasoura values West because of what his novels say

---

[24] DiTommaso (1999: 93–94) gives a good summary of the novel's proliferation of faker-
ies, disguises, deceptions and uncertainties.

about causeless suffering, a matter of importance for the novel as a whole (ch. 7, 113). Bewildered and humiliated by these supersubtle and subtly contemptuous Orientals, Childan falls back on his patriotism as an American, but he even expresses this in acculturated Japanese terms, as his interior monologues reveal. In the novel the Japanese are given to telegraphese and a rather literal resort to proverbial wisdom, and that is how Childan thinks to himself:

> And this is the straight dope, right here. *These people are not exactly human.* They don the dress but they're like monkeys dolled up in the circus. They're clever and can learn, *but that is all.*
> Why do I cater to them? Due solely to their having won?
> Big flaw in my character revealed through this encounter. But such is the way it goes. I have pathetic tendency to . . . well, shall we say, unerringly choose the easier of two evils. Like a cow catching sight of the trough; I gallop without premeditation. (ch. 7, 114)

Childan shows Paul Kasoura one of the jewels he has appropriated from Ed. Kasoura grasps the special authenticity of the curious bloblike abstract piece of moulded silver. He feels it is 'a new thing in this world' and in order to express this he has to think newly—though to do so he uses the terms which his culture offers him—and he has to act newly, 'ruthlessly' pressing his conclusions on his Japanese associates, contravening every rule of formality and tact (ch. 11, 174–77). The specialness of this nondescript thing, he says, is not a matter of 'wabi', that is, the historicity that accrues to some relic or vestige of the past (of the sort that the Japanese think they are collecting from the Americans); nor is it exactly a matter of the rarer, more elusive spiritual grace called 'wu', for that comes from the appreciating subject, who somehow instils it in, perhaps, a piece of trash, an *objet trouvé*—yet 'wu' it must be, but of a new kind. He ponders earnestly, and determines that the jewel represents and reflects on nothing; it is simply interesting and valuable in itself. Kasoura's interpretation arises from the circumstances of the novel's history and, as we shall see, that history inflects what follows; but this kind of new object is somehow also free of history. Tagomi will come into possession of the jewel in different and grimmer circumstances, and find it harder to interpret.

The outcome of Kasoura's declaration to Childan is vexed and uncertain. Kasoura puts it to Childan that he has a hit on his hands: this kind of object could be mass produced, and thereby made available to the many, not merely the elite. Kasoura could put Childan in touch with certain entrepreneurs, were he to want to take the matter further. Childan, insecure, bewildered by all the talk of 'wabi' and 'wu', hesitates, wavers, and at length rebels. Kasoura's proposal is an insult to honest

American workmen (workmen of the sort that Childan swindled and perhaps intends to go on swindling, we note); he rejects it, and, with a great effort, given that he is talking to one of the ruling race, and to a client, demands an apology. Kasoura inscrutably gives the apology. Childan feels victorious, and feels himself authenticated, though the terms of the combat have been entirely Japanese: insult and apology; power gained not merely from extracting the apology, but from being sufficiently 'high caste' in one's attitudes to detect the insult. But perhaps Kasoura intended this outcome all along, though he felt it his duty to let Childan be a crude profiteering American if he wished; if so, Childan was outwitted anyway, even in his victory. But then again, did Kasoura outwit Childan as a Japanese, or as one learning to appreciate American culture —better than the acculturated Japanese-American Childan can? To such questions, the prudent critic always answers 'both'; what is important is the sense of lived and ongoing history which prompts the questions.

In the context of American–Japanese relationships, what is at issue is a set of mundane dealings, those of customer and salesman here, employer and employee in the case of Wyndam-Matson and Edfrank, or middleman and worker in the case of Childan and Ed. The behavioural context is naturalization and *ressentiment*—cynical acceptance of one's historical plight, or frustrated anger at it. But the outcome is positive. A new thing is made by Edfrank and thought by Kasoura; Childan and Kasoura break from the constraints and distortions of the relation between salesman and customer. We can say that differences are relaxing, differences between Japanese and Americans, for instance, or that they are, so to speak, fructifying (variant potentials of the modern). This is significant, because the dissolution of difference is so often troubling in Dick, as was seen in Chapter 1, and will be seen again, particularly in Chapter 10. But this general condition in *The Man in the High Castle* becomes more problematic when we look at the relations of Tagomi and Juliana with the Nazis. The difference between themselves and the Nazis is not one that Tagomi and Juliana want to relax.

The outer edges of the novel's depiction of *ressentiment* are traced— more hazily, however—in the novel's depiction of the relationship between Juliana (Frank's estranged wife) and Joe Cinnadella, with whom Juliana is travelling to Denver, to meet the author of *The Grasshopper Lies Heavy*. (Ostensibly, Joe is a bored truck driver, and Juliana a lonely unattached woman he picked up in a diner.) Joe is moody, aggressive and disillusioned; formerly an elite soldier in Africa, he feels the Italians gained nothing but contempt from the war; once a believer in the Fascist ethos of labour, he feels the ideal has been degraded; and his efforts to justify the Fascist belief in the deed rather than the word are mocked by Juliana (as too wordy [ch. 10, 162]) and hardly even convince himself. In fact the whole persona he builds up during the journey, by means of a series of bitter allusions and justifications, is a fake: he is actually a German assassin, Abendsen is his target and Juliana he has merely brought along as his cover. But then Juliana almost certainly sensed this already, as she was attracted to Joe by the air of death he brought with him (ch. 3, 37), and when the time comes it is she who kills him, slitting his throat and leaving him to bleed to death in his hotel room.

Tagomi's killing of the German agents who had meant to assassinate Tedeki is clearly parallel to Juliana's killing of Joe Cinnadella, who had meant to assassinate Abendsen. With Tagomi we pass out of the realm of buying and selling, naturalization and *ressentiment*, however, because Tagomi's most testing relations are with the Nazis, and the feeling that is dramatized is not *ressentiment* but nausea. Nausea is Tagomi's repeated response to the nihilism and abstract evil of the Nazis.

3. Global History

In many of his other novels, Dick refuses sober extrapolation, as we have noted; the narrative must find some other basis, or celebrate its lack of basis; and as well as refusing extrapolation Dick will cut the novel off from history, breaking the world of the novel from its past and then depicting as shallow and stagnant whatever is supposed to have replaced the past. In *The Man in the High Castle*, Dick gives a great deal of careful scope to extrapolation, and parallels this with a strong sense of the historical specificities of behaviour and psychology—naturalization, acculturation, *ressentiment*. He maps a coherent space within history, we can recognize what happens in this space (there are ironic reflections on our own society) and even applaud its positive potential.

But the side of the novel which concerns the Nazis sets limits to this coherent space. The Nazis dominate history, but they are not of history in the sense in which history has a local rationality that can be reacted to and built on. It is certainly possible rationally to explain the growth of anti-semitism, petty bourgeois rancour, blood and soil nostalgia plus enthusiasm for technology: but having put the ingredients for Nazism in place, the rational has to be modified by a sense of the absurd and dreadful, because what ensues, the vastness of self-fuelling violence which takes over history, is difficult to reason about.[25] This is a reflection prompted by

---

[25] Rosenbaum's *Explaining Hitler* (1998) is an illuminating discussion of ways in which historians, theologians and film-makers have dealt with the problem or, sometimes, refused to acknowledge its existence.

the particular character of the Nazis' presence in history in *The Man in the High Castle*. As has been suggested, there is a lack of mesh between the novel's rich sense of local contingency and its apprehension of the global domination of mass forces. The Nazis represent this second aspect of history. Frank Frink sees them as ogres and automata, prehistoric men in sterile white lab coats—they have no stable temporal identity (ch. 1, 13–14). Tagomi feels that German totalitarian society is somehow adventitious, 'faulty' and 'pointless' (ch. 12, 200); the Nazis, for all their powers of organization and enterprise, are seen as improvisers, freaks, blind, possibly insane (ch. 6, 97)—incestuous, madly obsessive about their mothers (ch. 3, 36); the mind of the text itself tends to panic in their presence. As the story unfolds, however, it comes to be shaped by a strong desire for some sort of sublimation or transcendence, a jump to a new perspective, in which all will find its place. There are two claimants for this role: the complicated plot whereby Juliana and Tagomi both engage in killing, but Tagomi also saves Frank; and the *I Ching*.

The *I Ching* is a refreshing cultural presence in the world of the novel. It encourages us to think differently about textuality, and thence about the possibility that no received reality has supreme authority, and it does this even before we learn that Abendsen wrote *The Grasshopper Lies Heavy* with its aid, and even if we don't know that Dick said that he wrote *The Man in the High Castle* in the same fashion (Sutin 1989: 10). By its gnomic utterances, the *I Ching* suggests that the history one is apparently living has no existential primacy: the world of *The Man in the High Castle*, with which the characters have to cope, is not more real than that of *The Grasshopper Lies Heavy*, or than our own. It also suggests that this history is open, at least in the sense that each individual has a distinct place in it and a chance to understand it for himself or herself.

With its stress on 'the Moment' in which all are bound in interdependence by 'synchronicity', the philosophy behind the *I Ching* opposes a quality of horizontality to the remorselessly sequential and ongoing verticality of the history of events, controlled by the Nazis but issuing in a series of intrigues in our novel. So it may be, at least to the degree that the local and mundane, in which, for instance, Childan and Paul Kasoura interact, is given a little more scope. Because it is the virtue of the *I Ching*, as a 'good' text,[26] to be uncoercive, its activity in history is necessarily modest, and,

---

[26] Benign texts in Philip K. Dick are open and uncoercive, and they are often jokey in style (for instance, the messages in bottles that Glimmung sends Joe Fernwright in *Galactic Pot-Healer*, and the graffiti by which Glen Runciter communicates with his employees in *Ubik*); the bathetic style of the *I Ching* is analogous. Malign texts in Philip K. Dick coerce by foreclosing the future (for instance, the Book of the Kalends in *Galactic Pot-Healer* and Dr Bloode's book in *Lies, Inc.* tell you exactly what you are doing and are just about to do). See also Chapter 7, n. 6, below.

further, each moment in which a character consults the *I Ching* in the novel is overshadowed by the oncoming catastrophe of Operation Dandelion. Operation Dandelion is something alien to the *I Ching*, which it can intuit but not express. 'I open a book and get a report on future events that even God would like to file and forget', comments Frank Frink, when the oracle gives him incompatible messages regarding Operation Dandelion and the prospects of his jewellery business (ch. 4, 51). Indeed, at a crucial moment in the story, Tagomi suspects that the *I Ching* may have absconded from history, leaving human beings behind to make out as best they can (ch. 14, 222).[27]

Nonetheless it is true—again in a simple, mundane way—that the *I Ching* changes each moment in which it is consulted. The moment becomes different for the consulter, because he or she has to calm down and meditate on whatever the book teasingly supplies:

> His nose and feet are cut off.
> Oppression at the hands of the man with the purple knee-bands
> . . .
> For a long time—at least half an hour—he studied the line. (ch. 6, 101)

Further, the aleatory enters into the moment in which the oracle is consulted, since one comes up with a hexagram by manipulating stalks or coins, yet the idea is that the unique configuration of the moment enters into this seemingly random manipulation and thence the 'choice' of hexagram. The hexagram is thus the moment's report on itself. The working of the *I Ching* offers a fragile image of a way in which local history might mesh with and infiltrate the menacingly undifferentiated larger history. Being fragile, this image needs reinforcement, and that is supplied by its connections with Edfrank's humble 'squiggle' and with the two other texts, *The Grasshopper Lies Heavy* and *The Man in the High Castle*.

At the very end, when Juliana meets the author of *The Grasshopper Lies Heavy*, she establishes that this book is true, and was written with the assistance of the *I Ching*. The thematic point would be that the *I Ching* is the patron of the other two texts and all three share 'Inner Truth'. None is an imitation or replication of historical truth, to be judged by a criterion of accuracy; it is the Nazis who are condemned to repetition in their actions, just as their art, being representational, lacks meaning, as Baynes says to the Nazi artist Lotze ('I like the old prewar cubists and abstractionists. I like a picture to mean something, not merely to represent the ideal' [ch. 3, 39]). The Nazis have taken over history and reduced it to repetition and

---

[27] On the restricted role of the *I Ching*, see Rieder 1992: 225.

destruction. This alternative to representation and repetition can be connected to Edfrank's jewel, an abstraction, in whose making chance played a part—in the random shapes taken by the hot metal—and which, as we have seen, caused Paul Kasoura to recognize a new thing, requiring new behaviours.

As the plot develops, the outline of a redemptive movement can be discerned. Good comes out of evil; good perhaps comes by evil. Edfrank finance their business by blackmailing Wyndam-Matson, and they do that by terrifying Childan with the possibility that his artifacts will be exposed as fakes. Childan appropriates Edfrank's jewel; he accepts it back from Kasoura and eventually passes it on to Tagomi. His motivation at each point is morally dubious: duping Frank, defying Kasoura, gaining cheap power over the distressed Tagomi. But something good comes out of this set of transactions, as we saw when examining the significance of the 'wu' that Kasoura finds in the jewel. (The effect of the jewel on Tagomi will be considered below.) Again, Tagomi joins with Tedeki and Baynes in an intrigue whose Machiavellian rationale is that the good need to join with the 'most malignant' (ch. 12, 189) among the Nazis, because that element happens to be opposed to the surprise attack that the Nazis are planning. In the course of this, Tagomi has to kill, shooting down the hired assassins the Germans have sent against Tedeki.

He uses one of those 'antique' collectors' items, a Colt pistol—uses it with real skill and vim, in an exciting scene. The reader probably enjoys this scene, but Tagomi, who is an elderly bureaucrat, not a reader of thrillers, is horrified by what he has done. He had seen the pistol as a collectible (a thing for itself, functionless), and as part of a game innocently separate from the rest of social life ('Much fooled around in vainglorious swift-draw practicing and firing, in spare hours' [ch. 12, 192]). It turns out to be a piece of destructive technology—puny compared to an atom bomb, but shocking in the immediate circumstances. The sight of the dying SD man with his jaw shot off is sickening to Tagomi (ch. 12, 199).

> Whole situation confusing and anomalous, he decided. No human intelligence could decipher it; only five-thousand-year-old joint mind applicable. German totalitarian society resembles some faulty form of life, worse than natural thing. Worse in all its admixtures, its potpourri of pointlessness. (ch. 12, 200)

It is when he is in this condition that he accepts the jewel that Childan thrusts on him.

Meanwhile, Juliana has come to realize that Joe intends to kill the mysterious dissident author Abendsen. In her earlier dealings she had been confronting a mixed-up, embittered underling, a loser. The two of them had readily exchanged amateur psychoanalyses of each other's hang-ups (ch. 6, 84–90; ch. 9, 140–41). Now she realizes that Joe has been using her to get to Abendsen. She spends the day happily shopping with Joe, then he abruptly indicates that they will travel on to Abendsen at once; there is a kind of slippage, and she fugues into derangement:

> She said, speaking slowly and painstakingly, 'Hair creates bear who removes spots in nakedness. Hiding, no hide to be hung with a hook. The hook from God. Hair, hear, *Hur,*' Pills eating. Probably turpentine acid. They all met, decided dangerous most corrosive solvent to eat me forever. (ch. 13, 212)

Joe had got her a headache pill and made her have a shower: these simple things are transmuted by paranoid associations with Nazi crimes (hanging people on meat hooks, the deadly shower, the pill that releases gas). Presumably the shock of discovering what she had suspected but suppressed, that Joe is not a bitter, pitiable loser but the Beast itself, jolts her into this condition and nerves her to kill him.

We can say that she has been sickened, as was Tagomi, but what is disconcerting is that she appears to stay sick. She packs her new dress and the other things that Joe has bought her, and leaves him bleeding in the hotel room, without reporting the fact. The novel doesn't name her action as a killing until it appears in a newspaper she reads, and at this point we are told that she is 'Much less anxious now' and that she can make herself comfortable in a motel room and finish reading *The Grasshopper Lies Heavy* before contacting Abendsen (ch. 15, 247–48). It is hard to see why Dick has Abendsen praise her as something magical, a 'chthonic spirit' to whom the secret of the relation between the *I Ching* and *The Grasshopper Lies Heavy* has been entrusted (ch. 15, 258).[28]

Nonetheless there is a parallel between the two killings. An ambiguous redemption is brought to completion: through evil, some good is brought about. History is theologized, though disturbingly so, because the sequence under discussion seems as much Machiavellian as Christian. In addition, the parallel completes a structure of synchronicity. Tagomi and Juliana are synchronous; so are Edfrank, Childan, Kasoura and Tagomi, in the matter of the passage of the jewel from one to another. So, in a more poignant sense, are Tagomi and Frank, when Tagomi insults the German official Reiss and refuses to sign the papers condemning Frank to deportation as a

---

[28] Juliana's actions in the last part of the novel have been much discussed, and perhaps subjected to an interpretive pressure that they are not really equipped to answer. It is difficult to have confidence in any interpretation of her scene with Abendsen that does not also face the implications of the way she kills Joe Cinnadella and of her feelings about the killing —or her lack of them. (Contrast Rieder 1992: 225 and DiTommaso 1999: 112.)

Jew. This synchronicity is really the novel's self-awareness of what novels customarily do without seeming to advance a philosophy—or theology— of history. That is, the effect is not the invocation of a transcendent truth (that of Taoism), but the registration of the novel's enterprise at this point, which is a matter of telling a story interconnecting diverse characters, and posing that story against the grimness of history. This happens in a context in which history has been thrown into question (by the fact that three texts are on the scene, each imagining history), but not abolished. The reader has been made to see both the contingency and the terrible determinacy of history by the way her or his usual sense of synchronicity has been thematized as part of a view of history. The reader's habitual inference that separate episodes create meaning together because they are in the same novel feeds into an understanding that *The Man in the High Castle*, the *I Ching* and *The Grasshopper Lies Heavy* are all true.

Into the world of the novel there has been introduced a sequence of actions which has a coherent shape and which, because it does involve conflict with the Nazis, brings reasonableness to what is otherwise inchoately dreadful or nauseating. But this is not exactly the transcendence the novel sometimes reaches for. What is crucial, it seems to me, is Tagomi's experience. Here—more tellingly than with Juliana's lack of affect after killing Joe, for that finally seems a confused area of the novel, unlikely to yield productive discussion—the outcome is ambiguous.

In the course of a meeting of Japanese officials, Tagomi listens to the biographies of the Nazis who are candidates to succeed Bormann. He is bewildered and disgusted (ch. 6, 94–96). He experiences nausea: a sick response to a glimpse of the evil of those who now control history. Tagomi is literally sick; he has a heart attack. The reaction is renewed and intensified when he kills the SD assassins. It turns inward, becoming angst: Tagomi doubts his own philosophy, which involves not merely a quietist acceptance of the world but a faith in it—faith that there is always a Way, that seeming evil is part of a larger harmony. His life has lost its point. His third attack comes in connection with Edfrank's jewel, for which he had attempted to exchange the pistol he used to kill the assassins. He sits in a park and meditates; he interrogates the jewel. As is usual with Tagomi, every cultural resource is employed: Taoism, Aristotelianism, empirical description, stray tags from W.S. Gilbert, proverbs whose wisdom is not particularly obvious, allusions to Elijah and Paul.[29] And reality is abruptly transformed for him. At the moment when matters in his personal and historical universes are at their worst, he shifts into what we recognize as

---

[29] Wolk (1995: 106–109) traces the sources of this aspect of Tagomi in Dick's critiques of John D. Benjamin's Proverb Test in *We Can Build You* (1972) and *Timothy Archer* (1982).

the San Francisco of our history—dirty, noisy, racist. (Tagomi discovers the racism of this world when behaving with the racism of his own, that of a member of the ruling race—a racial structure which is of course rebuffed in the San Francisco of our history.) The experience is parallel to Juliana's intuition that *The Grasshopper Lies Heavy* presents a true history. But it is not really a happy one, not a revelation or transcendence. Tagomi is unsure whether he has had a mystical experience or a physical seizure.

At the end of the novel, we don't know whether the Nazi attack on Japan has been thwarted; and if it is thwarted the Nazis will no doubt break out in some other way, because they cannot do otherwise.[30] The actions that took place in the novel's ambiguously redemptive parallel plots are measured against this cloudier future. In addition, if they were synchronous, and thus interdependent, they were also performed in mutual ignorance. This ignorance figures forth the blindness of individuals in history, and suggests the narrow path left to individuals' free determination of their own and others' lives.

Whereas Marxist history often has trouble moving from the epochal to the quotidian, and contemporary cultural commentary tends to gaze obsessively on the dominant and ignore the exceptional and the residual, the novel, especially one that uses the procedures of realism, experiences a contrary problem. In the case of the treatment of history in *The Man in the High Castle*, this takes the form of a lack of fit between the local, the sphere of individual actions by unimportant people, and the epochal, dominated by the Nazis. To bring about, if not a meshing of the two levels or aspects of history, at least some glimpses of relation, *The Man in the High Castle* employs the resources of fantasy, of a textualist dissolution of the objective 'real', of a non-linear conception of temporality, and of a theologizing of history, or at least of the narrative that takes place within the alternative history. The modes of thinking of a novel are different from those of a work of theory or historiography; it is able to be experimental and 'nomadic'[31]—and, in this case, forced to be tentative and ambiguous. The Nazis are that element of evil and irrationality in global history which shocks the mind into uncertainty, and the *I Ching*, benign as it is, also takes us to the limits of reason. Just because it is careful about its extrapolation in a way that is unusual in Dick's fiction, *The Man in the High Castle* suggests the limits of reason in the treatment of history or society. The Nazis and the *I Ching* are outside the novel as well as inside it, in that they

---

[30] Frank's life is not safe, because he is Jewish; as for Abendsen, Dick planned a sequel in which he lies injured in the ruins of his house. (He discusses it in an interview, in August [?] 1974. See Williams [ed.] 1985: Side Two.)

[31] See Patton's exposition of this Deleuzian notion (1988).

remain unassimilated. Dick's other novels take a different course; they are more wildly and freely metaphorical or allegorical, but they contrive a whole series of different ways of suggesting how the making of connections and relations, whereby a text is given meaning about our history and society, runs up against baffling limits.

7. Eating and Being Eaten: Dangerous Deities and Depleted Consumers

In *The Country and the City*, Raymond Williams discusses 'To Penshurst', Ben Jonson's poem about the good life (1985: 28–33). The poem seems down to earth and straightforward: the good life is largely a matter of things to eat: fruit, cheese, fish, meat. Even people are seen as consumables, or as 'fruitful'. But nonetheless Williams enters a criticism; something is left out, because this is a good life of consumption. Williams proceeds to take a long view of the implications of this omission; Christianity, he says, has always been a religion of consumption, centring on communion, the love feast of believers. Production has received short shrift (1985: 30–31).

Certain themes in this strike a response in the reader not of 'To Penshurst', with its wholesome 'blushing apricot and woolly peach', but of Philip K. Dick, who creates worlds whose harassed inhabitants ingest nasty-tasting flakes of Proxian lichen, or tabs of Substance D, or, perhaps most dismaying, hamburgers made of 'turkey gizzards' and 'ground up cow's anuses'.[1] For Dick is aware (most tellingly in *A Scanner Darkly*, from which those last phrases are taken) that we live in a consumer society. He does try to rehabilitate production, in his many portraits of repairmen, potters or pot-healers, and craftsmen. These men and women are imagined as makers of special, 'wu'-invested things, humble antagonists of entropy. Dick tries to restore value to the individual thing, made or fixed, as against the non-thing, as it seems to be, mass produced and rapidly discarded or superseded.

Yet he is also inspired by the Christian ideal of fellowship and communion. He adheres to an ethic of kindness and empathy; he frequently centres his novels on a beleaguered group of ordinary people. These novels are often based on a stereotype of popular fiction (*Stagecoach*, *The Poseidon Adventure*, most of Agatha Christie): the random selection of ordinary people, thrown together to make common cause or to be rent by individual egos and individual histories. Dick is contributing to popular

---

[1] The Proxian lichen is in *Clans of the Alphane Moon* (1964); the substance D and the hamburgers are in *A Scanner Darkly* (ch. 2, 30).

culture's staging of the claims of the group against those of the individual. And in his case the effect can also be found where the group is less explicitly separated out; for instance, in *The Man in the High Castle* with the duo of Edfrank and the trio of Tagomi, Baynes and Tedeki.

Solidarity is a perennial hope for him; shared consumption might well be a value. As often with this novelist, it is a matter of balancing humanist values against perception of the condition of social life—in this instance, as it is dictated by postmodern consumption. In this condition 'the human' is hard to find or define. In the work of Baudrillard, to take an extreme instance, subjects are seen as objects, brought about by the processes of consumption. This chapter traces Dick's treatment of consumption, particularly eating, from its general social occurrence to its occurrence in those episodes in which a deity eats or consumes humans, in an inversion of the eucharist. This discussion will complement the picture of the phenomenological shape of Dick's megatext that was offered in Chapter 3, and extend the discussion of his sense of the situation of the producer and consumer that was opened in Chapter 5. The previous chapter concerned the testing of reason in the face of the irrational aspects of modern history; here we see Dick elaborating a kind of anti-eucharist, an inverted myth of consumption. The effect is ironical, exploratory: the feelings and possibilities expressed are ambiguous.

In those of his fictions that are concerned with being merged with or consumed by a deity, Dick's strong valuation of individuality, in people as in things, battles against his sense that ordinary people need help, and need to join in a fellowship or common purpose such as the superior being may offer—but at the risk of their individuality. In what follows, reference is made to deities: entities that can, for instance, manifest themselves in a variety of places or worlds, and appear to create new worlds; entities with a great deal of control over the bodies of others and a great deal of insight into their thoughts. It is true that powers like these are also possessed by freaks or psionics, by governments and strongmen and ruthless women in Dick's novels, in varying degrees, but one misses a point by defining deity too precisely

The high degree of overlap between outsiders—deities—and insiders such as strongmen suggests Dick's complex feelings about power. It appears that power to manipulate or know others is very much the same thing, whoever has it, and in whatever degree. Deities may be like dictators, so that there is nothing sacred or numinous about their power; dictators may be like deities, in having uncanny insight into others and the capacity to influence them. Each possibility is unnerving. Conversely, deities are often maimed or imperfect, and dictators are often clumsy and hampered in some way, or revealed to be subject to some other, more menacing power.[2] Power is ceaselessly dehumanized and rehumanized, and perhaps this is because in Dick's universe it is everywhere and nowhere: power is constantly being exercised, and its scope is vaster than even in our world, but it is owned by no individual, not even a dictator or deity.

This restless complexity reflects the difficulty of expressing power as process, as something systemic, through conventional fictional agents in the form of individual characters, even characters of a bizarrely variegated kind. It also renders advisable circumscribed critical discussion of a topic that is otherwise boundless: thence the linkage of consumption and eating, eating and the individual's relations to a deity, in what follows. But it has to be added that the problem is not just to do with power; it is do with the status of the individual. The whole treatment of consumption comes to a crisis at the point where a figure that is not individual, that is sometimes a blend of deity and android, offers to consume the protagonist. That this is a nightmare of consumerism ('if you go on trying to devour everything, something will want to devour you') is one thing, and obvious; that it jeopardizes the sense of individuality is another, and ambiguous. As was suggested, the 'something' is complex, fallible and hard to define as Other in a clear-cut way. It is neither nature nor the unconscious nor the alien, to name three things with which one might for instance identify Dracula, that famous, powerful devourer.

1. Wide Angle: Images of Consumption

Eating as it usually occurs is a distinctly material business. Indeed we might say that if eating is not material, nothing is, and in considering Philip K. Dick this aphorism, though probably erroneous like all aphorisms, is useful as a starting point. The eater very likely participates in the transformation of raw into cooked, and then of cooked into nourishment of his or her body by means of a physical activity, chewing and swallowing, that takes perceptible time. Then the residues have to be defecated, put through the Insinkerator, treated with indigestion pills and so forth.

---

[2] For example, Stanton Brose in *The Penultimate Truth* (1964), a vast bulk kept going by 'artiforgs' (he is described as a 'fat semi-dead organism' [ch. 5, 44]); the gross Willis Gram in *Frolix 8* (1970), wallowing in his bed as he transacts business (see e.g. ch. 16); Gino Molinari in *Now Wait for Last Year* (1966), apparently all-powerful because he can reinforce himself with new versions of himself from alternative presents, but actually subordinate to the aliens with whom Terra is allied. Analogous is the common case of a character who has impressive will and presence, but whose actual power is local and puny: Arnie Kott in *Martian Time-Slip* (1964) is a good example; so is Glen Runciter in *Ubik*, massive yet clumsy, able to manifest himself like a god, yet by no means omniscient (see ch. 14).

But another kind of ingestion is only minimally material: consumption of fast food is on the way to this, since the stuff is processed rather than cooked, and eaten quickly, leaving behind bits of greasy plastic that disappear into a bin, and a confused feeling that you must have eaten, since you are now feeling dissatisfied rather than hungry. Less tendentious examples of this second kind of ingestion include the consumption of a pill, a eucharistic wafer, a pinch of snuff,[3] a shot of heroin. In these cases that which is ingested is insubstantially material. Its effect is sometimes on the body, but often on the mind or spirit—drugs to affect mood, insight and fantasy, or even to make contact with the divine. It may be taken in at some other orifice than the mouth, by sniffing or injection.

It is probably manufactured, or pre-processed, or questionable in its origins. There is a scene in A Scanner Darkly (1977) (ch. 10, 161–63) where Barris, who has earlier tried to extract cocaine from Solarcaine, a suntan spray, is to be seen stuffing little scraps of mushroom into capsules and then working the phones trying to sell his product; he evidently feels that a drug should appear manufactured, not merely collected in the woods. Elsewhere in the novel there is talk of the secret formula behind Coca-Cola,[4] which is thereby seen as a drug of mysterious origins, like Substance D, the drug at the centre of the story.

Perhaps it is the case that the more the Material is attenuated or purged, the readier we are for contact with the Immaterial, the divine: an involuntary ascesis, such as sometimes happens in fictions of space flight, where the antiseptic feel of technology and the rationalized abstractness of its processes are accompanied by a disembodiment of the humans and others involved. 2001: A Space Odyssey (dir. Kubrick, 1969) is an example: there follows an encounter with a deity, itself of a very abstracted kind. For several reasons, however, this is likely to be a complex matter in Dick's imagination of it. He is strongly drawn to the thingness of things, as has been discussed; his fictions are full of nightmares of insubstantiation, in which things melt, fade, dissolve, attenuate, leaving nothing, or leaving horrible withered remains (Joe Chip's companions in Ubik), or a scrap of paper with a name on it. In his treatment of consumption by deities, Dick is likely to be uneasy at the prospect of losing that thingness or individuality which he often struggles to recover in his fiction, even allowing for his attraction to Gnosticism, Taoism and Platonism, with their various ways of expressing the feeling that the real may be elsewhere.

---

[3] Dick himself was a devout if heterodox member of the Episcopalian Church, a consumer of many prescribed medications and controlled substances, and a taker of snuff.

[4] The history of Coca-Cola, from its murky origins, has recently been published: see Prendergast 1993. (See A Scanner Darkly, ch. 8, 148).

Anthropologically speaking, forms of ingestion that attenuate the material and achieve contact with the immaterial depend on a 'normality' in everyday eating and consumption. This condition holds even if normality is relative. But the relatively stable contrast which gives definition to both kinds of eating is lacking in Dick's novels. His depiction of eating or being eaten by gods is coloured by his sense of the depletedness of 'normal' consumption in his own, contemporary society and in the societies he imagines. In the dystopian future societies in which Dick sets novels such as *Ubik* and *Palmer Eldritch* and in the facsimiles or images of present society in which he sets novels such as *Time out of Joint* and *A Scanner Darkly*, 'normal' eating has been shaken loose from the material and substantial, and from the connections it often has with the erotic; it is thinned, dessicated.

In these societies, dazzling futurist technology abounds, and occupies even the most banal areas of life: there is not only space travel, but there are robot taxis, obedient like robots but opinionated like taxi-drivers; not only 'psychotropic' darts that can home in on your individual brainwaves, but beds that insist on your having the regulation amount of sleep and what is more, if you are sleeping alone, experiencing the regulation dream.[5] It is true that perfection of the technology of surveillance and destruction is common in dystopian fiction, and is often accompanied by degradation of the quality of individual life: omniscient governments, vast cities, tiny apartments, dull jobs. But in Dick's case the combination of technological evolution and the degradation of life is problematic. It doesn't seem logical that technology should have advanced and the production of food and the means of comfort should have regressed at the same time, even when we take account of the fact that technology so frequently malfunctions in Dick's fiction.

Perhaps the combination is illogical as an extrapolation but telling as a metaphor. This metaphor would then reflect the arrival of a historical condition in which consumption, like production, has become dematerialized. We consume not foodstuffs but images, or items of information — and both Dick's characters and his readers put their most frantic energies into the processing of information. The metaphor has a critical edge. When they consume, his characters experience a lack, and this is the sign that things have gone wrong for them.

We notice that men with exceptional power and privilege in Dick's dystopian futures not only drink genuine whisky and coffee, and have big-breasted mistresses; they also have good hi-fi sets and collections of classical recordings. (These are the three common signs of power and privilege.) It is not only decent food that is lacking to all except the

---

[5] Taxis: *Now Wait for Last Year*; darts: *Lies, Inc.*; dreams: *Galactic Pot-Healer*.

powerful: also lacking to all except the powerful is the means of spiritual nourishment, chiefly, in Dick's view, music.[6] And we can notice that while whisky or coffee or cigars *are* occasionally available to the powerful (they are drugs, after all), such things as apples and steaks are not.

It is significant also that the breast—the place where nourishment and the erotic might be felt to converge—is revealed only to be de-eroticized. Women in Dick's fiction very often have jutting breasts, enlarged or artificially erected nipples; they also, often, bare their breasts, only to reveal implanted jewellery in the nipples, or even a kind of light show—things that rebuff the impulse to kiss or caress. Appropriately for my topic here, the light show is worn by a waitress in a restaurant, and, predictably, the luxurious meal to which the main character and a big-breasted mistress are ushered by the waitress is interrupted and unsatisfying (*Lies, Inc.*, ch. 5, 46–51).[7]

Again, there is a scene in a coffee shop in *A Scanner Darkly*: Charles Freck is eating a sugar-glazed doughnut, Barris is consuming patty melt ('melted imitation cheese and fake ground beef on special organic bread'). The two men usually consume Substance D and suchlike; today they are taking another road to poor health.

> 'The waitress we had last time was named Patty,' Barris said, eying the waitress grossly. [She has a name tag on her left breast.] 'Same as the sandwich.'
>
> 'That must have been a different Patty from the sandwich. I think she spells it with an *i*.' (ch. 3, 37)

---

[6] Radio is almost invariably benign, and television almost invariably malign, in Dick's fiction. Radio is seen as a source of music, television as a source of news and talk shows, both of them lying and intrusive. An example of the benignity of radio is the orbiting disk-jockey Walt Dangerfield in *Dr Bloodmoney* (1965), a marooned astronaut with a vast music library which he draws upon to console the post-holocaust survivors on Earth. A fascinating piece of evidence here is the scene in *Mary and the Giant* (1987) (ch. 11, 101) in which Coombs, a deranged and racist cameraman, waits in his car before attempting to kill the black blues singer Carleton Tweany; he listens to classical music, and the titles are carefully enumerated for us. Examples of the malignity of television include Buster Friendly's nasty talk show in *Androids*, and the extraordinary passage in *Lies, Inc.* in which the braying television image of President Omar Jones mutates into a cyclopean monster which proliferates dozens of eyes, itself consumes them, and begins to exude more eyes (ch. 10, 130; ch. 12, 142). This treatment of television relates to an emphatic unease about looking (the feeling that one is being watched is defined as the source of paranoia) and eyes (the title scene in *Eye in the Sky* [1957] 95–96]). The preference of the medium of music to that of 'news' also figures as a comment on the regime of signs and signification in which the texts are them-

occur in *The Simulacra, The World Jones Made*, and 'We Can Remember ...e'.

The one Patty is politely unavailable, the other is indigestible. Barris doesn't get any further with either; instead he and Freck talk gloomily about how they cut off your 'pecker' in drug rehab centres (the word itself suggests a meagre way of eating). This is depleted consumption and attentuated sexuality at their grimmest.

These pictures of consumption thwarted or depleted amid technological sophistication perhaps bespeak the modern condition. A brief historical survey is in order; an impressionistic one, because it is not contended that these fictions respond to a history that might be agreed on objectively. (For instance, the consensus[8] is that the fifties in America were a time of enjoyed abundance, but this is not what Dick's stories and novels convey.) The 1950s: a rise in wealth, unaccompanied by an abundance of good things to spend it on; a feeling of increased power, technological and financial, issuing in a kind of bewilderment or unease, as the power cannot be applied at the right points and the money cannot buy what one dimly remembers as a decent meal—this is the twist Dick imparts to the conventional view of the period. The cliché image for the fifties, say an advertisement for Hoover depicting a brisk young housewife with a shiny new vacuum cleaner, with which she may enjoy herself, if she can, catches a truth.[9]

Elsewhere, for instance in *Time out of Joint* (1959), the accent is on malnourishment: Ragle Gumm lives in a household whose idea of adventurous cooking is lasagne. He drinks warm beer; he *likes* it warm. Judging from his fiction, then, Dick enters the sixties as a malnourished, frustrated consumer. The shift from the scene in the Lucky Dog Pet Shop, in which Dick is buying the pet food to eat himself, in his poverty, and the owner knows it, and Dick knows the owner knows it, to the glimpse of Dick standing in front of his refrigerator shovelling in amphetamines by the handful is a drastic one indeed.[10] The sixties is the era of drugs, a new dimension in consumption, a time when consumption goes rebellious. It

---

[8] See for instance Hine 1986, Halberstam 1993, and Jackson 1985.

[9] *Confessions of a Crap Artist*, published in 1975 but written in 1959, presents in Fay Hume a tough but perceptive picture of a woman revolting against housework (several important scenes show how she is trapped in contradiction, wanting others to do the housework yet feeling men are unmanly when they do it; for instance, ch. 13, 166–68), strong and adventurous yet desperate to retain her expensive house. Fay could be seen as another of Dick's predatory females, but this would be a mistake: here we have a moment in the history of women that belongs with *The Feminine Mystique* and *Peyton Place*. See discussion in Chapter 4 above.

[10] See Dick's Introduction to *The Golden Man* (1980), xv-xvi; Sutin 1989: 169. Samuel J. Umland reminds me that the pet food in question was horsemeat, and that this is significant in view of Dick's later discovery that his own name could be punningly rendered 'Horselover Fat' (*Valis*). Images of self-consumption in *Lies, Inc.* are discussed below.

is mostly in Dick's novels of the sixties, in which drugs are often consumed or the effects of drugs are replicated in various ways, that people meet devouring deities.

2. Dangers of the Deity

In the course of *Ubik* (1969), Joe Chip and his friends gradually discover why things in their world are failing, regressing and fading, and why they themselves are horribly withering and expiring one by one. Things and people are trapped in a half-life universe fabricated by Jory, a vicious teenager with ugly spade-like teeth (ch. 5, 44). The things fade because Jory cannot sustain them, and it is Jory who is killing Joe's companions. He is eating them, absorbing what remains of their lives to feed his own, and he can do this because, having died young, he has more vitality and thus power, even in half-life. In something like a combat of good and evil deities, he is opposed by Joe's boss Glen Runciter, who intrudes into Jory's decaying world with gnomic, witty messages—graffiti on a toilet wall, interruptions to a television commercial for detergent. Runciter finally conveys something called 'Ubik' to Joe; 'Ubik' is not very solidly material, since its manifestations change and it is sprayed from an aerosol can, but it is material, and reassuringly linked to the banal, since it can be proclaimed by advertising slogans (the epigraphs to the book's chapters). It is also divine, if you can believe advertisments: 'I am Ubik. Before the universe was, I am' (ch. 17, 201: the ultimate epigraph).

Ubik the novel ends hopefully: the devouring adolescent deity of the 'half-life' world is thwarted by an aerosol with divine pretensions. We can ascertain from our survey of Dick's treatment of consumption that Ubik the spray satisfies certain conditions: it comes from a benign, non-coercive deity;[11] it is both magical and linked to the ordinary; it works to recover the thingness of people and objects.

In *Galactic Pot-Healer* (published the same year as *Ubik*, 1969) Joe Fernwright, a washed-up depressive, is rescued by a very powerful 80,000-ton being called Glimmung—or possibly 'the Glimmung', because he is the sole member of a race of one. Rather like Glen Runciter, Glimmung communicates by intruding witty and cryptic messages into Joe's world—a message in a bottle floating in Joe's toilet, for instance (ch. 2, 23). He proceeds to gather Joe and a motley collection of other failures and misfits from many systems in order to raise the sunken cathedral

---

[11] Several deities—Glen Runciter is allied to his wife Ella ('She'), young and sexually attractive. Consumption is again connected to sexuality; when he found Ella, Joe had actually been looking for a prostitute. (This side of Joe is discussed in Chapter 3 above.)

Heldscalla. The task seems a trifle pointless, but it is certainly positive. It may even be that Glimmung has invented it to give his team a purpose. Many things impede the task (Jungian doubles; a determinist text called the Kalends which adapts itself to and prescribes the exact future for each of its readers). Glimmung himself nearly dies. At this low point, when Joe seems more depressed than ever, Glimmung abruptly raises himself from where he lies wallowing in his own blood and the icy water of the lake (he is here comparable to the dying Christ, giving forth blood and water), rears up awesomely, and 'engulfs' Joe and his companions. Included in this mighty being, these individuals seem like worms in a cadaver; the voices of their individualities echo tinily, no more than background noise to Glimmung's 'mentation', which, however, is strengthened by theirs. This is the climax of the story (ch. 15, 166; ch. 16, 181–85). Thus enhanced, Glimmung succeeds in raising Heldscalla, transcending as it does so both gender (it becomes female, for the moment containing Heldscalla as a kind of foetus, which is then born onto dry land) and time (it becomes younger and stronger again, regressing). Having achieved all this, it invites the intergalactic team to stay within it, sharing in purpose and strength. Only Joe Fernwright and one other creature (a multi-legged gastropod) refuse, and are ejected onto the dreary shore.

Dick has played out a confrontation between the individual, ineffective and a failure, and the saviour whom the individual plainly needs, in this case a benign saviour. Yet the point of this final episode seems clear. The absorption of Joe and his friends by Glimmung, whereby both parties gain strength and purpose, must be refused.

Very early in the novel, Joe puffs a cigarette in his drab cubicle, and meditates:

> What do I really yearn for? [. . .] That for which oral gratification is a surrogate. Something vast, he decided; he felt the primordial hunger gape, huge-jawed, as if to cannibalize everything around him. (ch. 1, 10)

Joe is better off as we last see him, on his own, trying, and failing, to make a pot, a unique thing, trying to revive the métier of the craftsman (ch. 16, 188–89).

In *The Three Stigmata of Palmer Eldritch* (1965; an earlier novel than *Ubik* and *Galactic Pot-Healer*) the eponymous character returns to, infiltrates and begins to take over the two worlds on which the novel takes place: an intolerably hot Terra, and the colony planet Mars, a place so dreary that the inhabitants not only live in hovels but accept 'hovel' as the customary name for what they live in. Eldritch is an uncertain amalgam of human entrepreneur and nameless creature from the intersystem void.[12] Eldritch pushes Chew-Z, a drug which both traps the person who takes it inside Eldritch's creation, and is inflected by the taker's own desires and imaginings. By the end of the novel, Eldritch has possessed at least the bodies of most of the humans. They have become him and he has become them; they show his 'stigmata' (steel teeth, horizontal slotted artificial eyes, gleaming metal arm). They have not only become Palmer Eldritch, they have become partly non-human, but they have also attained, if not immortality, at least durability. They won't need glasses when they get old, because they have 'Jensen luxvid' for eyes.

In a travesty of union with the godhead, the human being gains durability, freedom from the strict bonds of time, and the capacity to create things from nothing—as in the episode in which Eldritch creates a 'gluck' which nastily bites Leo Bulero's leg, but Leo counters with a gluck trap which frizzles the little beast (ch. 6, 75–77). The exchange between human and deity seems grimly weighted in favor of the deity, however:

> *Who gets sacrificed?* Leo asked himself. Me, Barney, Felix Blau—which of us gets melted down for Palmer to guzzle? Because that's what we are potentially for him: food to be consumed. It's an oral thing that arrived back from the Prox system, a great mouth, open to receive us. (ch. 11, 155)[13]

There ought to be no doubt that Eldritch is evil, whatever species of being he is. But there *is* doubt. Eldritch is seen as ambiguous, perhaps suffering and trapped—'stigmata' suggests a kind of mutilation, rather than inhuman power, which is what his appendages might otherwise suggest (steel teeth, for instance). The explanation for this abstention from condemning the Eldritch thing as evil lies in the sterility of the world he threatens, which already depends on illusions nested in fakes.[14] Already people depend on a drug, Can-D, which has the effect of making the taker one with Pat or Walt, two dolls along the lines of Barbie and Ken, living in a miniaturized consumerist paradise which appears real when one is living as Pat or Walt in the state of fusion that Can-D brings. Taking Can-D is a group activity (the males fuse into Walt, the females into Pat; there don't seem to be any other options), but, like the group experience of 'fusion' in *A Maze of Death*,[15] it tends to bring out rivalries and fierce desires

---

[12] See Tolley 1980. Tolley also discusses 'Faith of Our Fathers' (1967, CS5), a story involving a very ambiguous deity.

[13] The Nazis are imagined in similar terms by Baynes in *The Man in the High Castle*: 'Man has not eaten God; God has eaten man' (ch. 3, 42).

[14] This part of the novel is anticipated by 'The Days of Perky Pat' (1963, CS4).

[15] This very interesting novel is briefly discussed in Chapter 9. (In *Galactic Pot-Healer*, union with Glimmung is also called 'fusion'. See for instance ch. 16, 181.)

within the group, rather than expressing solidarity or a ceremonial bonding. At the least, those who take Can-D cannot decide whether they are looking for 'transubstantiation', as some of them call it, seeking a religious dimension, or group sexual gratification. In the circumstances, they are vulnerable to Eldritch.

Two characters, Leo and Barney, do resist him—yet for most of the novel these two are in conflict not with Eldritch but with each other, and the theme of their conflict is sacrifice. Barney would not risk his safety to help Leo, Leo would not risk his safety to help Barney. These failures lead to enmity. Barney decides to 'atone' for his failure by having himself shipped to Mars; there, when Leo induces him to help him outwit Eldritch, the plot takes the form of having Barney ingest a drug to imitate the effects of epilepsy. (The effects will then be blamed on Chew-Z, and Eldritch will be held responsible: Eldritch's plan to subject the world to Chew-Z will be thwarted.) This plot fails. Instead of being the instrument of Leo's plot against Eldritch, Barney becomes an avatar of Eldritch, developing his stigmata.

At a nadir of self-disgust, stuck in a broken-down 'dredge' on the Martian wasteland, he is menaced by a specimen of the local fauna, a telepathic jackal.[16] The jackal is hungry, it approaches, then it retreats, rejecting Barney decisively.

> '*Unclean*,' it thought to itself; it halted at a safe distance and fearfully regarded him, tongue lolling. 'You're an unclean thing,' it informed him dismally. (ch. 13, 184)

Barney sees the refusal of a low life-form to eat him as the ultimate humiliation (ch. 13, 183–84). Consumed by Eldritch, one is unfit for consumption by anything else, and ashamed of the fact. This is not the end of the novel—it ends with Leo's resolution to carry on the struggle against Eldritch, even though Eldritch appears to have taken over everyone on earth—but it is a powerful moment.

Dick last imagines a god eating a human in his story 'Rautavaara's Case' (1980, CS5); this is an interesting story, but set firmly in a context of cultural relativity (the message is that the eating of the worshipper by the god is no more unnatural than the eating of the god by the worshipper).

In his religious, speculative novels of his last years, Dick imagines deities with very different qualities. The trouble with most of those discussed so far is that, though powerful, they are not benevolent as we hope gods will be. The trouble with the gods of the late novels, the child Sophia

---

[16] Carlos Castaneda's first book, *The Teachings of Don Juan* (1970 [1968]), features a bilingual coyote; in *Palmer Eldritch*, telepathy solves the language problem.

in *Valis* (1981) and the child Emmanuel in *The Divine Invasion* (1981), is that, though benevolent, they are not powerful, as gods need to be if they are to save us. Emmanuel is suffering from amnesia and cannot remember that he is God; Sophia sickens and dies. These are impaired gods; they certainly leave humans their autonomy, but not in the witty mannner of Glimmung's and Runciter's cryptic messages; humans are left to speculate feverishly, to search for meanings in a world in which everything has become a sign, like the label on Patty's breast and the sign on Ragle's drink stand; and the search for meanings is eventually a distraction from action of any kind.[17]

There is much more to be said of these late novels; in Chapter 11 I shall discuss the way in which *The Transmigration of Timothy Archer* (1982) ends with the return, not of an ambiguous, menacing deity like Eldritch, but of the all-too-human Timothy Archer—a return to humanism for Dick, as Norman Spinrad has said (1990: 198, 216). Here we may recall that Archer dies on a crazy search for a holy mushroom which, he has come to believe, the early Christians ingested in order to become God: the eucharist given a literal, material meaning. Moreover, he dies because he takes nothing more nourishing than a couple of bottles of soda water into the desert with him. The irony of submitting to consumption on a transcendent level when one cannot or will not consume satisfactorily on a mundane level is again underlined. And Dick's late, ambiguously religious novels are immediately preceded by *A Scanner Darkly* (1977, discussed in Chapter 10), which offers the most moving and detailed presentation of the fate of the depleted consumer in postmodern society.

In ambiguously melding consumption and the divine, Dick is playing with the notion of consumption as transcendence, that is, as the only transcendence we can now expect. This is clearest in the treatment of Ubik —a commodity, a god, a poison (at one point), an elixir, a device with a scientific rationale, an object of quest: the drastic overdetermination expresses, surely, an uncertainty. Are we being suckered by commodities, in the most obvious way, or (and?) is submission to this suckering the best chance we have of finding value? To put the question in a broader context, are Warhol's Campbell's Soup cans even emptier and blander than the things we put in the supermarket trolley, or are they icons?

Ubik is, however, an object of consumption rather than a thing which consumes. It seems that the religious element in Dick's novels up until the late theological novels is best seen as a way of allegorizing the nature of consumption in modern society. By means of this allegory, Dick denies

---

[17] See Chapter 12 for discussion of *Valis*'s obsession with signification and credulousness about texts.

that consumption is what identifies the subject, as might be the case in postmodern society; rather, it is something done to the subject by a power that threatens identity. One could not even say that consumption 'inter-pellates' the subject in consumer society, if this implies that, having been interpellated, he or she is able to act stably in that society and feel part of it. It might seem that the individual is simply left in desolate islation, like Joe Fernwright at the end of *Galactic Pot-Healer*, who is at least free of absorption in the collective that the deity allegorizes. But the matter is less clear-cut than that: Joe is in fact accompanied by a 'multi-legged gastro-pod' which has also refused Glimmung, and which wisely advises Joe to turn to production (the making of pots); in *Palmer Eldritch*, Leo and Barney have in fact co-operated in their struggle against Eldritch. There is usually some 'sodality', to borrow Suvin's word, inhabiting a shadowy space between a threatening collective and the lonely individualism that is asserted against that collectivity. The sodality is always present, but its place is always on the margins of the novels, largely, perhaps, because sexual warmth and affection between individuals are never present. Sexuality, again in the form of consumption, is thwarted in the individ-ual, for instance Joe Chip, and is enacted by the deity with shameful effects for the individual, for instance in the case of Palmer Eldritch and Barney Mayerson.

8. Critique and Fantasy in *Martian Time-Slip* and *Clans of the Alphane Moon*

Martian Time-Slip and *Clans of the Alphane Moon*, which are among the novels Philip K. Dick published in 1964, are alike in several ways, but sufficiently different to provide striking illustrations of his procedures as a novelist. In both novels Dick attempts to fit realist delineation of mundane lives and struggles, and fantastical, sometimes whimsical, reality distortions into the same text. *Martian Time-Slip* and *Clans of the Alphane Moon* are 'anti-psychiatric' novels. Both suggest that the socially powerful are more dangerous—since prevailing ideology both encourages their destructive behaviour and blinds them to their own condition—than are those who are labelled insane and rendered powerless. Both parties live by fantasy; social 'reality' is not readily available as a norm. In this respect these novels corroborate the contemporary anti-psychiatric politics of Thomas Szasz and R.D. Laing.

Clans is largely a novel about a bitter marital break-up, and *Time-Slip*, extensively concerned with parents and children and the inability of adults to protect children from the evil abroad in their society, is pervaded by aridity and degradation. These observations may lead in two different directions. We may be reminded of how solidly both novels are concerned with things we can all recognize, and fear: the strains of divorce, the difficulty of committing suicide when all the neighbours in your apartment block know what you are up to, the difficulty of understanding your children when the passage of lived history means that they are alien to you, the strains of life in the suburbs. (Silvia Bohlen and Erna Steiner and their kids, beside the banks of the dull Martian canal, are living in the suburbs —or a better comparison would be with one of the trailer-park settlements on the outskirts of small towns in the American West.) Or we may feel that both novels are intensely concerned with sterility (see Chapter 5 above), and that this sterility has an ontological dimension: although we can explain it as a reflection of social forces (wastefulness and destructive competition), this explanation does not seem fully adequate. It signifies the encroachment of entropy, which is at once that which destroys life and that which, alone, underlies reality. The fiction moves from representation and critique to something like myth, as was noted in the previous chapter in relation to Dick's imagination of consumption by deities. The key here is Dick's sense of modern society's co-operation with the entropic forces of waste; to redress this, he goes outside society (which is deconstructed anyway in the course of *Time-Slip*) to aliens and misfits, and in the same motion goes outside the terms of the realist novel.

In Dick's fiction, individuals' actions, commitments and entanglements with each other express perceptions about social forces. The forces that compel the characters and transform the patterns of their relationships are recognizable as those that relentlessly form and reform modern societies. This is what determines who loves, fights, deceives, owns, rescues, is alienated from or momentarily allied with whom, and, furthermore, impels the characters' hectic lurches through several or all of these actions, commitments and entanglements. The dynamism of the plots is Dick's seizure of the dynamism of modern society. Yet, although these perceptions about social forces are extremely pessimistic, the characters whose actions are impelled by them occasionally, by their actions, resolve the problems set up, if only because genres of popular fiction, with which Dick is expertly working, encourage this resolution. The ruthless battle between the big organization and the honest loner, involving both labyrinthine conspiracy and sudden violence; the wise advice of a dispassionate outsider (Lord Running Clam, Helio, Doreen Anderton); the culminating shoot-out (personal conflict transformed into interpersonal discharge of laser bolts); the reunion of estranged husband and wife, chastened and happier; the escape of the imprisoned, vindication of the victimized: all these can be found in thrillers or romances, and found also in *Clans* and *Time-Slip*, in the context of radical criticism of social sickness. Neither novel reaches the sort of simplistically happy resolution suggested by these remarks; nonetheless, we begin to appreciate the vectors shifting and tugging Dick's characters through such bizarre alignments and exchanges: in *Clans*, Chuck Rittersdorf's movement from his wife Mary, to Joan Trieste, to Annette Golding, to Lord Running Clam, and back to Mary; in *Time-Slip*, the interplay of Arnie, Otto, Manfred, Jack, and Helio which results in Arnie's death, Otto's death, Manfred's escape and Jack's escape (from Arnie *and* from Manfred). In *Clans*, Dick finds moments of mutual assistance and kindness in the midst of the prevailing aggression and conspiracy which expresses his sense of the psychopathology of the powerful. In *Time-Slip*, patterns of ironized sacrifice, by which the powerful become victims and the victims escape their bondage, are drawn out of relationships of exploitation.

This discussion concentrates on the relations between political critique and the element of fantasy in these two novels. Here and in the next chapter, we turn aside from the confrontation of humanist and postmodernist which has structured the discussion so far. In Dick's fiction, the postmodern appears as the extremity of the modern; it is modernity that he critiques, and at certain moments, as in novels such as *Ubik* or *A Scanner Darkly*, postmodernity shows through as modernity pushed to its limits. Similarly, humanist ethical concern is important in Dick because of the confrontations and contortions he is put to as he simultaneously expresses his hopes of individual responsibility, kindness and solidarity with others, and expresses his intuitions about a modernity pressed to postmodernity.

Nonetheless, structuring the discussion around this confrontation has its limitations, because it runs the risk of replicating the very split between the individual (seat of value and small group affirmations) and society (arena of system, of domination and of transforming historical change) on which liberal modern society is founded—a split which has repeatedly thwarted its own ideals.[1] Indeed, we saw avatars of this split in the division between global and local histories in *The Man in the High Castle*, and we will see it again in the formal vicissitudes of the empathetic scene from middle to late Dick. With *Clans* and *Time-Slip* in mind, it could be said that psyche and society come into existence in the same instant and that neither can be thought, or has meaning, without the other. This formulation does catch the interpenetration of different fields of existence that we find in Dick's novels, the sense that what we usually see as social manifests itself in some inner quirk of the psyche and what we usually see as personal is to be found shaping some large aspect of the whole world. Yet in its turn it misses the conflict and collision that is the life of the interpenetration.

In the discussion that follows, 'fantasy' has been chosen as a term sufficiently ambivalent to help define how these fields of existence collide and conflict in two of Dick's novels. As was observed in Chapter 5, fantasy can be a value (creative imagination); a force that shapes societies to the wills and desires of the powerful; and also a force that shapes stories to the will and desire of the writer, by way of, for instance, wish-fulfilment. To define it more rigorously, as 'the fantastic', something that exceeds and negates realism, is to overlook the messy struggle by which the fiction reconciles the potentials of representation and fantasy. Dick's manoeuvres between realism and fantasy are attempts to see past the limitations of realism, as the ideology behind the split between individual and society that does structure modernity, without abandoning realism's potential for relevance, the ways it can speak directly to mundane experience. *Clans* takes the form of satiric fantasy; the novel proceeds not by criticizing fantasy, however, but by acting it out and transforming social possibility.

---

[1] This is the theme of Melley's *Empire of Conspiracy* (2000), which briefly discusses Dick's work.

Time-Slip is much closer to the novel of inwardly developed character and social detail, yet its procedure is critical of the premises of this kind of novel, and it eventually abandons them.

1. Lord Running Clam Reproduces

At the centre of *Clans of the Alphane Moon* is a story of divorce and marital combat, involving Chuck and Mary Rittersdorf and a variety of women, men and aliens. At first it appears that the clans of the title and their affairs on the moon of the title frame the story of the Rittersdorfs. The frame is ironic: while the notion of a moon inhabited and co-operatively governed by former mental patients, organized into clans of 'Pares' (paranoids), 'Heebs' (hebephrenics) and so forth, seems weird, and the notion of husband and wife struggling over jobs, money, and kids seems ordinary, it turns out that the members of the clans are sane, whereas those involved in the main story are insane. Thus the novel's anti-psychiatric message.

The inhabitants of the Alphane Moon, accepting their status as unbalanced, attain insight into their condition, and on that basis have built a society—co-operative and functioning, though tending to stagnate. They are not going to infect anyone else with their illness; this is not true of Mary Rittersdorf and Bunny Hentman. Mary and her allies do not see that their actions are psychopathically aggressive and insanely conspiratorial; their world is competitive, not co-operative, and any activity in it (marriage, the law, friendship, art) can be perverted into ruthless competition. Completely outmanoeuvred by Mary in their marital dispute, Chuck begins to share this insanity: he takes two jobs (16-hour workdays supported by 'thalamic stimulants of the hexoamphetamine class' [ch. 5, 49]); he plans to use a 'sim' to assassinate Mary. He loses possession of his own dreams, as his secret intentions are echoed in the script ideas his colleagues come up with—and their ideas are very banal. His future is pre-empted so that his enemies know his intentions before they occur to him, as when people burst in to photograph what he *will* do with Joan Trieste, to use in the divorce proceedings (ch. 5, 55–57).

There is a clear distinction between those on the asylum moon—at worst, reflexive and self-victimizing in predictable ways that provide a stability to their lives and give their society an order—and Mary, Bunny and the other plotters in the 'sane' world, whose actions bring about a breakdown of social order and coherence—mutual exploitation, plotting, owning others, appropriating their realities. So far, we have a satirically schematic novel which avoids ambiguities. We have a frame (the clans) which offers us a perspective on the mad restlessness of the conflicting characters on Terra.

This relatively static structure is unusual in Dick's novels; it does not last in this one. The story of the Rittersdorf marriage itself expresses paranoia and fulfils wishes. This conclusion is not a tendentious one; it is one that the reader would have to work very hard to avoid. Paranoia: Mary is a castrating female, who divorces Chuck not to get rid of him but to hurt him while still possessing him—possessing him in the only way that counts to such a woman, by owning his labour. Though Mary is a woman in (one would suppose) a man's world like ours, institutions and power structures further her designs at every turn. As matters develop, she will own Chuck more thoroughly *after* the divorce than before: he has to take the two jobs not merely to her and the children, but to subsidize her ambitions and malign schemes, which involve leaving the children behind and travelling to the Alphane Moon, which she intends to reduce once again to subjection to Terra, thus eliminating the inhabitants' hard won freedom. Wish-fulfilment: by the end, when Chuck and Mary meet again on the Alphane Moon, she has been humbled, Chuck is vindicated, the marriage resumes. Her aggression, no longer rationalized and expressed through the manipulation of institutions and social codes, as it was on Terra, bursts openly forth in a grotesque scene in which desire takes the form of a cannibalistic attack on a bewildered inhabitant (who, poor schmuck, had planned to seduce her as a way of thwarting her attack on the moon's independence [ch. 10, 132–34]). At the end she accepts that she is indeed psychotic (ch. 13, 18).

If Dick sets out to write a satiric novel contrasting the sanity of the 'mad' and the insanity of the 'sane', he does not maintain the necessary detachment. A novel about derangement becomes a deranged novel; Mary's aggression towards Chuck is capped by the author's aggression towards Mary. This is a return of Philip K. Dick's repressed. Looking back from this point, we can see the strength of the non-SF novels which Dick wrote in the late fifties, grim and trapped as they are. The demands and constraints of realism in these novels mean that we take a long look at the twists of mood, impulse, suspicion, aggression, that shape marital conflict or simply, as in *Mary and the Giant*, the behaviour of a restless young woman; not much is settled, there is not much scope for strange or transformative actions, though there certainly is some scope (for instance, in *Teeth*).

To return to *Clans*, as long as the only alternative to uncontrolled, almost insensate aggression is stagnation and impairment (the world of the Clans, harmless though it seems), then Dick must go with the former: the mode of this part of the story (the punishing of Mary Rittersdorf) embraces the behaviour (ruthless aggression) for which she is punished. The treatment of Arnie Kott in *Time-Slip* is, as we shall see, more controlled, because Dick shows clearly that if Kott destroys social bonds (he is the equivalent of Mary in the novel's scheme) he also *makes* society, using his energy and extraversion. But much more happens in *Clans*.

Between the early scenes in which the hapless Chuck is victimized by Mary and the come-uppance she receives at the end, the novel riffles through a series of possible replacements for Mary. The procedure is still fantasy (wish-fulfilment) but the quest is for goodness, an alternative to the violence and deceit in which Chuck has become embroiled.

The first person to be considered is Joan Trieste. As well as being gentle and attractive, she has paranormal powers—but then this hint that the bureaucratic (the mode Mary works through) might be countered by the paranormal is mocked by the modesty of those powers.

> Joan broke in, 'I have a very meager power, but look.' Turning, she raised the lapel of her shirt. 'See my button? Bona fide member of Psi-men, Incorporated, of America.' She explained, 'What I can do is, I can make time flow backward. In a limited area, say twelve by nine, about the size of your living room. Up to a period of five minutes.' (ch. 4, 35)

She has a humble, poorly paid job with the local police department, re-timing (and thus preventing) traffic accidents: this is more than any of us could achieve, however, and she is beautiful besides, with a beauty that connotes goodness, as is underlined just after the passage quoted. Nonetheless, Chuck moves on to the Alphane Moon, where he meets Annette Golding, gentle and kindly also, but ill, impaired in some way. She too is, hesitantly, passed up.

> 'Annette Golding,' Chuck said. 'Polymorphous schizophrenia.'
> 'Yeah, but even so won't she do?'
> After a pause Chuck said, 'Possibly.' He was not a clinician, but Annette had not seemed very ill to him. Much less so, in fact, than Mary. But of course he knew Mary better. Still—(ch. 12, 168)

That Chuck tries Joan and Annette and returns to Mary is one thing; after all, sisters of Joan and Annette can be found as often as sisters of Mary in other novels by Dick.[2] But that Chuck tries Joan, Annette and Lord Running Clam is another thing, a leap right beyond the parameters human society offers. For Lord Running Clam is a Ganymedean slime mould.

---

[2] The usual pattern involves an aggressive, unscrupulous but attractive 'other woman' and a gentle, passive or dull wife; Dick inverts the arrangement in this case, as he does in *Puttering About in a Small Land*. Examples can be found in *Frolix 8*, *Palmer Eldritch*, where Barney has already left his gentle wife, and *Martian Time-Slip*.

The Ganymedeans, who communicate telepathically, locomote by oozing, reproduce by sporing, and reproduce not only offspring but themselves (a Ganymedean may die yet be reborn when it spores) certainly seem to elude the Terran gender division, or any division. Seldom has a personage been more fluently liminal than Lord Running Clam. He is an alien, estranged from earth culture,[3] yet able to draw on the assured wisdom of an ancient race. There are, however, also elements of the stereotypical female (the gossip, the eavesdropper, using telepathy in this case), and the biological female (ability to give birth). And there are elements of the male: not only because of the character's title (as Ganymedeans are ungendered, 'Lord' is plainly a Terran mistranslation, but it sticks), but because the story distinguishes him from the women who befriend Chuck. Chuck's relationships with Joan and Annette are cut short by his feeling that if they are to go any further they must become sexual, and he is not ready for this; since this is not a factor with the Ganymedean, much can follow: friendship, the acceptance of counsel, assistance in reproduction. But it is significant that the scene in this novel that embodies co-operation and hope, and affirms fertility against mechanism and destruction, centres on such an anomalous personage.

Lord Running Clam sacrifices himself for Chuck by stepping in front of a laser bolt intended for him, having earlier, interferingly but firmly, prevented him from suicide. Joan Trieste kills the assassin, but in doing so loses too much time to revive Lord Running Clam by exercise of her talent. Nor does she revive the assassin; instead Joan and Chuck grope in the 'dirty, much-used carpet' for the alien's spores, released when he was hit (ch. 9, 116–22). Perhaps his offspring can be saved. The Ganymedean (like a mushroom) needs moist conditions to reproduce, so Chuck conveys his spores to the Alphane Moon. This, then, is the narrative means by which the main point-of-view character is moved from Terra to the Alphane Moon. The frame and its contents are melded together, the climax of the story may now take place. Chuck's action is at considerable personal inconvenience, given the nerve-shredding complication of his life by now, but it is more than successful. In reproducing, Ganymedeans are reborn! Lord Running Clam is back, to ooze sluggishly and therefore perilously, to dispense his gnomic counsel, as the final climactic battle, which pits each of the novel's characters against all of the others, rages around them.

Reciprocity is established, in this comedy of kindness; one helps and is helped. Chuck's enemies tried to kill him, but they injured Lord Running

---

[3] Aliens on Terra, whatever their status, are confined to seedy residences like that into which Chuck moves after Mary throws him out (ch. 2, 23).

Clam, thus precipitating premature sporing; Chuck had already sent an android assassin to the Alphane Moon to kill Mary (Lord Running Clam approved of this: revenge is in accord with Ganymedean ethics [ch. 5, 48]), but found himself instead on the moon, struggling to help his exotic friend. It seems that living creatures will death, yet somehow make for life. (The android is detected, turned against others and eventually nullified.) At the same time, however, a fantasy is pursued, to the extraordinary point of a male giving birth. Females have somehow reneged on or suffered the impairment of their own capacity to nurture;[4] so it is with Mary, Joan and Annette in the scheme of the novel. Things are so desperate that males must assume the role: Chuck acts as midwife-gardener, assisted by Annette, and Lord Running Clam reproduces himself.

> Already the first-buried sphere had begun to grow; in the light of the handtorch Annette saw the ground quiver and bulge, tremble as the diameter of the sphere radically increased. It was an odd, funny sight and she laughed. 'I'm sorry,' she apologized. 'But you scuttled about, popped it into the ground, and now look at it. In a while it'll be as big as we are. And then it can move on.' Slime molds, she knew, were the sole mobile fungus; they fascinated her for that reason. (ch. 11, 141)[5]

No doubt the fiction can be seen as impelled by Dick's desires, anxieties and resentments. Feelings that are powerful at the beginning are never ironized or disowned; they are extravagantly pursued until, with Lord Running Clam, they are transformed. The transformation is not complete, since Mary is humbled at the end, in a further but less interesting wish-fulfilment, but it is sufficiently spectacular for us to ask what prompted the invention of this particular alien.

We are dealing with a knot of fears and desires related to women: so the evidence of a lot of Dick's stories and novels suggests; but these fears and desires are part of a set of insights into the whole nature of modern civilization.[6] Dick's strong intuition is that the ground of reality in

---

[4] See the discussion of similar matters, again in the context of the ambiguities of fantasy, in Chapter 5 above. Very relevant is the ferocious conflict between Walt and Sherry in *Teeth* (see Chapter 4 above).

[5] Paul Levy writes of '*Cordyceps robertsii*, an organism that appears to be a fungus, but seems to have the property of locomotion (its Chinese name means something like "summer grass–winter worm". In fact, the fungus invades the bodies of caterpillars)' (*Times Literary Supplement*, 5001, February 5 1999: 11).

[6] 'A specific biographical pathology [. . .] constitutes under certain circumstances a recording apparatus for a unique historical content that it alone can disclose and bring to objective expression'; Jameson (1994: 121) on Andrei Platonov.

a subjective world, perhaps the only thing that has 'objective' existence behind the veil of human imaginings and constructions of reality, is entropy, the tendency of things to decay and degrade. His horrified observation is that modern society, considered both as industrialism and as capitalism, releases and increases the power of entropy, whereas the purpose of society ought to be to keep entropy at bay. Industrialism involves routinization and mass production, making actions and things into repetitions and replications; capitalism involves 'progress' and planned obsolescence, leading to a vast piling up of waste, causing things, again, to lack or lose phenomenological substance, since they are made only to be superseded or discarded. It involves competition, destructive civil war within household and society (Mary versus Chuck; Arnie Kott versus everyone who gets in his way).

The sources of the Dickian worldview are complex. The above summary involves the political (matters relating to historical conditions to which the author responds) and the ontological (matters which he connects to 'the nature of things', outside history). The opportunities and constraints of genre also operate: vindication and come-uppance, shoot-out and marital reconciliation. The brew thickens, and also goes sour, in the opinion of many, if we add to it Dick's feelings about women. Entropy is sterility; things become false, depleted, degraded.[7] Women ought to offer nurture, kindliness, fertility; they have turned aside from this potential in them. But in *Clans of the Alphane Moon* a whole complex of feelings to do with sterility and fertility, violence and kindness, has interacted to produce the exhilarating scene of Lord Running Clam's sporing on the embattled satellite, assisted by the madly shovelling Chuck Rittersdorf.

2. Helio Prescribes Nembutal

Martian Time-Slip is a grimmer novel than *Clans of the Alphane Moon*. The pressure and counter-pressure of genre and social indictment issue in a much more troubling series of substitutions and displacements when things come to a shoot-out on Dirty Knobby than happened when the lasers flashed around Chuck and Annette on the Alphane Moon.

Time-Slip concerns Jack Bohlen, a repairman with a history of schizophrenia. Jack is pulled into the orbit of Arnie Kott, an aggressive, corrupt union leader who is trying to exploit Manfred Steiner, an autistic child

---

[7] Similarly, a set of observations about consumption and exploitation in modern society interacts with a set of intuitions about transhistorical phenomena, both natural and sacred —eating and being eaten. The result is a rewriting of the myth of communion: the deity (ambiguously ruler, purveyor of consumer goods, bringer of purpose and unity) incorporates the worshipper (see Chapter 7 above).

with strange powers who may help Arnie to make a lot of money by fore-telling the location of an important Martian housing development. Forced to work with Arnie and Manfred, as well as Arnie's generous mistress Doreen and his gnomic servant, the indigene Helio, Jack begins to crack up. By contrast Chuck Rittersdorf is not schizophrenic, as Jack is; his stability is threatened from without, not from within, and the novel in which he figures sends him on a real, if bizarre, trip in search of human companionship. The episode is social, in keeping with *Clans'* schematic procedure. Chuck meets a lot of people—many are hostile, many are friendly, none are indifferent. Jack is threatened by the autistic Manfred and by the psychopathic Arnie, and so is caught between the most intro-verted and the most extraverted people in the novel, but what jeopardizes his sanity is that his struggle remains internal. He doesn't manage to relate concretely to anyone else; that is, he doesn't manage to love Doreen or hate Arnie or fear Manfred—or reject his wife Silvia. He is distracted by inner fears, memories and visions. Fortunately Jack's one decisive moment of empathetic, practical contact with others comes when he gives water to a party of desperate Bleekmen (indigenous Martians)—this one moment (ch. 2, 35–39) is enough to save him.

For Philip K. Dick, salvation is in sociability, but in kindness to strang-ers rather than to members of one's own, familiar social circle; this paradox is a reflection both of the need for society and of the sterility of society (the most arid of relationships in Dick are the most intimate—those with children, spouses, ex-spouses). Only those who are in effect outside society can provide the opportunity for empathy (the Bleekmen; Lord Running Clam; the black man whom General Buckman hugs near the end of *Flow My Tears*). This opportunity for empathy is peculiarly hard for Jack and for *Time-Slip* to achieve. That chance meeting with the Bleekmen is also almost enough to kill Jack. He speaks sharply to Arnie, who is annoyed by the delay (Jack has also called upon Arnie's helicopter pilot for assistance), and by Jack's obedience to the rule that Bleekmen must be helped. Arnie plans to take revenge.

Time-Slip is marked by an economy of intrigue. So often in Dick novels the contending forces are big organizations headed by gross vulgarians served by squads of steely henchmen (ready to betray and double-cross): *The Simulacra* (also published in 1964) is a good example. In *Time-Slip*, however, the contending forces are pared down to single, shadowy pres-ences. It is Scott Temple who bombs Otto Zitte's base; he does this on Arnie's orders, and leaves Arnie's name behind. (Otto is a small-time smuggler who has inadvertently entered into competition with Arnie.) Otto never learns of Temple's involvement, and he has no idea why he has attracted Arnie's malignancy, for Arnie has never met Otto. Arnie never meets Leo Bohlen, the solitary representative of nameless power-ful investors who thwart Arnie's plans in the FDR mountains. There is no chance that Arnie will ever hurt Leo, and Leo feels nothing about Arnie. The ascetic Mr Yee, who believes in salvage, and appropriately employs Jack as a repairman, is contrasted to the indulgent Arnie, who lets the water of his shower scandalously waste in the Martian dust (ch. 1, 20; ch. 2, 25), but he coolly sells Jack to Arnie, and we hear no more of Mr Yee. We first meet Arnie in the midst of that wasteful shower of his, address-ing a circle of his 'boys', indeterminate, and never seen again (except when the passage is repeated as part of Arnie's time-slip [ch. 2, 25–27; ch. 15, 217]).

What is true of the powerful is true also of the victims. The isolated indi-vidual is surrounded by a blur of faces, like someone coming out of a faint. The suicide of Norbert Steiner, Manfred's father, happens like other violent actions in the novel, abruptly and inexplicably, rather than as part of a connected intrigue, and it happens after a series of one-to-one con-frontations (with Anne Esterhazy, Arnie's ex-wife; Manfred; Milton Glaub, the psychiatrist; the bartender—the last of whom appears virtually as two schizophrenically disconnected people in the space of a few minutes). These are encounters of one monad with another. Then, when Steiner kills himself, we see only the frightened face of the bus driver for a second—Steiner is surrounded by a cloud of unknowing witnesses (ch. 3, 47–55).

Almost every character in *Time-Slip* is detailed so that we pause, empa-thize, plumb a helpless, ordinary human depth—Norbert, Otto, Silvia, as much as Jack, Manfred and Arnie, the novel's central trio.[8] The result of this detailing in *Time-Slip* is a human texture, so that this novel offers the pleasures of a good realist novel; but what is being registered is a deple-tion of the social. Dick uses the forms of the realist social novel to render society a husk—or it would be better to say, to find himself doing this, since he also gives explicit recognition to our need of social continuity (ch. 6, 75–76).

Much depends on our assessment of the child Manfred, who is plainly ambiguous, in contrast to the members of the clans on the asylum moon. In his autistic state, Manfred may be seeing an aspect of reality (entropic degradation), but he may be feeding it. He is victim and threat, manipulated, symbol of alienation, of capitalism's desiccation of time, yet

---

[8] Arnie's mistress Doreen might be an exception. For all her conventional wish-fulfilment qualities—flaming red hair and full breasts (but this is as Arnie sees her)—Doreen is really as much an alien as Lord Running Clam is. The clue here is provided by the passage on her nose (ch. 6, 100). Helio is discussed below.

form-destroyer, threat to Jack's sanity, destroyer of Arnie Kott.[9] Whatever Manfred is, however, he is not happy. Dick does not make the mistake made by some proponents of anti-psychiatry; to be 'insane' is certainly to be miserable in *Time-Slip*. This is perhaps why we are drawn to Arnie Kott, in spite of his selfishness, total lack of self-knowledge, and destructive capriciousness.[10] It will be to Arnie that Manfred transfers his nightmarish disgust and cynicism, becoming free of it himself, and also saving Jack.

Arnie fits into a pattern—the big organization (the UN and the speculators around Leo Bohlen) crushes the petty power (Arnie with his Union settlement) which crushes the small-time crook (Otto Zitte, black marketeer) who seduces the lonely housewife (Silvia Bohlen). But he is not sympathetic solely because, fitting into this pattern, he is exploited as well as exploiter (Robinson 1984: 56). He is sympathetic because he makes a purpose where otherwise there is introversion, timidity and prudence only. He is sociable; he gathers around him a kind of team, and bullies its members into usefulness by his extraversion. We might ask of the ideal society that it find a use for such bizarre isolates as Jack, Manfred and Helio, and because Arnie finds a use for them (without a project, any society is locked in monotony), we suspend for a time our judgment of the selfishness of that purpose.

Very often in Dick's novels society is already constituted, and not only that, but already oppressive, and yet also already disintegrating or failing, even in its own oppressive terms. All that the individual can do is attempt to escape, or to make some enclave of empathy within a small, beleaguered group. Dick is sceptical of the utopian premise of much science fiction, the premise that by taking a leap away from our own society in time and/or place, we can collectively remake society in a better form. *Martian Time-Slip*[11] certainly doesn't relax that scepticism, but it does imagine the need of society, the inescapability of society, by showing both Arnie's gregariousness and Manfred's and Jack's isolation, and by implication it recognizes that the poignant, passing encounters of empathetic individuals are not enough.

---

[9] The following chapter discusses this way in which Manfred is loaded with significance. The effect relates both to Dick's intuitions of the end of romantic individualism and to his reluctance to accept this.

[10] 'Doreen Anderton and Arnie Kott, Jack said to himself. The two people who mean the most to me, the friends with whom my contacts, my intimacy with life itself, is the strongest' (ch. 11, 159). Dick at one stage intended to entitle the novel after Arnie (Williams 1986: 94).

[11] We can fit this novel, and several others by Dick, into a genre of novels bitterly disillusioned with the idea that empire or settlement in a new land can be a new beginning for society. See ch. 3, 64–67.

Arnie is as defensive in his activism, however, as the others are in their inertia; he is able to construe all sorts of unrelated actions as personal attacks (Steiner's suicide, Zitte's scurryings, Leo's ventures). Arnie's grasp on reality is arguably shakier than Manfred's, and since he has not got the power to ensure that what he sees as reality *becomes* reality, he is condemned to psychopathic flailing. Paradoxically, it is Manfred who can infect others with his vision of reality. Arnie's psychopathology is most notable when he has his colleague Scott Temple destroy Otto Zitte's base. Having taken Steiner's suicide as a personal affront, because it terminated Arnie's supply of black-market Terran delicacies, Arnie sets up his own replacement. Then when he discovers that Zitte has continued Steiner's work, Arnie takes this as an attack, and reacts with a violence that Zitte can only see as inexplicable and malignant. Expenditure (only Arnie in the novel has the capacity to enjoy things for their own sake[12]) becomes consumption, becomes production, becomes competition, becomes insensate violence: seldom has a demonstration of the nullity of capitalism been delivered so ruthlessly. We see how appropriate the image of accelerated time is to the novel. But if Arnie now seems to the reader to be ripe for punishment (whereas the come-uppance Mary Rittersdorf receives is a matter between Philip K. Dick and his feelings about women) this is because he has offered something positive and then betrayed it.

Arnie's downfall is brought about by the ambiguous Manfred, but we will approach it by consideration of his native servant Helio, who presides over the incident at Dirty Knobby. Helio is aloof, proud and embittered. He is contemptuous both of the members of his race who have remained 'outside civilization' and of Arnie Kott who has, as the latter sees it, 'tamed' him and given him access to the benefits of civilization (such as preparing gourmet meals for Arnie Kott). We see him first, that is, as the member of a colonized race. Like the other Bleekmen, he has been given the alternative of subservient absorption into the colonizer's society, or bleak decline in a wilderness from which one can be expelled if anything should turn it from wilderness into source of profit, as is about to happen to part of the FDR mountain range. In keeping with the different procedure of this novel, he is historically specified as Lord Running Clam is not. Nonetheless, like Lord Running Clam, being of another race,[13] he has

---

[12] A reader who cites the passage in which Arnie happily screws Doreen while she is half asleep (ch. 8, 126–27) will put me to some shifts to justify my point about Arnie and 'enjoyment for its own sake', but this action is a betrayal of Arnie's own sociability, which is elsewhere of value. The term 'expenditure' is borrowed from Bataille; it is useful because it suggests the more positive aspects of waste.

[13] Actually Bleekmen and Terrans are related; Helio is alien in the way that a Bushman or an Australian Aborigine might be alien to a European or white American. The Bleekmen are

access to wisdom of a special kind. As with Lord Running Clam and other aliens the sign of this is a strange relationship to language: Helio is telepathic, and communicates in clipped, gnomic utterances.[14]

This only emerges when he meets Manfred (only with Manfred is he telepathic). He doesn't take the initiative, as Lord Running Clam does, but is drawn out by the child. His action is ambiguous: he sends Arnie and Manfred to Dirty Knobby, the Bleekman holy place, equipping them with a note of instruction that will enable Arnie to exploit Manfred's special power in order to go back in time. Arnie's plan is to use Manfred to forestall Leo Bohlen in the matter of the land purchase in the FDR range, and also to kill Jack Bohlen in revenge for an action which, in that time scheme, he will not yet have committed, and which reflects well on him in any case—helping some Bleekmen who are dying of thirst. Why does Helio co-operate? We note that the visit to Dirty Knobby leads to the child's liberation, since he is able to join the wild Bleekmen and circumvent the horrible fate he has foreseen for himself, that of coming to a long agony of senility in the as yet unbuilt AM-WEB building over whose site Arnie is struggling with Leo. The building will decay, while Manfred will be kept alive by force—a perverse care for the individual life in the midst of social desolation. And the visit to Dirty Knobby also leads to Arnie's death. The death is at the hands of Otto Zitte, whom he had capriciously injured, but it comes after the terrifying failure of Arnie's plan to go back in time. The extraverted, selfish and buoyant Arnie had been taken over by Manfred's frightening sense of reality as menace and decay: that was the penalty for his access to another time (ch. 15, 217–16, 229).

So the wise Helio has dispensed both justice and mercy. 'Helio' is the sun, but Mars has too much sun; 'Heliogabalus', his full name according to Arnie, who named him, was an unpleasant adolescent Roman emperor. Helio's action in the novel is very different from that of the jokingly named Lord Running Clam. To the incident of the slime mould's Chuck-assisted sporing, which combines the ridiculous and the poignant, the dramatic (the battle rages) and the pastoral (Chuck gardens), we can now compare the scene involving Arnie and Manfred in the cave on Dirty Knobby, presided over by Helio's instructions. The cave is a sacred place, an aperture in time, but the note is cryptic, prescribing Nembutal (reminding us of

Footnote 13 *continued*

not simply depicted as indigenes possessing a special wisdom; they also resemble the hoboes so often idealized in sixties fiction. Dirty Knobby, site of mystery, is given a very unexotic name.

[14] For example, Glimmung in *Galactic Pot-Healer* (1969), who communicates by messages in bottles; Morgo in *Frolix 8* (1970), also telepathic, uses idiosyncratic American English learnt telepathically from the space voyager Thors Provoni.

everyday suburban drug usage, as in the opening scene of the novel), taking the form of a recipe, like the cooking by which Arnie is 'civilizing' Helio: 'Take Nembutal (boy not take)' (ch. 15, 216).

Arnie does go back in time, but he now sees everything in Manfred's way as menacing 'gubble'. Manfred transfers his horrible disgust and fear to Arnie, becoming free of it himself. Arnie also stands in for Jack, who was threatened with absorption into Manfred's world because Arnie was forcing him into proximity with the child: Arnie begins to see other people as sinister mechanisms, as had Jack during his schizophrenic fugues (ch. 15, 220; ch. 5, 80). By this steely series of transferences Dick invents an antidote to the exploitation, the owning and manipulation of human beings such as Manfred and Jack, that Arnie practised and that is seen as typical of modern society in the novel. Having shifted people about as though he owned them—since he did own them—Arnie is made the creature of deeper forces.

The antidote is a grim one. It is appropriate that it is administered by the alien Helio, wise, but quite without Lord Running Clam's affection and enthusiasm. Manfred joins a party of the wild Bleekmen; but he joins as the aged Manfred of the future, having escaped his imprisonment in the AM-WEB hospital that will be built on the land Arnie is fighting over, so that when Arnie went back in time, to his doom, Manfred went forward, to his liberation. (Yet he also went back, since we think of the Bleekmen as archaic people.) We don't have a comic mushrooming of fertility,[15] but Manfred is given the chance to become a child, and to approach the other children who are adjusting to Martian life, and becoming like Bleekmen in the process (ch. 2, 32–33: Arnie's observation).

In *Martian Time-Slip*, then, a series of elements is brought together with ambiguous effect: political critique, with its grim reflection on our world;[16] the resolution of imbroglios that is characteristic of popular fiction; and the hint of new life that answers to an intense need on the part of Philip K. Dick. If the ambiguity is a sign of how hard it is to reconcile these divergent elements, it is also a reflection of Dick's sense of the social. The social is inescapable and desirable; indeed, it is us, and to think of the individual as something apart from the social is already a sign of how distorted our situation is. Yet our situation is indeed distorted, and as a result society as

---

[15] Comparable to the swift germination of Lord Running Clam's spores is the passage in which Jack shows a speeded-up film of the germination of a seed, to illustrate what experience is like for Manfred (ch. 9, 128–29); but that is as close as either Manfred (who finds human sexuality loathsome) or the novel can approach to reproduction.

[16] See Brian Aldiss's discussion of the novel (1975). As Aldiss points out, 'AM-WEB' is an acronym for the German phrase 'Alle Menschen werden Brüder', meaning 'all men become brothers'.

it actually exists is not at all desirable, and the individual has to be thought of as something apart from the social. Salvation for the individual comes ambiguously out of the conjunction of the powers of loners, misfits and aliens such as Helio and Manfred, and is articulated by means of an impure fantasy (time-shifts, a numinous native site, a banal drug).

Martian Time-Slip begins with a suicide that is prompted by the inhumanity of Martian society (revealing itself to Norbert Steiner in the proposal to close down the centres that care for children like Manfred) and that exposes the monadic isolation of most people in the novel: Arnie, the most sociable, society-making person in the novel, is a psychopath; and Manfred and Jack, two characters who are each in their own way sympathetic, are also painfully isolated from others. And insofar as it is Helio who supervises Arnie's doom, Manfred's liberation, and Jack's survival, then we read this outcome as a product of Helio's will (not as a product of Dick's wish-fulfilment, as seems the case with the ending of *Clans of the Alphane Moon*), and also take note of Helio's position on the extreme margins of the novel's society, as neither a settler nor a nomad.

There is a contradiction, then, at every level, including the conceptual, between the social and the individual. It can only be imaginatively resolved by introducing an outsider, an individual who is not social or is at least on society's margins. This is very frequent in popular fiction,[17] which commonly implies that the ruling structures of society are inadequate or corrupt and that average people are helpless or incriminated, so that a superhero or—what is much the same thing—a private investigator must come to the rescue; but this is an extreme and complex case. In this chapter, I have discussed Helio as the outsider, but in fact the novel is constructed in such a way that we end up seeing its society as both imprisoning and non-existent at the same time. So many of the important characters are insane or psychopathic, or both, that *everyone* seems to be an outsider and the society seems to have no inside. Individuals, such as Manfred and Jack, disintegrate; the social is deconstructed. It is significant, however, that there is no wholesale collapse of space-time, as happens in *Ubik* and *Palmer Eldritch*; the time-slip of the title is confined to a demarcated area of the novel, and the blurring of boundaries is worked out in terms of the fates of individuals—and of the social itself.

---

[17] A good example is *Total Recall* (1990), a film loosely based on Dick's story 'We Can Remember It For You Wholesale' (1966): a superhero, played by Arnold Schwarzenegger, allied with assorted misfits, mutants and aliens, battles squads of faceless corporate henchmen in uniforms or suits, and eventually brings blue skies and fresh air to arid Mars—or seems to, since all this may be illusion and wish-fulfilment.

9. Critical Reason and Romantic Idealism in *Martian Time-Slip*

How does a genre energized by immediate, desiring transformation and going-beyond, as SF is, come to terms with reason and with historical conditions? What kind of relations does SF maintain with the untranscendent democratic ordinariness that the realist novel has often affirmed as a value but which SF tends to denaturalize? This chapter pursues these questions by considering Dick's depiction of children, concentrating on *Martian Time-Slip*. The discussion then broadens to take in the grim prospects of the social and of the ordinary in the world of the novel, before coming to rest on the survival of the schizophrenic but decent Jack Bohlen.

As regards the image of the child, what romantic innocence or power can survive in an age of psychology? Dick has profound affiliations with Romantic poets of childhood, in his sense of the subjective variety of human time, though he connects this with a particular critique of modernity and in so doing makes it very problematic and disturbing. Still, he is like Wordsworth in his sympathy with the notion that prevailing reality is a cover for a lost or forgotten world of value, sometimes a childhood one, that may be recovered or redeemed, and he is like Blake in his ambition to rewrite the Christian myth so as to restage its reconciliation of transcendence and incarnation.

Yet, among SF writers, he is the most thoroughgoing in his embrace of the Freudian notion that to define our innnermost personhood is to define the way in which we are all, adults and children alike, at best neurotic. If so, children are not distinct from adults and will not easily stand as images of values that adults have lost or are busy extirpating in children—a view of children that the romantic side of Dick is otherwise drawn to.[1] Children are more likely to remind us of what determines the instability that adults exhibit: that is, the adults' childhoods. And among SF writers Dick is also one of the most explicitly diagnostic. When he does not himself classify this or that character as schizophrenic or paranoid or autistic, this or that behaviour as regressive or infantile or insane in some way, he often clearly

---

[1] After Freud, it is difficult to recreate the romantic image of the child, as Coveney argues (1967, ch. 11).

invites his readers to do so. The diagnosis and the range of symptoms offered may be idiosyncratic, but they are definite. For all his zany fantastication, and the flippancy of his explanations for, say, 'half-life' states or drugs that unbind time, Dick in fact extends the supervisory role of reason further than more hard-headed rationalists among SF writers, who stick to physics or astronomy. He extends it into the quirks and depths of human behaviour, where other writers of SF use 'normal' characters as means of entry into radically changed worlds.

Either children are not different from adults, since we are all neurotic together, or a given individual, child or adult, is suffering from an identifiable disease and so is distinct from others. The two approaches, one emphasizing that we are all neurotic together and the other that we are each isolated in our particular disease, may clash with each other, but they both cancel out the romantic possibility that the child be a source of value —or (if it comes to that) of malignancy. The crux is arguably that of liberalism itself: each individual is unique, but we have common humanity. Manfred, a totally asocial, monadic person, whose relation to society is only that of victim, is to be reconnected to society in the course of the narrative, and, as was argued in the previous chapter, *Martian Time-Slip* is intensely concerned with sociality.

Further, if a character is a case (that is, someone to be diagnosed, perhaps treated, then restored to society, to the group of those who don't need treatment), then they cannot be a metaphor, a sign of the general condition of society. In a story by Ian McDonald called 'Fragment of an Analysis of a Case of Hysteria' (1992), a young woman suffers repeated dreams of a train journey and a fearful fate awaiting her when she gets off the train; she is treated by Freud, analysed, cured, marries happily. Then, at the end of the story, she is put on the train by the Nazis and arrives at Auschwitz—this last segment of the story being an exact repetition of those early dreams, now revealed as unbalanced only insofar as European history was itself unbalanced to the point of nightmare. Her dreams were social, symbolical and visionary, rather than individual to her. Her symptoms were not distorted memories but lucid premonitions: psychiatry gives way to history. Dick's treatment of the issues is less clear-cut: he wants his children to be at once metaphors, sources of value, cases, and sharers in the common neurotic lot. This breadth of ambition, or overdetermination, puts SF's mingled adherence to fantasy and reason under a significant pressure.

1. Prophetic Children and Childish Adults

Two short stories, 'Jon's World' and 'Autofac', give the scope of the case. The first illustrates affinities with the romantic view of the child, the second the complications that start to gather as soon as we look at Dick's view of the adult as, if not childlike, certainly irrational.[2] In 'Jon's World' (1954, CS2) the main character is a young boy, strange and feeble in his environment, who has visions of a different world, green, peaceful and happy. This child doesn't fit into the society he actually has to live in, which is stressed, urgent, organized and militarized. In particular he doesn't get along with his father, a functionary engaged in time travel for military reasons. Jon, then, is child as visionary and also victim, in classic romantic fashion. His father, stereotypical figure of an utterly rationalized and desensitized adult world, has him lobotomized before departing on the time travel mission on which, by certain unintended actions, he brings about the changes for the better in the world of the story which transform it into the green and pleasant world that his son had precognitively envisaged. The moral of the story is clear enough. Jon could be classified or diagnosed as clinically odd, a sort of mutant, by way of scientific pseudo-explanation of his talent, as is often the case with psionics in Dick and other authors, but nonetheless his vision is real and the lobotomy was a horrible error. Time *can* loop and alter. The child is open to certain dimensions of reality that are, to use a Dickian word, occluded for the adult, though they have the authority of the SF megatext, in which precognition (psychic) is as real as time travel (technological).

There are no children in 'Autofac' (1955, CS4), only adults and robots, but both parties behave childishly. In the world of 'Autofac', humans are confined to consumption, served by homeostatic factories which were set up before the usual SF destructive war and are now working independently. 'Autofac' can be read as an allegory of the situation of consumers in modern society, who are served by a totally efficient productive system which promises to bestow anything on them, if only they could make it acknowledge their desires. Consumers are infantilized. The story is structured around three incidents sharing a similar quality. In the first, a group of consumers become so exasperated by a robot's moronically bureaucratic reponse to their complaints that they throw a tantrum, first spitting out the milk it has offered (which is perfectly good milk), then, more cleverly, complaining that the milk is 'pizzled', a deliberately meaningless response and one which seems at first to work, since it finds a gap in the robot's program. In the second, when a home visit from a robot agent of the autofacs shows that their first plan has failed, they descend to mob violence and tear the machine limb from limb. The humans recover and take thought; this time they hatch a plan to incite neighbouring autofacs to

---

[2] A group of stories about children as victims and/or sources of value is discussed in Chapter 5 above.

fight for scarce raw materials. They pile prized items precisely on the boundary between several factories. It works; instead of the humans regressing, as in the incidents of the tantrum and the lynching of the robot, the autofacs succumb to an atavistic hoarding and competing instinct, start to war for the prized materials, and tear themselves apart—or almost, for the story has a twist in its end, which is not relevant for our purposes.

The irrational outbreaks which structure 'Autofac' reveal in schematic form why the classic romantic depiction of the child as visionary and victim that we found in 'Jon's World' is not going to be easily available in Dick's more complex works. There is too much that is unstable and driven by impulse and anxiety in the adults, or, more importantly, in the constitution of modernity in those worlds, for it to be possible to idealize children's visions and pity children's sufferings. When we get to Manfred, we meet someone who is diagnosed, just as Jon was, but diagnosed by the novel as well as by the novel's arguably prejudiced society, and whose visions (which are, like Jon's, dependent on a destabilizing of time itself in the fictional world) are ambiguously registrations of the future *and* manipulations of it. Meanwhile he is himself manipulated by adults in his world, and pitied, and seen as evil. This ambivalence which collects around Manfred and thence shapes our varying judgments of the adult characters has to do with the relations of reason and unreason in Dick's mature novels.

2. Wide Angle: Modernity, Time and the Psychic

Zany inventions and arresting inversions of the normal and the expected abound in Dick's works. It is helpful to relate this aspect of his writing to the quality of affect—the immediacy, abruptness, and brutality of changes of feeling and allegiance, as well as changes in the condition of things and environments. This emphasis pulls things away from Dick's wonderful imaginativeness and towards the kinds of experience people undergo in these novels. Feeling, will, desire and anxiety seem to have been let loose to work without hesitation and at close quarters.

In specifically psychological terms, we can mention the number of bad mothers we meet (often actively devouring mothers with predatory kisses), the frequency with which the main character is stalled, trapped and frustrated, and, if he is a father, is a weak one, or if he has a father, has a boomingly overbearing and not particularly helpful one. There are suggestive resemblances to, say, the Grimms' fairy tales. The alternation of episodes of stunning transformation with episodes of nightmarish stagnation or clogged repetition is also fairytale-like.

An interesting example is *A Maze of Death* (1970), because in this novel the link between form, content, and affect is made clear. In *A Maze of Death* a group of ordinary misfits and failures, beleaguered on an unknown planet, begin to self-destruct, while their environment mutates (buildings shift position, animal and artificial beings become confused).[3] Sudden envies, enmities and unsparing psychological diagnoses of others, expressed crudely and acted on without hesitation, are rapidly followed by killings. The final explanation for what is going on (and for who and where the characters are) is that all we have just witnessed is the product of a collective fantasy (but, clearly, not a smoothly co-operative fantasy), in which the crew of a marooned spaceship are engaging to pass the time, their thoughts, impulses and resentments co-operating by means of a 'polyencephalic' link-up (ch. 15, 177–82). That is, most of the narrative itself was written by a deranged collective; what is more, the question of what if anything frames this part of the text is given an ambiguous answer.[4] It is unsurprising, then, that all these declarations and betrayals and mutations, uncloaked by social niceties, have the direct quality of things in dreams—that is what they are.

Dick's novels seem both to challenge romantic conceptions of fantasy as a mode of liberation, and also to challenge reason, the faculty of extrapolation and explanation. Further, it is quite difficult to find in Dick's novels either characters or general qualities of affect that are 'adult' as the term is usually, consensually understood—firmly individuated, socially co-operative, and to some degree (we do not ask for too much here) shaped by reason. The characters and qualities of affect are easy to recognize and sympathize with—that is not the problem. The problem, as regards children in Dick's novels, is that in a society of neurotics the visionary child may have some trouble standing out.

The subjectivity of Dick's worlds, that is, the sense that the external and material is something dreamt or fabricated, can be related to his imagination of what modernity has done to time and to the relations between person and world. Modernity has unfastened or dislocated linear time, the sequence of events or experiences on which cause and effect depend, on which narrative depends, on which meaning appears to depend, and on which growing from childhood to adulthood depends. Since modernity feeds on—since it is—perpetual change and transience, nothing has objective existence, everything is a phase or phenomenon, existent only in order to be replaced. Modernity is perpetual change, a kind of system

---

[3] For instance, ch. 6, 70; ch. 7, 81–83; see Chapter 10 below.

[4] After the revelation that the story we have been reading was the collective fantasy of the marooned crew, one of the crew members meets—or appears to meet—'the Intercessor', a supernatural figure from the religion prevailing *inside* the collective fantasy (ch. 16, 187).

for making us constantly accept its newest phase as natural and as what we can happily live with, and then making us accept the necessity and excitement of the replacement of that in turn by something else. All this bears on the fate of Manfred in *Martian Time-Slip*, because his extraordinary and sometimes visionary relation to time is what distinguishes him.

If we try to sum up the view that is implied, and intricately ramified, in Dick's fiction, modernity as relentless change seems to have rendered insecure, if not demolished, the premises on which modernity as science, technology, calculation and rationality depends. This is the situation about which many a poststructuralist or postmodernist thinker is blithe or triumphant. Dick is not blithe or triumphant, because he has not abandoned the human subject and humanist ethics to which, evidently, he cannot imagine an alternative. For him, the situation leads to problem, conflict: just what novels are suited to staging.

It also exacerbates in him a visionary romanticism. For instance, if we think of romanticism as involving imaginations of the recovery of time, the recreation in memory of a kind of original purity of experience such as we believe we had as children, then a classically romantic moment occurs in Dick's *The Cosmic Puppets* (1957; otherwise a notably unsuccessful novel). This is when the main character and the town drunk, striving to recover the small town of their childhood which has been overlaid with a tawdry, sterile fake, combine their powers and by sheer devotion of thought (helped by an SF-type gizmo which they are close to recognizing as purely a placebo) reconcretize something out of their past (ch. 7, 66–74). The moment is wonderful, but its context is ironic. Actually it is only Aaron Northrup's tyre iron that they recover by this poignant effort of memory, and this appliance lacks the poignant resonance of a madeleine or a daffodil. It's a banal thing, and one involved in public rather than personal life (Aaron used it to knock a bank robber on the head: that is why it is famous in the town). It never existed in nature, only in history.

3. Manfred Steiner: Multiple Characterization Disorder

Martian Time-Slip is a more complex case. Although it is set on a future, colonized Mars, it is a novel about ordinary contemporary society: bored pill-popping wives allowing themselves to be seduced by oilily seductive travelling salesmen; aggressively demanding bosses and inarticulate dominated employees; family troubles, stale marriages. The plot is largely generated by two things, one pulling backwards (the suicide of a man who could no longer bear his responsibility for his autistic son), and the other pushing forwards (the competition of various parties for a certain block of land that, as inside information has it, is to be bought and developed by the government). That is, the plot involves a kind of time derangement of an everyday, non-fantastic kind. (Modern or postmodern time derangements are accepted as non-fantastic when they are part of the consensual world: nuclear deterrence and investing in derivatives are examples.)

The grimly ordinary does not, it seems, make such a poignant guest appearance as did Aaron Northrup's tyre iron in the earlier novel. And it is necessary to talk of ordinary, not normal in the sense of providing a norm. In fact, when we take a second look at the cast list, we notice a whole crowd of specimens of the Other, that is, persons who are not stable white males but might have access to some alternative insight: the madman (for the main character Jack Bohlen is schizophrenic), the Woman (Arnie's mistress and Jack's love, the idealized Doreen); the indigene (the native inhabitants, called Bleekmen[5]); the aged (Jack's father Leo; the Bleekmen, an archaic and expiring people; Manfred himself as old; simply the land as the figure of oldness). These can all be regarded as having access to some special insight. This is characteristically Dickian—a process of overloading, in which the misfits outnumber those who fit.

In fact it is not hard to show that there is no fit, no normal and moderately stable way of behaving in the novel, and therefore no ready way for the novel to define Manfred's abnormality. The characters do not exactly behave like the affect-ridden dream figments of *A Maze of Death*, but their perceptions are usually shaped by a low-intensity subjectivism, and their actions are marked by instability.

The following summary picture of adult behaviour in *Martian Time-Slip* might suggest a twisted grimness. This is not the effect of the novel as one reads it. Nonetheless it is startling how often people respond to each other with envy or enmity, suspecting others, rejecting any hint of dependence on others, projecting feelings of hostility or threat or longing onto their interpretations of others. Manfred seems to concentrate and simplify an aspect of everyday social life on Mars. The adults are all given to sudden moods, accesses of guilt and denial and blame, and then astute analysis of their feelings. This is most painfully caught in the episode of the suicide of Manfred's father, Norbert: his dismay at the news that Camp B-G where Manfred is cared for might be closed down, swinging to angry assertion that this might be a good thing, because 'reality' should be faced, disgust at the prejudice of the barman in the scene that immediately follows, then the sudden almost whimsical seizing of the impulse to kill himself:

> Suddenly it came to him that he should kill himself. The idea appeared in his mind full blown, as if it had always been there,

---

[5] See the discussion of Helio in the previous chapter.

always a part of him. Easy to do it, just crash the 'copter. He thought, I am goddamn tired of being Norbert Steiner; I didn't ask to be Norbert Steiner or sell black-market food or anything else. [. . .]

In fact, he thought, why wait until I can get back to the 'copter? Along the street came a huge, rumbling tractor-bus, its sides dull with sand; it had crossed the desert just now, was coming to New Israel from some other settlement. Steiner set down his suitcases and ran out into the street, directly at the tractor-bus. (ch. 3, 54–55)

We can see how Norbert undergoes a kind of time-slip of a subjective kind, as anyone does in moments of intensity ('suddenly'; 'easy'; 'why wait'; 'just now'); we can see how Norbert's decision comes to him as completely individual (he thinks in terms of 'what I am' and 'what I can do'), though the scenes leading up to it have shown how thoroughly social it is. Then each of the other characters, responding to the news, also responds as an isolated monad, their interpretation of Norbert saturated with their sense of themselves and what, if anything, they wanted out of him. Any simple phrase uttered in a moment of normal stress (such as 'I wish I was dead', 'I feel as if I'm going insane') begins to be pulled into the currents of extreme behaviour released into the novel by Norbert and Manfred; we become very alert to everyone's dealings with time, which can of course seem to halt or race for anyone in moments of impatience, boredom or expectation.

The novel is not suggesting that Manfred is no more neurotic than the ordinary adults in the novel. They are often perceptive in a rational, self-critical way; more interestingly, they are often shown to have powers of intuition that are hard to distinguish absolutely from those that Manfred more weirdly exhibits. A couple of remarks about Jack Bohlen's father, Leo, will establish the variety of this. He is a hard-headed old guy, come to Mars more to clinch his land deal, perhaps, than to visit his son. He is so caught up in his own projects that he literally does not notice the landscape of this new planet until Jack forces him to (ch. 9, 129). The landscape of Mars only exists insofar as it plays a part in his project, and we can see that as neurotic. But, then again, he intuits that Jack's marriage has gone bad; and this is associated with his cleverness as a businessman —a form of instinct, of intuition (ch. 8, 123). To return to Manfred's relation to the other characters, the novel is suggesting that the others, as it were, open a space for Manfred. He is a freak, isolated and unconnected to anyone else, and also a development of their own desire-oriented, temporally floating, monadic side. They find a use for him. Arnie takes him out of the institution—he doesn't belong there, he belongs in the wider world. Arnie will use Jack Bohlen to develop some means of contact with the child, and then profit from the child's access to the future.

Given these general conditions it would seem that the novel could do with a few children. Are not children lively and playful, expressing the feeling—the human necessity—that things should be done for their own sakes, and in their own moment, as in games, not for some desiccating future purpose, such as outwitting your competitors and buying a tract of land that you expect to make you a profit? Are not children very commonly gifted with healthy, unselfconscious self-centredness? There is such a child in the novel, the Bohlens' son David, and he is unfazed by the fact that his father is on the brink of miserable psychosis and his mother is the pill-popping seduced housewife referred to earlier. But he makes only fleeting appearances; Manfred Steiner is a very different case.

He is autistic—diagnosed as such, to the accompaniment of an intriguing description of the condition as involving a disorder in the sense of time which, as people conjecture, is speeded up for Manfred, so that he is out of contact with others because he is literally on a different time-scale to them. He does not talk or interact or respond. Yet there is some strange grace about him, sprinting about 'on the tips of his toes, as if dancing to some unheard music, some tune from inside his own mind whose rhythms kept him enthralled' (ch. 3, 50). At least, this is how his father sees him; people in this novel are fallible, projecting onto others their desires as well as their suspicions, and Norbert is shortly going to kill himself. Manfred will seem very different when we are actually taken inside his head.

When we first meet him he is institutionalized, but he is well treated. Those who care for him are trying dance and music; they plan to try science and technology too: Westinghouse, for instance, are going to make a kind of artificial environment that will slow down his sensory input and perhaps put him in touch with the external world as consensually experienced (ch. 3, 46, 52). These details seem to fit the faith in diagnosis that defines him as autistic, a person with an ailment, and therefore curable by specific means which modern civilization makes available.

In this early scene, set apart from Martian society in an institution for people like Manfred, the novel seems to pause. Manfred is autistic, yet he has a special grace to him; music might help him, so might science and technology. Later in the novel this hopefulness is lost: music figures as malfunction (horrible squawks from a hi-fi) or cover for Arnie Kott's nasty —in fact psychopathic—plan to attack a business rival who has never even met him and doesn't know that he is a business rival. (Arnie encodes instructions for this attack in a tape of avant-garde music.) As far as technology is concerned, we have the life-support machinery which Manfred foresees as waiting for him in a miserable, extended senility; we have the machines (artificial people, 'Thomas Edison' or 'Mark Twain' or 'Kindly

Dad') which are entrusted not merely with teaching but with the trans-mission of human culture, a process that Jack plausibly sees as absurd; and we have the machines into which people are transformed, first as Jack sees it, in a schizophrenic episode, and then later as Arnie Kott sees it (his natural healthy selfishness somehow tainted by Jack's or Manfred's way of seeing things).[6] Conversely, when time travel is accomplished, it is done not by means of technology, but by an alliance between Manfred's special powers and the holy place of the degraded indigenes of Mars, the Bleekmen.

As it happens, people in the novel are more conversant with psychiat-ric accounts of unusual behaviour than one might have expected. They use these terms of the main character Jack Bohlen; so does Jack himself. He is said to be schizophrenic. As for Arnie Kott, the other important char-acter in the novel, by the time the story reaches its climax, and he is killed in the course of a time reversal that he has brought about by using Manfred, the reader feels encouraged to define him too as unbalanced—immature for all his success, repressed for all his extraversion, capable of thoughtless psychopathic violence.

If everyone is neurotic, or worse, then it becomes difficult to single out particular sick individuals. The whole society might be said to need treat-ment. But Dick does not retreat from his definition of Manfred in partic-ular as insane, and in consequence needing help and pity. He refuses the pure, countercultural, anti-psychiatric view of Manfred. Instead he adds other categorizations to this one.

Arnie takes Manfred out of Camp B-G, and sets Jack (a repairman, a tech-nician) to work to devise a way of communicating with the child, not to cure him so much as to see whether his insight into the future can be turned to some practical profit. In the process, utterly asocial as he seems to be, Manfred becomes an agent; he starts to affect and even merge with others.

Dick devises a stream-of-consciousness style to express the effects of Manfred on Jack and Arnie in particular. Manfred would seem to be down there on the pre-rational level, the level of, in Kristeva's term, the semi-otic. His thoughts are babble, circling round the word 'gubble', which is for Manfred a key to the universe (though children do commonly invent expressive, multi-use words of this kind); babble that is sensuous, disgusted, deliquescing, degrading in both senses of the term. This kind of

---

[6] The horrible squawks, ch. 10, 149; Arnie's use of music for a coded message, ch. 7, 113; Manfred as machine, ch. 16, 238; the teaching machines, ch. 5; Jack's vision of humans as machines, ch. 5, 80; Arnie's vision, ch. 15. Anthony Wolk has pertinent things to say on this episode in the context of the importance to sanity of human solidarity, and the threat of reduction to the mechanical (1995: 113, and 110, with reference to similar passages in *We Can Build You* [1972]).

writing, then, leaks into the novel and expresses Manfred's plight; we no longer see that grace or strangeness of movement which others had sensed in him. Manfred repeats himself—the same incident, a scene at Arnie's house one evening, is repeated several times in his gubble talk. 'The autistic child's overall behaviour is governed by an anxiously obsessive desire to maintain sameness', writes Bruno Bettelheim in his essay on autistic and feral children (1990: 176); a psychotic person is one to whom nothing new can happen, says Jack Bohlen in our novel (ch. 11, 160).[7]

Because he sees through and beyond sensuous physical life to what it will become, decay and death, Manfred sees only decay and degeneration. He is the victim of his time ailment, which, instead of projecting him into a new future, simply returns him always to the same process, that of decay and death. Yet he is right—he is prophetic, the decay and death are not simply reflections of his illness. (This point is also trite, if taken literally. We are all going to die, therefore visions of our rotting bodies are true but redundant—if pathetic in a child. It is the social context that gives the vision its point.)

Further, Manfred feels things in a direct, uncomprehending way that makes him vulnerable:

> Seated on the carpet, snipping pictures from the magazines with his scissors and pasting them into new configurations, Manfred Steiner heard the noise and glanced up. He saw Mr Kott hurry to the tape machine to shut it off. How blurred Mr Kott became, Manfred noticed. It was hard to see him when he moved so swiftly; it was as if in some way he had managed to disappear from the room and then reappear in another spot. The boy felt frightened.
>
> The noise, too, frightened him. He looked to the couch where Mr Bohlen sat, to see if he were upset. But Mr Bohlen remained where he was with Doreen Anderton, interlinked with her in a fashion that made the boy cringe with concern. How could two people stand being so close? It was, to Manfred, as if their separate identities had flowed together, and the idea that such a muddling could be terrified him. He pretended not to see; he saw past them at the safe, unblended wall. (ch. 12, 182)

The same set of actions is retold several times; on this occasion, we have Manfred's point of view, but not his unpleasant 'gubble' idiom, except in

---

[7] According to Adorno and Horkheimer, late modernity is marked by 'the exclusion of the new', the abolition of change (1979: 134). They are referring to 'mass culture'—but as victim of 'the universal triumph of the rhythm of mechanical production and reproduction' (134).

that suggestive use of the word 'muddling'. We pity him; we guess that this is how such an isolated, disconnected life might really be.

The other retellings, in the gubble idiom this time, with many images of physical decay, people melting and rotting in front of the speaker's eyes, are clearly also from Manfred's point of view. But in the other retellings Manfred seems to overlap with others; it is as if he were operating, staging, Jack's or Arnie's or Doreen's experience as he himself sees it. The melting, blending and muddling that he feared in the passage quoted is projected in the gubble passages. As Doreen comments, Manfred appears to be manipulating rather than simply registering the future (ch. 10, 153). Not that this is simply a matter of evil-infant horror material. Manfred foresees his own old age as a senile wreck, kept alive by pointless medical procedures. This combination of a kind of premonitory disgust (like a backwash from the future) at what is to become of him, and a neurotic version of the ordinary child's fascination with the bodily and the grotesque, expresses very painfully how Manfred is trapped in a time loop, the pre-rational of infancy and the post-rational of senility cancelling out both joy and constructive thought.

Manfred is trapped, exploited, and frightened: therefore pitiable, the child as victim. He is unwell, diagnosible as autistic: able to be contained within a reasoned therapeutic system. He is visionary: the future that he sees is true. But although he is trapped and is emphatically an isolate, he is not alone. He is unusual, but everybody in the novel is at least a trifle neurotic, and from time to time several of the main characters are much more than that. Further, he begins to merge with, to infect, the minds of others; perhaps—so others come to feel—to manipulate, rather than simply to register in an uncensored childlike fashion. He may be sick in the colloquial sense: evil. We can see him as evil, as visionary and as victim, and as psychiatric case. We can judge him, value him, pity him and diagnose him.

An extensive repertoire of romantic and post-Freudian views of the child seems to be exhibited. Recalling Lacan's own seminar on the case of an autistic child, one could read Manfred as trapped in the imaginary. The repetitious looping of the Manfred stream-of-consciousness sections is a threat to the narrative, which is well under way in half a dozen plots involving numerous lives, just as their gubble-based idiom is a threat to meaning—to the symbolic. Manfred is both overloaded with meaning and a threat to meaning and to forward movement through time. There is a real question whether the narrative resources of the genre will be flexible enough to give coherent form to these possibilities; the temptations of the horror story, and those of the tale of romantic escape from society, beckon to an already busy plot. Philip K. Dick often seems restless with the assumptions of SF as a genre and with the delicate negotiations of reason and fantasy characteristic of SF at its best. His tendency is to embrace and exacerbate, and we have begun to see how problematic this is in the case of Manfred.

As the story proceeds, the question becomes, will it be Jack or Arnie who is infected by Manfred's sinister vision? The narrative will be worked out at the level of individual character, though the twist is that it is the *sanity* of the individual character that is at stake. The answer ought to be easy. Arnie is the most extraverted, enjoying and energetic person in the novel; surely his selfishness, which is patent and admitted, is just plain selfishness, not neurosis. Jack, for all that he is the 'ordinary guy' main character often found in Dick's novels, is stalled in unconfidence and inarticulacy; moreover, he has a history of schizophrenia, and under the influence of contact with Manfred, this begins to resurface. Indeed, according to the view of the disease that people in the novel hold, schizophrenia is incurable anyway. Jack will be driven further into breakdown, further into his past. The chief symptom of Jack's illness is a recurring vision of humans as machines, soulless repetitions. This is not very far from Manfred's tendency to see people as sacks of skin, containing horrible soon-to-decay organic matter. The irony is that if we can see Manfred's illness as perceptive or prophetic (because he sees into the future), so we can see Jack's. People really are, very often, soulless machines.

Jack acknowledges this, both as regards himself and as regards Manfred. But this awareness doesn't help him much. His worst moment comes when he and Manfred visit the Teaching Machines at the High School. These are 'people' who really are machines—the satiric point is plain. The Teaching Machines always make Jack feel distinctly unwell; but Manfred makes them into nothings, into repeaters of his favourite gubble word; or rather (the episode is ambiguous) he makes Jack hear them as saying only this (ch. 11, 168–70).

4. Manfred and Jack: Survival of the Ordinary

To oppose the child to the adult world is very often to oppose the child to society, since adults control society and can be seen to have shaped it to their own excessively rational measure. The child as either alternative (visionary) or victim is thus going to present as asocial, even though actual children are very sociable in their own way. Manfred is extraordinary, a complete isolate. But he has special powers. He is telepathic. It is not usually his thoughts that are communicated, however; his feelings and perceptions infect or combine with the feelings and perceptions of others.

He already sees the future, or at least its grimmest aspects as they affect him. Just as he does not exist in the 'normal' one-to-one relation to others, but is at once agonizingly isolated and threateningly, sub-rationally merged with others, so he does not exist in the normal relation to the sequence of time. He experiences the condition of modernity, as Dick imagines it: suspension of the sequence of time, suspension of the differences between things, loss of the distinctness of things in time (everything for Manfred is already in decay, things are crumbling before they are built). We could say that the text experiences this condition also, if modernity means that any value or description is relative and to be improvised. Manfred, who slips between childhood and senility, and in another way is trapped in a dead non-time, is only graspable by the novel in momentary, changing, and (in rational terms) incompatible ways. The novel's skill as a narrative, however, as distinct from a metaphor or allegory, is that it finds a set of behaviours and differentiated characters by which it can test and clarify Manfred's significance.

The story resumes its onward movement, after the repeated renditions of the scene at Arnie's apartment, and it enacts an ingenious solution to the threats Manfred presents to others, and others to Manfred. Manfred and Arnie embark on a time trip. As was discussed in the previous chapter, the outcome is grim. Arnie is punished. He is absorbed into an inflection of Manfred's frightened, degraded world, experiencing things as both causelessly hostile and inertially clogged; and then, when he re-emerges into 'normal' time, he is killed by Otto Zitte, victim of that earlier act of violence. The story makes it clear that this earlier attack on Zitte was evil and unbalanced. Yet when Zitte attacks Arnie the whole action appears insane, just as the attack that Arnie organized on Zitte's base appeared insane to Zitte. The menace that seems to emanate from the consciousness of Manfred, whom all agree to be unbalanced, is transferred by the narrative to Arnie and Zitte, engaged in a business contest that has gone sour. The latter reveals the potential for insanity in the normal dealings of Martian society, and the threatening complexity of Manfred's activity in the world of the novel is somehow exorcised. Manfred no longer serves as a kind of sump for the instability and brutality of the society in which he is an isolate, but which, nonetheless, he has earlier merged with.

Arnie dies; Manfred, for his part, moves through the time-slip into the world of the Bleekmen, for whom time passes differently, as they are pre-modern nomads. This departure from the social space of modernity is also an escape from the time to which it had condemned him. On the very last pages of the novel he returns from the future as the senile wreck he had foreseen himself as becoming, *and* comes out of the desert as the happy member of a Bleekmen tribal group. The narrative outcome thus extricates Manfred from his time ailment and from modern society, while delivering Arnie to a justified fate and in effect transferring the element of psychosis to him. Further, in a subtler way it frees the other main character, Jack Bohlen, and this is significant because the effect is to broaden the scope of the novel and offer us some hope.

Jack is left free to develop as the novel's ethical centre. Schizophrenic and barely fit for modern society as he is, he emerges as the book's reasoner. He soberly thinks out what human culture needs for its transmission, that is, the right form of connections with the past (ch. 5, 76). This meditation takes place at the school, where Jack comes closest to succumbing to Manfred's illness, in the presence of the Teaching Machines. Jack also articulates the necessity for change, that is, for a future that makes a difference, as Manfred's previsioned future does not. He arrives at a notion of *sociality* that no one else in the book's society can reach (though various characters do try for it)—a notion that is contrary to romantic and anti-psychiatric views of the social.[8] Jack's meditations, which, however, do not win him anything like happiness or stability, figure as the novel's brief recuperations of a Habermasian reason from the postmodern flux of rationalization and irrationality. Jack is a misfit, but he is also—exhibiting Dick's inclusiveness and duplication of characterizations—the ordinary person given ethical weight as normal.

The outcome cannot be separated from the strands of the rest of the text, which, as we saw in the case of Manfred, are sometimes tangled and knotted. What is affirmed (or, better, 'rescued') is a kind of careful decency. Whether you decide that this is, after all, a revival of liberal humanism, or that what is remarkable is the way in which any firm sense of wholeness or singleness of personality is jeopardized, and the social is deconstructed, is a question of emphasis.

---

[8] We can say that, to a limited but moving degree, Jack overcomes that false division between the individual and the social that Melley (2000) sees as basic to 'the culture of paranoia in postwar America', to cite the subtitle of his book.

10. *A Scanner Darkly*: Postmodern Society and the End of Difference

A Scanner Darkly was published in 1977 and is set in 1994.[1] It is thus a novel of the near future, and lacks the crazy reality-distortions of Dick's earlier novels of the far future, and the hectically driven, breakneck plots those distortions fuel. The chief item of technology by which the world of the novel differs from our world is the 'scramble suit' (discussed below). In Dick's *oeuvre*, *A Scanner Darkly* is the novel that offers the most thorough conspectus of the nature of postmodern society, with emphasis on the social. It is not the dissolution of the boundaries between subject and object, nor the groundlessness of knowledge that is highlighted here, but the kind of social group and social experience that is significant of the conditions of postmodernity. What shapes events, characters, behaviours and things at the deepest level in this case is not dissolution, or stagnation, but something like deprivation: a narrowing down and stripping away.

Dick is here, as he sees it, writing an anti-drug novel; he is writing about what happened to himself and his friends. The different purpose and setting of the novel have prompted a different take on characteristic features of Dick's imagined universe. It's as if we have a recoil into reason: let's slow down and take a steadier look at the circumstances of life in postmodern society. Let's detail, item by item. A slowing, and thence a nightmarish stopping of time is, however, what overtakes the novel's characters. The steady pace of the narration has to be seen in relation to what happens to the people whose story is being told. In the end, this is Dick's most powerful narrative of the loss of differentiation: Substance D, the drug that all are seeking, is with them all along, and Substance D is, obviously, Death—the catch being that they don't find death in the sense of an ending, but reach a stalled cessation of time and experience, exactly what was feared but averted for Manfred in *Martian Time-Slip*.

---

[1] 1994 is actually misprinted as 1944 on p. 9 of the Granada paperback edition—a nice trace of the malfunctioning of machines of reproduction and communication so frequent in the novel.

Between the 1950s and the 1990s, cultural critics had to revise their ideas of the social totality, and even to question whether the concept of the social totality is good to think with. An emphasis on uniformity, homogeneity, conformism and incorporation (mass culture, the welfare state, the national security state, the organization man) has been displaced by an emphasis on heterogeneity and fragmentation (blip culture, fragmented demographics, benign or malign neglect, niche marketing, modular man). The distance between Adorno and Horkheimer, on the one hand, and Baudrillard or Jameson, on the other, illustrates the change of emphasis. *A Scanner Darkly* starts from a development unforeseen in the fifties: the phenomenon of neglect and rejection, by which society as a whole decides not to bother with certain marginal groups, which are judged not worth incorporating, either by coercion or blandishment, and are cast aside. Those who thought they were dropping out, in a gesture of liberating cultural dissent, were willingly cast out as dispensable. This is not the end of the process, however. Registering this socio-economic situation, the novel proceeds to rethink the whole matter of totality, and restages a dialectic of exclusion and inclusion. Those who seemed discarded and neglected, whose economic situation and marginal culture is sympathetically delineated, are part of a whole after all: their lives on the margin replicate the conditions of exchange and consumption that prevail throughout society, and the shapes of those lives are part of a total pattern, which brings about not incorporation but a failure of difference. As a disillusioned meditation on the sixties, *A Scanner Darkly* is comparable to Pynchon's *Vineland* (1990), another demonstration that the counterculture, joyful and zany as it seemed, existed inside grim, totalitarian circuits of power.

The four novels that follow *A Scanner Darkly* are all set in the near future as this one is, but all investigate the possibility of something like salvation by self-surrender, perhaps surrender to the wills and purposes of a benign extrahistorical, extraterrestrial organization called VALIS. The idea offered in these novels of a small group of the faithful, a 'saving remnant' explicitly compared to the early Christians, completely revises both the paranoid sense of hidden, competing but overarching organizations that we find in *A Scanner Darkly*, and also the more positive sense of a small group of humanly decent but helpless individuals that is important in almost all of Dick's earlier novels. In this novel, the humanly decent but helpless group is that of the dopers who share Arctor's house. *A Scanner Darkly* ends with a sense of the impotence of sympathy or knowledge to help others. (It is true that there are passages late in the novel in which the hope of transcendence is poignantly expressed, without there being any grounds for this hope in the novel itself; these are unsuccessful passages, their failure connected with ambiguities in the novel's presentation of Donna, one of the main characters.[2])

Contemporary social reality is not extravagantly transformed here, though it is certainly exacerbated; and social reality is all we have — there are no visitations, revelations or intrusions from other realities, unless we count the dopers' drug trips. The novel is set in California, familiar as the pioneer and outpost of the postmodern culture of information and simulation, the site of Hollywood and Silicon Valley, not to mention Forest Lawn Cemetery, Disneyland and San Simeon, the locus of the genre of fiction which engages with this always-about-to-engulf-the-rest-of-us condition from *The Day of the Locust* (1939) to *Virtual Light* (1993). The implied prehistory of the novel is not merely Hollywood and Disneyland, but the big port and industrial complexes which Mike Davis discusses in *City of Quartz* (1990), sites of manual or production-line work. *A Scanner Darkly* mixes modern and postmodern cultures and economies, and suggests how they might overlie and disrupt each other.

The novel offers a density of information, anecdote and incident. In this respect it is in the mode of realism, building a recognizable plausibility by accumulating mundane details and behaviours. We have a blend of anecdotes having the feeling of personal experience and report about social practice (they are called 'Items', as in the parts of an inventory), with shifting doper fantasies, drug hallucinations, and elements characteristic of the private eye/spy genre (conspiracies overlaid with conspiracies; cross and double cross, the likelihood that the person who employs you to find the murderer is himself the murderer, or that the espionage organization that you serve intends you to be captured, as in Ross MacDonald or John Le Carré.)

The dopers are definable as a sub-class[3] in this society and economy: how they relate to matters of production, consumption and exchange can be specified. This is a world of machines and of consumer products identifiable by their brand names; the exchange and production of drugs, especially Substance D, which the dopers live for, but which is by degrees killing their brains, takes place in this recognizable context. Yet what *A Scanner Darkly* arrives at is the breakdown of the main character's self. Indeed this situation is present, as it were impending, from the beginning. The first couple of pages deal with the psychic disintegration of a character called Jerry Fabin, and the novel is littered[4] with images of the end

---

[2] See the discussion of the end of *A Scanner Darkly* in the following chapter.

[3] The Author's Note begins by saying, 'This has been a novel about some people . . .', suggesting that Dick intended that the novel should concern a group, not simply the main character Bob Arctor (276).

[4] See ch. 1, 17; ch. 4, 64; ch. 5, 81–83; and ch. 10, 174.

result of the process whose inexorable stages it is at the same time tracing with Bob Arctor: brain death, the situation in which you are still alive, but not as a person, simply as a thing, compared to an insect whose life is purely reflexive or to a machine with charred circuits, wrecked, now producing nothing more than a low-voltage hum. In dealing with the breakdown of identity, of self itself, *A Scanner Darkly* treats a theme, and arouses a terror, important to much of Dick's work. This can take the form of schizophrenia or autism; of coming to see the world and its inhabitants as reduced to entropic mess—what is called in this novel 'slush' or 'murk', and is vividly neologized in other novels. It can consist in the discovery that one exists not as a distinct self capable of one's own actions, dreams and nightmares but as something permeated and possessed by the nightmare of another, in whose universe, usually a limited and uncreative universe, one now exists. Yet these obsessions and fears find expression here in the context of Drano and Coke.

It is necessary to work with terms of discussion sufficiently open to embrace both this terror and the map of postmodern economy and society that the novel also offers. By means of a fictive meditation on the place of drug culture in society as a whole, based on the apprehension that it is neither marginal nor alternative, Dick arrives at an analysis of the conditions of the postmodern consumer society. Later I shall comment on formal matters, without claiming that the novel is other than subtly realistic in its form. Here, however, there is an obvious point to be made about affect: the novel deals with suffering and breakdown, dismay rising to a terror which is not permitted to lose itself in the vertiginous sublime but is always returned to Coca-Cola, fast food, supermarkets and Ford Torinos. This is Dick's most penetrating critique of postmodernity, and the terror is part of the critique. In fact, the terror stands for the moment of historical transition, the shift from modernity into postmodernity—a moment of transition that is conceived as the moment when what was menacing in modernity now completes itself.

1. Humans and Machines

Basic to industrial society is reproduction, replication: each product is exactly the same as the previous one, or rather, the previous million. None bears any mark of individuation or difference—difference would be defect. We could put the matter in Dickian terms by saying that objects in this society are replicas, copies, fakes—or impostors, if we extend the discussion to people.

This aspect of modern society has for a long time been recognized as threatening, especially to workers, who can become or be replaced by robots. How can an economic system whose processes of production make for perfect uniformity consist with the liberal ideal of individuality which has grown up at the same time? Surely the processes of production must affect the relations of production: replication will be done by replicants, to use one of the SF terms, alienated labourers who might as well be machines themselves. In *Lies, Inc.* a character works as a quality controller, checking for defective items on an assembly line; he says that his job might as well be done by a pigeon, tests have shown that pigeons do it more reliably, when he retires he will be replaced by a pigeon and indeed he already has a pigeon checking on his quality controlling (ch. 5, 59).[5] In *A Scanner Darkly* this sort of satiric recourse, with its touch of whimsy, is unavailable, because those we meet have been removed from the processes of production anyway. The novel and the characters in the novel repeatedly image people as machines, their processes—memory, conjecture, speculation, fear—in the terms of film projection or the operations of computers.[6] This pattern of images, which can often be read as a pattern of social observation, is intensified by the narrative, in particular by the fate of Bob Arctor.

A key feature of postmodern society extends replication into information. What is made is likely to be not a thing, an object, but an item of information, produced, disseminated, exchanged, and in fact, in the purest model of this form of economy, circulated, through a variety of receptors and transmitters, in a closed loop. The function of the 'workers' in this information economy is to pass the information on, rather than to use it in some fashion outside the circuit of communication. The product has become like money in its endless, restless circulation, abstract and as it were merely operative, existing only in order to set off further transmissions and exchanges. (It is true that before the arrival of computers automation advanced most quickly where the product existed as an unbroken stream, for instance oil in an oil refinery, so the model of industrial products as discrete items such as plates or cars is a trifle misleading.[7])

---

[5] He decides to emigrate, a characteristic recourse in Dick's novels and, as usual, one that is stymied. Whale's Mouth, the planet he emigrates to, is far worse than Earth.

[6] See for instance ch. 1, 19: 'a fantasy number [. . .] it was a documentary re-run, actually'; ch. 4, 57: 'Great overpowering runs for which there had been no previews. With the audio always up too loud inside his head'; ch. 9, 156: 'I've got that taped in my memory banks' (and see *Valis*, ch. 3, 23). Wolk (1995: 122, n. 29) discusses a possible source for this kind of imagery in Dick, referring us to Dick's story 'The Electric Ant' (1969).

[7] See the interest in the discovery of plastic—an almost endless chain of molecules—in Pynchon's *Gravity's Rainbow* (1973). It is notable that David Ireland's *The Unknown Industrial Prisoner* (1971), one of the best, and funniest, novels about alienated industrial workers, is set in an oil refinery.

What kind of workers function in this postmodern economy? The theorists of postmodernity have inferred major changes in human ideals and behaviours.[8] In order to fit into, or perhaps to cope with, postmodern society, the individual must be adaptable, flexible, 'protean'. What is prescribed, what indeed is produced by a society that produces psyches as well as things, is the free-floating individual, the subjectless subject, the nomad, the person whose ego is permeable (to borrow terms, almost in one free-floating breath, from Jameson, Adorno, Deleuze, and Marcuse), affectless or of 'neutralized' affect (to borrow one of the Dick's terms in *A Scanner Darkly*), of low-intensity, uncontentious expressive and conversational style; able to decouple from a relationship, a job or a political position with proper flexibility because it represented a phase rather than a commitment.

There is much in the novel that expresses these aspects of postmodern society. The dopers as a community still relate to industrial society: this is what they are trying to use to anchor their lives, though their conversations and emotions are certainly free-floating in the postmodern style. It is Bob Arctor, the main character, who is caught up in the circuits of information, the imperatives to flexible adaptation.

It may be observed that the preceding sketch of modern society emphasizes a conflict between economy and ethos, and the sketch of postmodern society emphasizes a very neat fit between economy and ethos. It might appear that the fit betweeen economy and society, always subject, in the earlier phase, to lags, pressures of alienation, contradictions, is becoming perfect.[9] Postmodern society is an aspect of the completion of capitalism. If this is true, and is not merely the result of an excess of totalizing zeal in the theorists of postmodernity, it must be due to the way in which the relations of economy and culture have changed in postmodernity. If postmodernity is the absorption of culture by capitalism, the embrace of culture by commodity, then indeed the terms of the game have altered, and it may be that the relation between economy and culture produces this tight fit between economy and ethos. It is significant that in centring his novel on the dopers, Dick chooses something between a class and a subculture. Since the sixties (and this is very much a sixties novel,

---

[8] Theory has its limits in this context, since the protocols of the genre sometimes operate as mechanisms for excluding problematic evidence. Other kinds of writing can therefore be very useful; in this case, for instance, a work of sociology, Steven Tipton's *Getting Saved from the Sixties* (1982). See also Lipton 1970, and Bauman 1997.

[9] See Perry Anderson's comparison of modernism and postmodernism in 'Marshall Berman: Modernity and Revolution' (1992: 25–55). Modernism comes about at a time when modernity is actually incomplete in certain important ways, and postmodernism is the expression of a completed modernity.

though published in 1977), society thinks of itself not in terms of classes but in terms of groups, interest groups or groups engaged in micropolitics.[10] The dopers are a group that still has some of the characteristics of a class, because their relation to the blue-collar work they used to do is still important to them, and yet if they are counter-cultural in their self-definition, they are counter-cultural as consumers, and thus part of the overall culture and economy in spite of themselves, just as the postmodern theorists have posited.

The dopers constitute a sub-class as well as a subcultural group; though they have presumably decided to drop out of 'straight' society, the impression we get is that they have been discarded. And they cannot go back: the shopping centres where the real wealth of consumer society is on sale are off limits to anyone who lacks a valid credit card (ch. 1, 10). The dopers are left with the cheap and boring goods, and this is important because it is by their material circumstances that they are defined. The only attractive consumable mentioned in the novel is the bottle of good Californian wine on which Charles Freck splurges when he decides to kill himself because he can no longer bear what is happening to his friends. For the rest, they are welcome to Coca-Cola, 'Solarcaine' (a brand of suntan spray), Drano, 'Yard Guard', McDonald's.[11] All of these are either poisons or drugs or both (as Substance D is a drug and a poison) and the dopers believe that both Coca-Cola and Solarcaine contain cocaine, if they could only extract it. (They are relying on hearsay, as the excluded must—an ironic situation in this society, where the police who monitor the dopers are drowning in unusable information.)

The dopers have menial jobs (one works at a brake-relining place, another at a centre for the redemption of Blue Chip stamps); as we mostly see them they sit around in a drugged daze losing themselves in long circular discussions. They do not work making things and, as we shall see, they fail in their attempts to repair things and to understand simple mechanical processes, although it is by means of these attempts, more than anything else, that they want to establish their place and identity as people. In addition, no one knows where Substance D is made or grown: this is what Bob Arctor is ultimately to be used to find out. But for all this alienation and impotence, they are part of a fierce, simple economic system, an exchange system. Goods enter this circuit not when they are made, but when they are stolen ('ripped off') and then bartered.

---

[10] See the discussion of the ambiguity of the consciousness of social groups as part of postmodernity and of postmodernism in Jameson 1993: 318–31, 345–55.

[11] Dick's vision of the plight of the ordinary consumer, subject to scarcity, thwarted, is discussed in Chapter 7 above.

> He [Charles Freck] lit up and turned on the car radio, to a rock
> station. Once he had owned a tape-cartridge stereo, but finally, while
> loaded one day, he had neglected to bring it indoors with him when
> he locked up the car; naturally, when he returned the whole stereo
> tape system had been stolen. That's what carelessness gets you, he
> had thought, and so now he had only the crummy radio. Someday
> they'd take that too. But he knew where he could get another for
> almost nothing, used. (ch. 1, 11)

The circulation of stolen goods is sufficient to supply everyone in this
world, and you simply have to accept that you may be stung occasionally,
as you are in the legitimate economy.

The exchange of drugs for money is different, tougher. Even the ingenuous Freck never 'fronts'—he never puts up the money before he sees the
goods. No credit, no casual barter of 'ripped off' goods. It is because drug
dealing constitutes the determining instance in this economy, besides
which other exchanges, based on barter or theft, are marginal, that Bob
can use it to explain to Donna how the legitimate economy works. (Donna
is herself a very 'economic' person, always stealing, collecting, hoping to
make use of things, as the anecdote about her theft of a stamp machine
makes clear [ch. 8, 131].)

> '*Buy*?' She studied his face uncertainly. 'What do you mean by
> *buy*?'
> 'Like when you buy dope,' he said. 'A dope deal. Like now.' He
> got out his wallet. 'I give you money, right?'
> Donna nodded, watching him obediently (actually, more out of
> politeness) but with dignity. With a certain reserve.
> 'And then you hand me a bunch of dope for it,' he said, holding
> out the bills. 'What I mean by *buy* is an extension into the greater
> world of human business transactions of what we have present now,
> with us, as dope deals.' (ch. 8, 147)

Donna is not as innocent as she may seem here, and near the end of the
novel she will, in effect, exchange Bob, or what remains of him now that
he is brain dead, for the chance of information about where Substance D
is made. In the world of *A Scanner Darkly*, you can exchange anything—
stolen goods, sex, information, a person—for anything judged to have
equivalent value. It is worth quoting from a letter Dick wrote at about the
time he was working on the novel; it concerns his own time in a 'rehabil-
itation organization':

> When a heroin addict confronts you, two insect eyes, two sightless
> slots of dim glass, without warmth or true life, calculate to the exact

decimal point how many tangible commodities you can be cashed in for. (Gillespie [ed.] 1975: 50)

In fact the novel is gentler than the letter, concentrating as it does on the pathetic exclusion of most of the dopers from the 'real economy' (though see ch. 9, 159). Nonetheless, it is neither as consumers, nor as functionaries in the post-industrial economy, nor, even, as members of the counter-culture that the dopers try to define themselves, but as workers concerned with making things.[12] In their case, then, there is a lag between consciousness and society.

Barris, Luckman and Bob try to repair Bob's car when it has almost lethally malfunctioned, probably as a result of sabotage; the suspects for this sabotage are, logically though insanely, Bob and Barris, who were riding in it. To repair the car is to retake control of a material reality that has insidiously turned wild. Such an action involves the use of reason; with a pre-electronic machine such as a car you can reason your way step by step to an understanding of what is faulty, since machines of this type work progressively—this pushes that, this connects to that. In this context to reason about machines is genuinely to exercise the lucid, higher faculties.[13] In addition, to repair something is to combat entropy.[14]

Capitalism is often seen as requiring built-in obsolescence for the

---

[12] It is interesting to compare the depiction of the dopers as failed or discarded blue-collar workers with the depiction of the 'unks', the unclassifieds, in Dick's first novel, *Solar Lottery* (1955). The 'unks' are drab, spiritless, rejected, and in all this they are not much different from the dopers in *A Scanner Darkly*. And even in this early novel their plight is associated with the changed relations of production and consumption, though the imagery drawn on for their depiction is derived from stereotypes of the Depression. The problem of production has been solved, at the expense of these workers, who, being unclassifieds, are in effect nonpersons; the problem of consumption remains, and is attacked by the organization of waste: bonfires of unconsumable goods (ch. 2, 18–19). The difference is that *A Scanner Darkly* centres on this social group, whereas in *Solar Lottery* it is merely glimpsed, by Cartwright, a character who is himself, however, an electronics repairman ('everything about him breathed obsolescence and age' [ch. 2, 18]), and who helps to end the situation of stagnation and oppression that grips the novel's society by using his skill as a worker to alter the operation of the 'bottle', the lottery mechanism that controls everything.

[13] See the conversation about the motor car and the oil leak in *The Transmigration of Timothy Archer* (Chapter 11 below, and *Timothy Archer*, ch. 8, 126–28), clearly a conversation concerned with kinds and uses of reason.

[14] For Dick's valuation of repairmen, fixers and tinkerers, see Chapter 5. The social scene in the short stories is split into private and public, and repairmen have scope only in the latter. *A Scanner Darkly* is very much about a household; these scenes involving broken machines usually have a domestic setting, though the most sinister, the scene in which Arctor's car breaks down on the freeway, is set in an urban wasteland. *A Scanner Darkly* is a remorselessly totalizing novel: there are no free spaces, no secluded places.

relentless expansion which is its life. Not merely is a certain product or model invented and marketed only to be superseded, but ephemerality is inscribed in whole processes, whole industrial ages, such as the age of steam or that of the car. Culturally speaking, we may now recognize more clearly than earlier observers that it is possible for people to naturalize what seems at first an unnatural process: the *esprit de corps* of the railway-man, the mystique of the Orient Express, the model train set for Christmas, Casey Jones, Sherlock Holmes' encyclopaedic knowledge of timetables. Yet at the same time we can see the futility in this work of culture; the faster economic change happens, the more likely it is that this naturalization takes the form of nostalgia, a welcoming of that which has already gone.[15]

To repair malfunctioning machines is urgent in this society because the failure of a machine is not the triumph of nature over mechanism, but the advance of entropy. Further, a machine is an image or replica of ourselves, made by the human mind in its own image as something which processes in logical steps. To repair a malfunctioning car or a damaged 'cephscope' is to repair and reassure ourselves. (A cephscope projects images from one's brain in coloured form.) The characters in the novel, the dopers, have damaged brains, and they never succeed in repairing their machines —let alone improving them, as when Barris's attempt to invent a better silencer only augments the noise of his pistol (ch. 4, 61–63). Conversely, machines are seen in almost human terms, for instance in the episode of Donna and the stamp machine: 'The machine was dingey and just kept cranking out stamps' (ch. 8, 131; 'dingey' in this idiom signifies mean and misbehaving).

In an important scene in the novel, Bob is being tested for the possibility that Substance D has burnt out the connection between the left and

---

[15] In *Of A Fire on the Moon*, Norman Mailer meditates (1971: 57–62) on the rednecks and blue-collar workers watching the moon launch across the Florida salt marshes. Their cars, customized, exchanged, eroticized, or simply talked about with relaxed knowledge, mark their naturalizing of a moment of industrial progress. ('Machines—all the old machines he has known—are as unreasonable as people' [60]). Now they sense that this is superseded: they have no understanding of the technology that is going to send a man to the moon and it has no need of them. Two other relevant novels are Primo Levi's *The Wrench* (1978) and Michael Ondaatje's *In the Skin of a Lion* (1987). Both celebrate breakdown, technical failure, even (in the latter book) the prospect of sabotage, because this is the sign of the heartening presence of nature or human nature, something distinct from the technical, a worthy contestant and a medium in which the worker lives, into which he may disappear (the workers lost in an Alaskan storm in *The Wrench*, the images of disappearing into the elements in Ondaatje—diving, being dyed in the dye vats; the prisoner painting the prison roof, who has himself painted blue and escapes into the blue sky). Nature is not available in this way in *A Scanner Darkly*.

right halves of his brain; the technicians replay to him a conversation, recorded on the scanners now monitoring his house, in which he and his friends try to understand how the gears on a bike work. It is meant to be a ten-speed bike but it seems to have only seven gears. They count, repeatedly, sometimes coming up with different totals, but never ten. They speculate that the people who sold it to them (having stolen it, naturally) somehow appropriated the missing gears; if so they will rip our heroes off again by offering to sell them the gears. They need another opinion.

> LUCKMAN: Who should we ask? Who do we know that's an authority on racing bikes?
>
> FRECK: Let's ask the first person we see. Let's wheel it out the door and when some freak comes along we'll ask him. That way we'll get a disheartened viewpoint. (ch. 7, 117)

A young black man comes along and gives them a perfectly lucid explanation of how the gears work on such a bike: two at the front, five at the back; by moving back and forth the chain gives you two times five, i.e. ten gears.

This is an image of how the two-sided brain should work; it comes into the text when Bob's brain is ceasing to work, and his brain's failure is imaged as that of a burnt-out machine. To be sane is to be able to function, as a good but simple machine can function; to be sane, to be a person, is to be able to understand how a simple machine works, or to be able to perform a simple process whose logic we don't usually have to think out. This model for the human itself, by its simplicity, suggests the pressure the modern is under in the world of the novel. (In earlier novels, the terror of reduction, of becoming a mechanism, is equally strong; but the text itself compensates, or reacts, by an overloaded complexity. The style and form of *A Scanner Darkly* are different, though the plot is certainly complex enough.)

Charles Freck talks of the clinics (in which Bob Arctor will end up when his brain is at length reduced to a reflex arc):

> One time I was there visiting a guy, he was trying to wax a floor— they said he couldn't wax the floor, I mean he couldn't figure out how to do it . . . What got me was he kept trying. I mean not just for like an hour; he was still trying a month later when I came back. Just like he had been, over and over again, when I first saw him there, when I first went to visit him. He couldn't figure out why he couldn't get it right. I remember the look on his face. He was sure he'd get it right if he kept trying to flash on what he was doing wrong. (ch. 1, 17)

What happens to this nameless doper is the same as what happens to Charles Freck and eventually to Bob Arctor. It is a brain death, a suspension of time and activity, a kind of cruel parody of actual death.[16] We can say this is inevitable—it has, virtually, already happened at the beginning of the novel because the novel is so saturated with images of people as mechanisms. Machine rationality is a dead end in *A Scanner Darkly*. One can become a machine, but only a deranged one, endlessly repeating the same action, as if the switch were stuck.

2. Postmodern Society and the End of Difference

Bob Arctor, who is supposed to be a police agent, becomes a doper, subject to the conditions of the dopers' existence as a sub-class of failed workers and failed machines. His fate is the most painful thing that happens in the novel; this section considers how that fate expresses the conditions of social reality in the world of the novel.

Out of the convergence of the knowledge that we can naturalize technological progress and the knowledge that the ability is futile, there comes, very likely, the suspicion or fear that from now on only a person whose basis is adaptation will be able to cope with change. Further (for much might depend on the *kind* of process in which a person made or became his or her self) this process is determined from without—the person is, so to speak, the lines around him which shape his space, not the inside which pushes on these lines. In Bob Arctor, Dick gives us a cipher, a space that 'should have' been traced around such a processual type. The novel delineates Bob's loss of identity; identity is left behind in the movement from Bob to Fred to Bruce (with a brief interval as Pete). Either this man is not mobile enough, or such mobility is impossible.

In an older style of society, your first name might helpfully individuate you, because you have a lot to do with your family, from whom your surname does not individuate you, and because only your intimates call you by your first name. You are Bob not Fred. In more recent society, one's family is less important, and the use of first names denotes only pseudo-intimacy. The name becomes a mere label, like 'Patti' on the waitress, which Barris confuses with the name of the food. As the patty/Patti

---

[16] Elsewhere Dick sees this suspension of time as a sign of madness: the mad are those to whom nothing new will ever happen (*Time-Slip*, ch. 11, 160). Perhaps this shift reflects the fact that the world of *A Scanner Darkly* is strictly limited. Extraordinary episodes and manifestations, such as a time-slip, are not possible, hardly conceivable, in *A Scanner Darkly*. Even at its grimmest, madness is an alternative, another way of being, in *Time-Slip*. In *A Scanner Darkly*, however, though people are cut off from the ordinary and everyday, they are not somewhere else, but nowhere.

confusion hints, it is useful to analogize these empty first names with brand names: Coca-Cola, Drano, Solarcaine. This latter kind of name pretends to be a proper name, but is actually a common name. It is a guarantee of uniformity: every can of Coke, every McDonald's hamburger, is identical to all the others.

Every time we eat and drink this sort of product, we eat and drink *the same thing* and this, which might seem a trick of logic to those who retain sufficient cultural and economic freedom not to consume these products, gives rise to intense existential unease in Philip K. Dick.[17] He sees it as the sign of an encroaching entropy, because the end of difference is the logic of this process.[18] If we come to eat, all of us, only one food, and drink one drink, then in the long run, we will all have the same phone number (there will be only one phone number), there will be only one law, only one punishment, and so forth (ch. 2, 30; ch. 16, 268). Donna believes that the formula for Coca-Cola is known only to the members of one family, handed down from generation to generation, a secret, until 'when the last of them dies that's memorized the formula [. . .] there'll be no more Coke' (ch. 8, 148). These eruptions of paranoia may not be entirely convincing, but they do point to subtler manifestations of uniformity. Perhaps Coke or a McDonald's hamburger are other manifestations of Substance D. Perhaps the police and the dopers, and beyond them the police agencies and the forces producing Substance D, are effectively the one organization.

This meditation began by relating the main character's empty names and the importance of brand names in the novel. In one way the products that bear these brand names are distinctly, organically present (hamburgers are made from 'turkey gizzards' [ch. 2, 30]); in another way, because lacking in difference, they are like abstractions, or voids.[19] Any name is a label, a mere signifier, especially in a novel, and actively in a novel that is concerned with clues, and this seems emphatically true with brand names.

---

[17] In the introduction to *The Golden Man* (1980), he recalls how he and his wife subsisted on Lucky Dog Pet Food in his earlier years as a writer (xv-xvi).

[18] See Chapter 7 above, where there is a fuller account of its relation to contemporary consumption: consumption become incorporation.

[19] William H. Gass on the plastic cup: 'It is an abstraction acting as a glass, and resists individuation perfectly, because you can't crimp its rim or write on it or poke it full of pencil holes—it will shatter first, rather than submit—so there is no way, after a committee meeting, a church sup or reception (its ideal locales), to know one from the other, as it won't discolor, stain, craze, chip, but simply safeguards the world from its contents until both the flat Coke or cold coffee and their cup are disposed of. It is a decendental object. It cannot have a history. It has disappeared entirely into its function. It is completely what it does, except that what it does, it does as a species' (1985: 204).

It is as if the thing drops away, and we are left with the name.[20] Thus, in the dopers' fantasy about the Maylar Microdot Corporation, where everything has become reduced to the microdots that are the product, and the employees are all outside on hands and knees looking for the product, and the factory—amid all this, the sign for Microdot Corporation remains full size (ch. 12, 192).

Things become their names, or people shift their names, because they lack thingness, or personhood. After all, they were only signifiers in a novel, signifiers indeed in the manner of clues in detective stories, but for Dick this is not to do with the fiction's consciousness of itself but with the vitiated phenomenological status of our world. The interpretation must be phenomenological; it must be in terms of the action of the society's conditions on the existence of things and people. This perceived drive towards entropic elimination of difference does jeopardize the novel's own desire for unity. This desire for unity could be seen as manifesting itself in perceptions of uniformity; each constitutes the other; the unease that results is in danger of blurring important distinctions between uniformity and a more dialectical unity.[21] The text's way out is not by means of an appeal to its own artificiality, as would happen in self-conscious, formally postmodern texts. This text never implies that it is concerned not with a world but only with its own play and structures as text. Nonetheless it is self-conscious of the act of paranoia—that is, of the act of unification of the contingent that can be high art on the level of texts but can be madness on the level of social life. Further, it constitutes a grim scrutiny of the act of recording and witnessing: there are several helpless observers in the novel, and the novel hints to us that novelists are helpless observers.

3. Dopers and Narks

It was remarked that the only dazzling futurist device in this thoroughly undazzling and very often malfunctioning world is the 'scramble suit', a piece of equipment used by the authorities but, typically enough, invented

[20] The historical implications of brand names from Balzac to Chandler to Warhol are defined in Jameson 1970: 638–40. In *Valis*, the act of finding a suitably arcane name—'entelechy', 'ajna', 'the plasmate'—generates a good deal of excitement; the problem is finding a signified for this signifier. See below, Chapter 12. Also relevant is the work of Bret Easton Ellis, especially *American Psycho* (1991), which depicts the tendency of all things to become their brand names, or descriptive labels that have the vacuity of brand names (as with the descriptions of restaurant dishes): naming itself becomes repetitive and interminable, while the main character loses identity (people fail to recognize him, his actions leave no traces) and his actions become at once unreal and sickeningly violent.

[21] It is in contexts like this that postmodernist criticisms of totalizing as a conceptual operation, associating it with the totalitarian, have most force.

by a police agent on the inspiration of a ferociously vivid drug experience.[22] The passage describing this offers a specimen of the low-intensity paranoia which has become the usual way to respond to anything puzzling in this society:

> For about six hours, entranced, S. A. Powers had watched thousands of Picasso paintings replace one another at flash-cut speed, and then he had been treated to Paul Klees, more than the painter had painted during his entire lifetime. S. A. Powers, now viewing Modigliani paintings replace themselves at furious velocity, had conjectured (one needs a theory for everything) that the Rosicrucians were telepathically beaming pictures at him, probably boosted by micro-relay systems of an advanced order; but then, when Kandinsky paintings began to harass him, he recalled that the main art museum at Leningrad specialized in just such nonobjective moderns, and he decided that the Soviets were attempting telepathically to contact him. (ch. 2, 22)

The paranoia, skipping from the Rosicrucians to the Soviets, is free-floating and not, so to speak, integral to Powers as an individual; in the morning he finds a simple organic explanation for the phenomenon, and gets the idea for the scramble-suit, which, from the memory-banks of a computer storing a million and a half 'physiognomic fraction-representations of various people' (23) projects an endless, randomized blur of part-images of human beings onto a membrane which the wearer assumes. As is rather obvious, this is a striking image of loss of identity. Its practical function in the world of the novel is to do with disguise of identity, most often when two police agents interview each other for purposes of report and planning. The narcotics agencies are infiltrated by 'the forces of dope' (ch. 2, 24), 'the S. D. agency' (ch. 2, 33)—another instance of the convergence of the worlds of order and disorder that is inscribed in the origins of the scramble-suit. Wearing the scramble-suit is a way of preventing an undercover agent working among the dopers from being betrayed by a doper working undercover among the police.

So it is that Bob Arctor, as he is known in his life as a doper, assumes his scramble-suit when reporting, and is then known as Fred. It follows that Fred can then be detailed to investigate Bob with particular care, in fact to oversee the complete surveillance of his private life that becomes possible when his house is bugged (with things called 'scanners'), since it is not known—it must not be known—that Fred actually is Bob. Bob

---

[22] The experience is in turn based on one of Dick's visions (Sutin 1989: 213–14); the narrator of *Valis* (Philip Dick), quoting the above passage from *A Scanner Darkly*, ascribes the experience to Horselover Fat (ch. 7, 96–98).

arouses suspicion because of his unexplained sources of income, which are in fact due to rewards for having informed on various dopers in his role as agent. He then uses these sums to buy dope, hoping by this to establish a role for himself as a small dealer, and thus to make contact with the big dealers who are the ones whom it is useful to arrest; but meanwhile, initially as part of his cover as a doper, he takes drugs himself, thus affecting his brain, so that when he is called on to discriminate between the Bob whom he is monitoring and the Fred who is monitoring Bob, while bearing in mind that they are the one person, he cannot cope. Up to a certain point, the episode keeps touch with the novel's bases in sixties' drug culture by having the structure, at least, of a very weird joke. Then it passes beyond this point and becomes much grimmer.

Fred's dismay comes because he wants to keep his roles separate and then to make a choice about which role expresses himself. The fact that the novel accompanies this dismay about his identity with encroaching brain death caused by Substance D means that when his brain does seize up and he becomes a vegetable ('Bruce') the novel expels from itself its moral consciousness. Apart from a few fragmentary musings by Mike (another inmate/agent, but still conscious) towards the end of the novel, this moral consciousness can only find a place in the Author's Note.

The inclusion of the scramble-suit in the novel focuses a whole series of elements of quite different types which have to do with the convergence of the dopers' world and that of the authorities. The two worlds indeed seem not merely to converge, but to form a vicious circle, a closed loop; and the common term for the suspicion or conviction that things are thus is paranoia.

For instance, it is customary in the world of the novel for police who wish to arrest undesirables speeding in souped-up cars to disguise their cars as souped up and themselves as undesirables; logical, though for the ordinary citizen there is then no difference. But the police, at least, do need to know the difference in order to know whom to arrest out of the mélange of speeders. Their car radios are specially modified to signal their presence to other police cars; but in turn others come to know of this:

> The pseudo-clever stuff that Barris continually alluded to about his own vehicle probably bore some resemblance to reality, the reality of Arctor's own modified car, because many of the radio-gimmicks which Arctor carried were SOP and had been demonstrated on late-night TV, on network talk shows, by electronic experts who had helped design them, or read about them in trade journals, or seen them, or gotten fired from police labs and harbored a grudge. (ch. 8, 139)

Dick is depicting a potentially totalitarian society where two very powerful organizations (drug manufacturers and police) have come to feed off
and resemble each other, leaving little space for the rest, those who are part
of neither social group.[23] But the situation is open in that it is permeable
and shifting; information, rumour, legend, some of it reliable, speads
quickly, since there are malcontents and publicity seekers. (When Barris
believes he has found a way of synthesizing cocaine from a suntan aerosol,
he proclaims his intention to 'write a best-seller eventually' [ch. 3, 47].)
Dick expresses a certain optimism about popular resistance to the tying up
of knowledge and thus power in 'The Android and the Human' (1972; in
Gillespie [ed.] 1975: 60); he says we have a new, technologically adept generation which can rip off or sabotage the apparatuses of power. He imagines
the police calling at a suspect's house and emerging a couple of minutes
later to find their car stripped, radio gone, and so forth. A relic of this hope
in the novel is Donna, ripping off the stamp machine, jamming dozens of
bent coins into the fixtures at the drive-in, shooting up the back of the Coke
truck. It's the kind of disseminated technological anarchism about which
some postmodernist commentators have also fantasized,[24] but it is stifled
in the rest of the novel, in which Donna is either a junkie who will die
before she is old enough to buy herself a drink legally, or a police agent who
will allow Arctor's brain to die in order to get him into New-Path.

It is to New-Path that a dealer resorts when he badly needs to shake the
police off his tail (ch. 3, 48). In these places every patient sheds his or her
clothes, papers, identity. In order to do their work by severing addicts from
their way of life, indeed from the rest of society which is seen as dangerous for the addict, these places are allowed to be off limits to the police.
As a result they are safe for fugitive dealers. At the very end of the novel
we discover that it is here that Substance D is produced, able to exploit the
position of the rehab centres as sanctuaries—and prisons—for addicts
and to profit from the fact that reliable workers for the production of the

---

[23] It is notable that the only 'straights' we see in the novel, after the early scene in the
Anaheim Lions Club, are the old couple who have to share a building with the likes of Dan
and Kimberly (an addict and her abusive partner), and the locksmith and his sister in the
episode of the forged cheque: terrorized, bewildered, humble, able to focus only on some
randomly selected aspect of the degradation they are aware of—dog shit on the stairs (ch.
5, 78), the possibility of choking on your food (ch. 11, 176). This social situation might seem
to resemble that in cyberpunk SF, where there is no middle class; in Gibson, for instance, the
field is left to streetwise punk cybernauts and immensely wealthy corporate recluses. In *A
Scanner Darkly* the field is left to dopers and cops, trying to make do, but in Dick's novel no
one penetrates alternate spaces, as Case enters cyberspace and Case and Molly enter the Villa
Straylight in *Neuromancer* (1984).

[24] See Louis Menand, quoting Ian Angus, in the *Times Literary Supplement*, 21–27 July
1989: 796.

drug may be picked from those whose brains have been ruined by it. New-Path is not an alternative space, such as is often glimpsed in cyberpunk novels; it is the ultimate point at which all becomes one, and becomes nullity. The twist certainly fits the double-cross structure of the genre Dick is using, and fits popular paranoia as well, but it is worth reiterating how much in the novel makes the ending plausible.

The novel observes a resemblance in the way the dopers and the police behave (see ch. 5, 81–82). The loose hippy idiom of the dopers ('freaky', 'funky', 'rinky-dink', and so forth), and the tight, neutralized, affectless jargon of the agents are different in style, but they have the same function: a smoothing away of affect, of difference.[25] It is right that the funniest example of impersonal jargon comes from Barris, the doper who wants to serve the police and is betraying his friend Arctor, the agent who is becoming a doper; he says that Arctor goes over to Donna's place and 'colludes regularly' with her (ch. 12, 206), meaning that he has sex with her (which he doesn't).

Second, Barris and Donna, the two important people in Arctor's life, converge in their treatment of him. Donna is the only person whom he can love, feel as human and use to reassure himself of his own humanity (ch. 6, 102); Barris, it plausibly seems to Arctor, is a creature of a particularly small malevolence, plotting against him. But Donna lets happen to Arctor what in his most human moments he wants to stop happening to her; Barris may in fact be trying to save Arctor by getting him put away before he destroys himself.

The convergence of dopers and police, in the matter of the car modifications or New-Path or the scramble-suit, can be schematized neatly and in the terms of a weird sixties-style joke, but with characters such as Donna and Barris we have a more dangerous blurring. This is summed up by the moment (ch. 9, 159; ch. 10, 173) when Connie, a doper waif whom Arctor goes to for sex, becomes Donna, and then becomes Connie again: not only in Arctor's hallucination, because the scanner records it too; not only as the result of some editing or feedback in the scanners, because Arctor has seen it in his bedroom: that is, an episode that neither a 'subjective' nor an 'objective' explanation will explain, like several other crucial moments in Dick's novels.

As regards the paranoid subplot with Barris, the main point is not what conjecture, if any, will explain what Barris might be up to; the main point is the pressure Arctor is under because the 'he' that is attempting the explaining is beginning to dissolve.

---

[25] 'The counterculture possessed a whole book of phrases which bordered on meaning nothing' (*Valis*, ch. 1, 6; and see ch. 10, 156).

While they are out driving, Barris reveals that he has bugged the house with a tape recorder, at the same time leaving the door unlocked so that anyone who enters will enter by the door and be bugged, though now that he has left the door unlocked anyone, including thieves, can enter. Arctor took them out driving to give the police a chance to install scanners in his house, so the bug setters working for the police may now be bugged by Barris; but, Arctor speculates, Barris is sure to do something dumb like leaving the plug of the recorder out; but then he will claim that the intruders have aborted his bugging by removing the plug, so that they will never know whether the removed plug—for when they return home the plug *is* out—signifies that Barris is incompetent or that there were intruders there anyway. (And in fact Arctor already knows that both these things are true.)

The dotty complexity of this, further embroiled by the discovery that Donna is the one who has entered and left a roach in the ashtray, is a pleasure for the reader, but we can see that it is hard on Arctor, since he is no longer sure whether he is 'really' a doper or an undercover agent. The strain of being Fred monitoring Bob and Bob being monitored is going to split him into two, in parallel to the split between the two halves of his brain which Substance D is bringing about, which in turn is going to make him into Bruce, fit only for New-Path.[26]

The dopers' days are filled with long, curling fantasies, in which the speakers, forgetting where they began, lacking purpose, cannot reach an end. Again, what might be amusing to the reader becomes threatening to Fred as he watches the scanners replay it. Time stops for the dopers; if Fred fast-forwards a few hours he finds that the dopers, ravelled in repetition, are just completing the sentence begun a few hours before (so that a fellow agent says that the only way one can tolerate this stuff is to run the tapes backwards [ch. 12, 199]). The images the novel finds for this effect are of a tape loop, a playback, repetition; and finally, when Bob/Fred has become Bruce, echolalia:

> 'Mountains, Bruce, mountains,' the manager said.
> 'Mountains, Bruce, mountains,' Bruce said, and gazed.
> 'Echolalia, Bruce, echolalia,' the manager said.

---

[26] Paranoia is sado-masochistic: reading or speculating about the world it presents is enjoyable but frightening. The novel catches this very well. But the pleasure and pain of degradation, of hurting yourself and also being hurt by others, has a different dimension in Bob Arctor, as in many other characters in Dick, beginning with Ragle Gumm of *Time out of Joint*, who both desires and is a victim of his situation. The sign of this different dimension is a crisis of the self. We entertain the thought that modern society depends on our desire to be slaves, concealed from us by our feeling that we are victims; then we realize that characters such as Arctor and Gumm are in danger of becoming neither slaves nor victims, but non-selves.

'Echolalia, Bruce—'

'Okay, Bruce,' the manager said, and shut the cabin door behind him, thinking, I believe I'll put him among the carrots. Or beets. Something simple. Something that won't puzzle him. (ch. 17, 273, and see ch. 12, 194)

All that a machine like a scanner records is what it is given to record, and if this is all redundancy, no information, then it reflects everything, blankly, without depth. Bruce himself becomes a camera, a dead eye, a scanner, as it were (ch. 14, 243; ch. 15, 266; and ch. 17, 275). The same dynamic rules things and people. Thus the episode of Arctor's bounced cheque. Maybe Barris forged it, Arctor thinks; but if so, he can't see any sign of this. Maybe he himself forged it, he finds himself thinking. Can you forge your own signature? Can you be so radically discontinuous with yourself as to sign your signature and yet not be yourself (the self that will think about this cheque)? There comes about a split between 'I' and 'Arctor' in Arctor's speculation about his actions:

What if I made it out myself? What if Arctor wrote this? I think I did, he thought; I think the motherfucking dingey Arctor himself wrote this check, very fast . . . (ch. 11, 178)

The matter comes up again when the dopers fantasize about impostors:

'The guy never posed as any of these [that is, surgeon, physicist, Nobel Prize-winning Finnish novelist, etc.]. He never posed as anything but a world-famous impostor . . . The guy pushed a broom at Disneyland, or had until he read this autobiography about this world-famous impostor—there really was one—and he said, "Hell, I can pose as all those exotic dudes and get away with it like he did," and then he decided, "Hell, why do that; I'll just pose as another impostor." He made a lot of bread that way, the *Times* said. Almost as much as the real world-famous impostor. And he said it was a lot easier.' (ch. 12, 197)[27]

Once the speculation begins to curve in on itself, there is no limit to the spiral; maybe the LA Times, by which Luckman authenticates the anecdote, faked the whole thing; maybe Luckman did. In this spirit, the dopers speculate about 'narks' (undercover narcotics agents), till Bob asks whether someone could 'pose as a nark', pose as one posing. This brings

[27] This fantasy brushes up against Warholian celebrity, which frees the subject to be an 'icon' in which fame relates only to fame; and the business with the cheques reminds us of the mundane way we can be 'not ourselves' with money: but these are reminders of other possibilities, no more.

them all up short as just too zany, but Fred, watching this on the scanners later, feels he understands what Arctor was saying—that is, that Bob is now a man posing as a nark rather than a nark posing as a doper. He empathizes with Bob, but he cannot include himself (Fred) in the proposition.

To come to fear that other human beings are not human but, say, (in an SF context) androids is one thing, comprehensible as a metaphor; to fear that you are not a human but an android yourself is another, worse thing, since you no longer have any standpoint from which to talk of human and not-human. This is the discovery that the main character makes in Dick's story 'Impostor' (1953, CS2), and it is in effect what is happening to Arctor. (He goes from being an actor to being a reflex arc.) There is a congruence between the material (the drug has charred his brain), the social (Bob/Fred becomes Bruce) and the personal (Arctor has discovered that he is posing as an impostor, a sort of self-cancellation).

This is a unity, indeed, a unity spiralling down and inwards to a point, an entropic singularity, both in Arctor's story and in what is observed of the society in which it takes place. What might be desirable in a fiction (whereby everything is tied together at the end, and everything reflects or replays everything else) is distinctly undesirable in a society.

4. Paranoia and the End of Difference

At one point Arctor discusses how the police sometimes broadcast instructions to agents mixed with 'typical boring DJ talk'; other passengers in his car seldom notice, 'Or if they noticed, they probably thought they were personally spaced and paranoid and forgot it' (ch. 8, 137). Everyday paranoia of the sort here referred to (a general assumption of plots and secret connections) puts those given to it in a bind. The suspicion that a series of contingent events forms a menacing pattern is, perhaps, ridiculous, though the fact that it is ridiculous does not invalidate it: we should know better than that. The suspicion is then dismissed, but the alternative is almost as dismaying: the subject is faced with the prospect that these events which endanger him are simply random. Either Barris is engaged in an unmotivated plan to disrupt Arctor's life, the more cunning in that it looks accidental (ch. 6, 97–98)—or he is simply freewheeling, hardly letting himself know what he is doing. There is either too much purpose or none.

This bind is a common one in Dick's novels and, it is true, one that owes a lot to the genre tradition from which he is borrowing. At a certain point the main character comes to hope that he is mad, that is, hallucinating occurrences or subjecting them to paranoid distortion (most commonly, both), since the alternative is that the universe is malign. Its actions are coherent, but coherent in a distortedly destructive way, like the malfunctioning machine to which Donna compares it (ch. 13, 236). To put the matter another way, either surface is without depth, or the depth, the hidden meaning and connection, is all one plot and inexorable tendency—the tendency of Arctor towards the state he reaches by the end of the novel.[28]

Genre fiction is often more explicit than 'literary' fiction; it is a common experience for the reader to draw some inference ('Maybe Bloggs is really about to double-cross our hero!'), only to turn the page and find it spelt out, often in italics (*'What if Bloggs . . . !'*). *A Scanner Darkly* intensifies this feature. It is extremely easy to interpret; virtually everything that has been said here on the level of specific observation is obvious and could have been illustrated by other quotations. Thematic material (the notion of brain death, for instance) or imagery (reference to machines, for instance) proliferates. This is not, of course, to say that *A Scanner Darkly* exhibits a pellucid knowledge of itself. Much of its awareness of Donna for instance is (as the novel itself might say) 'murky'; Dick had distinctly unworked-out feelings about funky young things of her type.[29] But the novel *is* self-reflective; very many things that it engages with are, as it were, lifted to the surface and made obvious, even exhausted and burnt out.

So it is, to some degree, with the novel's treatment of paranoia, and rather more with its treatment of empathy. Paranoia turns back on itself, and to have information, to know, to witness, to sympathize, is to be impotent. This is a general condition (the blankness of what the scanners so perfectly give to their viewer, the mood of drift in which everyone in the novel seems to live), but it receives a number of vivid illustrations. There is the way Fred witnesses, on the scanners, Luckman's near death (choking on fast food), which Barris appears psychopathically to permit. Later Bob can only repress this, when he tells the locksmith's wife how a friend of his died: 'He choked to death, alone, in his room, on a piece of meat' (ch. 11, 176). But no one suffers alone, unwitnessed, in the book, though no one can be helped, and no one actually succeeds in dying. It is as if dying is not a postmodern act.

The first character we meet in *A Scanner Darkly* is the doper Jerry Fabin, who believes he is infested with 'bugs', aphids of some kind:

---

[28] This can also be inferred from recent writing about postmodernity, such as that of Baudrillard. The offered generalizations concern the first aspect (heterogeneity, lack of depth), but the mode of generalization—for instance, the refusal to consider exceptions—imposes the second (a total system). And see for instance Pynchon's *The Crying of Lot 49* (1979 [1966]: ch. 6, 117–18).

[29] His letter to Bruce Gillespie (printed in Dick 1993: 69–73) is a good example; he achieves a coherent investigation of these feelings in his non-SF novels of the fifties, especially *Mary and the Giant* (written c.1953–55).

Most of all he felt sorry for his dog, because he could see the bugs landing on and settling all over him, and probably getting into the dog's lungs, as they were in his own. Probably—at least so his empathic ability told him—the dog was suffering as much as he was. Should he give the dog away for the dog's own comfort? No, he decided: the dog was now, inadvertently, infected, and would carry the bugs with him everywhere.

Sometimes he stood in the shower with the dog, trying to wash the dog clean too. He had no more success with him than he did with himself. It hurt to feel the dog suffer; he never stopped trying to help him. (ch. 1, 4)

The novel thus begins with a distinctly ironic specimen of empathy, and a great deal of the rest of it suggests the impotence of this human feeling, even its impotence when the novelist responds to it by writing a novel about the sufferings of his fellows. Later there unfolds a train of images of domestic animals (dogs, rats, dog shit [ch. 5, 78, 83; ch. 7, 113]) sketching the fading of this possibility of kindliness; eventually it is Bob Arctor who is 'given away' for his own good, or society's, and who sees Jerry Fabin as a rat named Fred, living under the sink (ch. 16, 267). (Before this he also entertains the paranoid fantasy that his pets might be against him, robbing him secretly, making long-distance phone calls when he's out, and so on [ch. 8, 133].)

The most poignant of the stymied deaths in the novel is that of Charles Freck. In these circles, we are told, it takes little work to organize the means of suicide: 'The planning part had to do with the artifacts you wanted found on you by later archeologists' (ch. 11, 186). The death is to be labelled, then; but the 'artifacts' Charles Freck selects, to signify the meaning of his death, have nothing to do with its real cause, which is that he is depressed by what is happening to all his friends. He chooses a copy of Ayn Rand's *The Fountainhead*, to show that he is a misunderstood superman, and an unfinished letter of protest to the gas company, to show that he is a victim of the system. By this he collapses his suicide into banality, concealing its real motive, since he evidently feels that it cannot be signified in the terms available to him.

Not that this matters; he discovers that he has been ripped off by the dealer from whom he obtained the tablets with which to commit suicide; he is in for a very long trip, a thousand years or more, during which his sins will be read to him, in shifts.

No doubt we can see *A Scanner Darkly* as itself a more successful selection of signs for those who come after, ourselves, than was Charles Freck's selection of Ayn Rand and the Exxon letter, yet it is interesting that this scene parodies the notion of judgment that Dick works with in his Author's Note. We are left with a chilling list of dead and injured (a list that includes himself), who have been commemorated in the novel, but not really helped, just as Fred cannot help Luckman when he sees him choking, on the scanners.[30]

Bruce's last action in the novel is to pluck a flower and hide it in his shoe: not a functionless, lyrical act, as it might seem, but a sign, a clue for those who have let him end up here, that this is indeed where Substance D is made. But not a purposeful act, for Bruce simply acts as a camera, recording information without motive or understanding (ch. 17, 275).

The ending of *A Scanner Darkly*, then, consummates its sense of post-modernity as a closed loop, but does this so thoroughly as to make empathy, or bearing witness, almost impossible, though we may feel that the novel was written partly to express empathy and to bear witness. Here is a challenge to Dick's humanism, and the next chapter discusses how he attempts to deal with it, not only in *A Scanner Darkly*, but in other late novels, such as *Flow My Tears* (1974), and *The Transmigration of Timothy Archer* (1982).

[30] See Chapter 11 below for further discussion of the Author's Note in relation to Dick's feelings about the potential for empathy in postmodern society.

11. Gestures, Anecdotes, Visions: Formal Recourses of Humanism

It is in its content—the themes, the imagined institutions, practices, devices and objects—that SF is radical; prose style and narrative forms usually remain more conventional. This separation of form and content is likely to be unstable: either those new or weird institutions and practices will in effect be presented as harmless, put within quotation marks as 'entertaining SF idea', or the form itself will alter to accommodate their political and existential implications. This chapter examines some formal issues to which radical content gives rise in Philip K. Dick's SF. The overall quality of action in Dick's novels tends to give system more power than individual agency, but this is an outcome that he resists. The focus of discussion will be on certain expressive units of narrative: incidents that can be classified as gestures, visions or anecdotes. These units of narrative are best seen as Dick's attempts to embody an alternative to the regime of system.

The complexity of the issues and effects under discussion can be suggested by the ending of *Ubik* (1969), a novel in which the grounds of reality and knowledge are drastically destabilized, both for the characters and the reader. The story ends with a twist: Glen Runciter's discovery of Joe Chip's head on a coin in his pocket (ch. 17, 202). We interpret this in relation to the novel's imagery of coins, coin-in-the-slot appliances and heads on coins: Fidel's head, Disney's head—and Runciter's head, inserted into the world of Joe and his companions to signify that he is alive and they are not.[1] This last twist has a wonderful dual effect: it ties the text together (because of its relation to earlier bizarre but meaningful information about the general and special conditions of this world), but it deconstructs the story. We thought we had finally pinned things down with the conclusion that Joe and his friends were actually dead, with Runciter finding various ways to manifest himself to them in half-life, including putting his head on their coins, and now we see that Joe is manifesting himself to Runciter, which ought to mean that *he* is alive and Runciter is

---

[1] See Chapter 1 above for further discussion of coins in *Ubik*, and of the novel's dissolution of existential grounds.

dead. The implication would seem to be that Joe, like Runciter before him, has attained autonomy (the ability to pop up anywhere) by becoming a kind of system himself. He is perhaps a kind of Joe effect, free of his previous confinement in his failing or merely inept body, and his limited and wavering knowledge.

1. Wide Angle: Process, Delirium and the Absence of Events

As with earlier discussions, I shall begin by characterizing a general feature of the kind of world that Dick frequently imagines in his novels, one that will help define the particular aspect of his fiction that is to be considered. It will be found that this feature is unfriendly to the concatenated sequence of events (and decisions, actions, commitments and so forth) that can make for a meaningful, rationalizable plot, and also to the distinct, differentiating event or action by a character (or several characters) that significantly changes the overall situation or that affirms human values. We can then examine Dick's attempts (at the level of form, the way the story is told) to resolve or at least gain distance from this (for him) threatening outcome.

The depiction of war in several of Dick's novels offers a clue. We might think of war as emphatically event, working by dramatic, decisive sub-events—battles. Of course, since the mid-twentieth century this is no longer necessarily the case—think of the 'war against terror' declared by the US after the events of 11 September 2001—and it is not the case in Dick's novels. In *Time out of Joint* (1959) war is routine, a condition rather than an event. The Earth is fighting rebels on Luna; sporadic bombardment takes place and that is all. In fact, as far as the story is concerned, the war is conducted by the novel's main character, Ragle Gumm, as a tedious day-to-day job. He is alienated, so that this job does not feel like real work and he is inclined to be shame-faced about it among his friends and neighbours: indeed the whole point is that he doesn't know that his work is to do with the war at all, and doesn't want to know. The community in which he lives is a humdrum routinized one, in which events in the sense of incidents that make a difference do not happen.

Ragle's small-town world seems real because it has all the characteristics of what is taken to be the real (domesticity, dullness, routine; the TV set, the living room, the child's playhouse), but it is an elaborate simulacrum. The world outside this fake is real because it is the source of power and violence (but it is also unreal, according to our commonsense view, because irrational). Ragle's world has been fabricated solely in order that he may not know that what he 'works at' is not competing in a guessing game in the local newspaper, but trying to determine the targets of missiles launched against Earth from the moon. These attacks are apparently random—thus Ragle's job is somewhere between guessing and predicting, interestingly analogous to the situation of Slothrop and the V-2s in *Gravity's Rainbow* (1973). There is no sign in the novel that the war is going anywhere or has any historical shape. Nothing is happening in Ragle's world, which is pure routine, nor is anything happening outside his world in the war, which consists of random incidents. Ragle thinks he is doing one thing (guessing the solution to a silly competition) when he is doing another (guessing the targets of missiles), but even in the first case he feels alienated. He feels that his job is pointless. The action of the novel, which is exciting and does gather momentum, takes the form of a series of clues and revelations to Ragle of the emptiness of the simulacrum in which he is living: the simulacrum crumbles from within. The most striking of these revelations (the incident in which a commuter bus dematerializes, and the incident in which a soft drink stand dematerializes but leaves behind the sign of itself in a label with the legend 'Soft Drink Stand' [ch. 6, 81; ch. 3, 40]) are effective images of the fact that the whole town is a simulacrum, but they resist rational explanation.

Something similar is true of conditions in *The Penultimate Truth* (1964), but whereas in *Time out of Joint* Ragle's apparently peaceful and secluded small-town existence was a fabrication, in this novel that is what the whole war is. In *The Penultimate Truth* most people live in underground factories to which they retreated at the outbreak of the war; the elite left on the surface now devotes itself to fabricating the simulacrum of an ongoing war.[2] The war is nothing more than the production of images of war. There are newsreels, announcements and exhortations, all striving to maintain the special urgency of war fever, which is based on the sense that events in war—for instance, the fall of a city—have a special meaningfulness and decisiveness. This illusion is kept up so that those below ground will continue to manufacture the robots on which the elite's comfortable way of life depends.

Although the fake that keeps the underground characters oppressed doesn't exactly crumble from within in *The Penultimate Truth*, as does that which cocoons Ragle in *Time out of Joint*, the above-ground elite does begin to split into factions and to engage in assassination, conspiracy and dissent, and in addition it becomes clear that the fabrication of the war is itself inept, riven with anachronisms and stupid faults (the appearance of a jet

---

[2] The influence is perhaps Orwell's *1984*. Dick's SF, especially that of the fifties and sixties, borrows a good deal from Orwell (the sense of surveillance and of perpetual war; the sense of regimentation; the sense of the ordinary guy as victim), though he also moves away from Orwell's depiction of the totalitarian state as unified and remorselessly effective.

plane years too early in a newsreel, and so on). This is characteristically Dickian: a ruling system that had seemed dominant in a totalitarian or paranoid way begins to break down, and we are left with only local enclaves of complete dominance or conspiratorial control, as in the assassination by a robot 'gesaltmacher' which deposits fake clues in one incident in *The Penultimate Truth*: bizarrely watertight, but influential only in a narrow area of the novel's plot and the novel's space (ch. 18). No individual, not even a formidably powerful and cunning one, retains overall control.[3] An emblem of this in Dick's work is the stigmata of Palmer Eldritch: a sign of his power when they start appearing on others, as though they have become Eldritch, but a sign also of his own victimhood, a kind of maiming.

As every reader notices, this regime of fabrication is general in Dick's works. To consider it in the context of the depiction of war in *Time out of Joint* and *The Penultimate Truth* is useful because this context suggests a link between the regime of fabrication and the dissolution of event into process. In Dick's works, whole environments, situations and people (androids) are manufactured, transient, able to be dissolved or manipulated. The result is a condition of non-differentiation; things converge or melt into each other rather than attaining and retaining distinction—whether the things in question be environments, subjects, objects, animals, times, or deities. An individual is often better seen as a process, his or her experiences, memories, moods not so much punctual expressions of individuality, will and so forth, as staged, free-flowing, processual.

The ramifications of this condition in relation to postmodernity were discussed in Chapter 1; what are its implications for Dick's narratives? This undifferentiating regime of process and fabrication provokes extreme instability in the characters. The characters perceive their world, in which everything blurs into everything else, as a total system; nor is this paranoid response wrong, because the people and things in it do indeed act with ingenious and ruthless calculation, often coalescing in conspiracy. In reaction, however, individuals act on impulse, abruptly and violently, subject to sudden alliances and desertions, repudiations and betrayals. They often quarrel with each other—the husband betrays the wife, the employee defies his boss—rather than with the powers that be, who are themselves locked in internecine conflict.[4] Thence the characteristic

---

[3] Two related characteristics of ruling groups in Dick's novels are that they are technically incompetent (they cannot repair the hypertechnological devices that they dispose of; see *The Penultimate Truth*, ch. 13, 102), and that their rule has archaic or regressive qualities (for instance, the territories of individual members of the elite in *The Penultimate Truth* are called 'demesnes').

[4] This conflict among ruling groups happens for instance in *Solar Lottery* (1955), *The Simulacra* (1964), and *The Penultimate Truth*. Other examples could be given; Dick's societies

quality of these novels: entrapment coexisting with anarchy. There are plenty of things happening, but they tend to flare and fade rather than cohering into courses of action, and the area of effective power or conspiratorial dominance itself tends to narrow, as the ruling order splits.

Also relevant here is a simpler quality, which is an exaggeration of a common contemporary experience, urban or institutional. It may be illustrated with reference to *The Crack in Space* (1966). Everything happens in haste, in a mixture of urgency and fatigue; it is not certain who the central character is, or what the central problem or thematic point of the story might be. (No doubt this bespeaks a decentred world, but as readers of what is clearly a narrative we expect some things to be 'topic' and others to be 'tacit', to borrow Polyani's useful distinction.) Decisions are serious, but they tend to give rise to, or to flow into, new situations that require new decisions, so that earlier problems and purposes are almost forgotten.

At the beginning of *The Crack in Space* we learn that much of the population has had itself put into suspended animation in order to wait for better times; these people now outnumber the actively living. What is to be done about them? This is a problem to concentrate the mind, and one with stimulating metaphorical possibilities. One of the characters who faces it is Jim Briskin, who already has problems because he is campaigning for the presidency of the USA and, if elected, will be the first black person to hold the office. (Clearly, this is an interesting speculation in itself, and one that we can envisage the narrative following up.) Meanwhile, an opening into an apparently empty para-earth is discovered —this too is an interesting prospect, narratively and metaphorically. Then we learn that certain characters (with their own problems and agendas) have disappeared into the para-earth—then, that it is not uninhabited after all—then, that the malign inhabitants of an orbiting satellite, in effect another kind of para-earth, are intervening in the affairs of the first para-earth . . . and so on. In short, overload. If a certain situation or revelation seems very important, as all of these do, then readers tend to define it as the central situation or topic, around which the novel as an organized narrative will be shaped; but this tendency is defeated. Each situation or revelation is connected to the others, but the effect is that each supersedes the others, and the characters are hustled off their feet, improvising and jaded. They tend to travel long distances and have hard days.

Footnote 4 *continued*
are usually oppressive but seldom totalitarian, if the latter involves effective rule by a unified group and ideology. Styles of behaviour are similar in Dick's non-SF novels; there the wider society tends to be stagnant rather than oppressive. (An exception is *Puttering About in a Small Land*, which sets the characters' struggles and conflicts in a changing history—the US in the forties and fifties.)

No doubt the analogy is with busy, multi-plotted episodes of TV series such as *Hill Street Blues*, but the effect, again, is that incidents are sensational yet difficult to separate out of the spate of emergency. They lose that distinctness that would enable them to stay in the memories of readers, and characters, and that would enable them to stand for some significant alteration in the overall shape of things. The word 'absence' in the heading to this section is thus misleading; events seem absent because there are too many of them, as there are sometimes too many people in a crowd for individuals to be discerned. The result is a flattening of eventness.

This is not necessarily a defect.[5] In some cases, for instance that of *The Simulacra* (1964), it is a success. The decentredness has a liberating effect because it is anarchically non-hierarchical. A society which—yet again— imposes an oppressive order on ordinary people by means of elaborate fakery, and, again, infantilizes or makes neurotics of them, simply spins wildly into anarchy. There are too many species of personage, too many incongruous purposes and plots, for anybody to control anything. The effect is genuinely, and positively, delirious.

Yet it is possible to exaggerate this aspect of Dick's fiction. In *Palmer Eldritch* (1965), for instance, the kind of thing I have evoked in *The Crack in Space* is present, but at the same time we can identify the way in which Barney Mayerson, in particular, experiences a moral history in the events of the novel. There is time for that. At a certain point Barney refuses to help his boss, Leo Bulero, the other important and potentially decent character. To punish himself, to seek 'atonement' as he calls it (ch. 9, 131), he exiles himself to the grim Martian settlements (chs. 7–10). The episode illustrates the way in which characters in Philip K. Dick can have sufficient subjecthood to fail, movingly, and to know that they have done so. Once on Mars, however, Barney becomes involved in a Machiavellian plot to impersonate one suffering from the ill effects of the drug that is threatening society in the world of the book (he will do this by taking yet another drug), and eventually finds himself in a situation in which Palmer Eldritch, the pusher of this drug, whom the plot was intended to destroy, will avoid assassination by occupying Barney's body and himself assassinating Barney in Eldritch's body. At which point (and I do not guarantee that I have perfectly understood the plot here) we find ourselves back in the world of multiple, overlapping simulacra in which it is difficult to single out events that make a difference.

Later in the novel Leo is projected into the far future—so far into the

---

[5] It is possible that its origins are in the hectic improvisations of potboiling; what Hunting (1987) calls speedwriting and Huntingdon (1988) ascribes to the influence of Van Vogt. The topic here, however, is its effect, what it might catch in common experience.

future that humans have evolved very different bodies. He comes across a monument to Leo Bulero, the heroic assassin of Palmer Eldritch: but then Eldritch himself—if that is the word—materializes as a small dog which urinates on the monument (ch. 6, 91–92). If a monument is something that commemorates and even immortalizes a person or action that made a difference, then this episode seems to ironize monumentality.[6] You don't need a monument when you can live forever, though living forever in the world of Eldritch's Chew-Z, or even as Eldritch himself, is not much of a life. (And it is probably significant that a minor but sinister character in the novel is named Dr Denkmal [ch. 5; 'Denkmal' is the German word for 'monument'].) The conditions in which a person has to take responsibility for his or her life coexist with conditions that make it uncertain that the life is his or hers.

The antagonistic conjunction of Mayerson and Eldritch in the same body (which is partly a mechanism) is an emblem of the situation of the individual in Dick's fiction and indeed in much popular fiction. Eldritch is a character, in that he is distinct, strongly marked (literally), and sure of himself. Yet in him character has been exteriorized; he resembles the monsters of horror fiction, the hideous returning repressed of individualism, people become 'creatures' who have answered the imperative 'Be Yourself' altogether too loudly. Mayerson is an ordinary guy, sympathetic, not very easy to distinguish from other ordinary guys, fallible and ineffective; he resembles those pallid 'normal' characters of horror fiction, who seem to lose individuality in retaining decency.[7] Because it is so painful

[6] Any monument is a kind of time traveller, with potentially ironic consequences, as we can see from Shelley's 'Ozymandias' (1818); there is another time-travelling monument in *Dr Futurity* (1960) (ch. 7, 62), a novel in which Dick parodies the project of travelling through time in order to redress history, in this case, the European conquest of the Native Americans. (See Chapter 3 above for fuller discussion of time travelling in *Dr Futurity*.) There is an interesting discussion of modernism, postmodernism and monuments in Krauss 1983 (see 33–36): the monument depends on a linear sense of time, and, once that fades, the space in which the monument is set becomes open, or empty. Contemporary monuments can be postmodernist, as Krauss shows—or reactionary, as the work of Ian Hamilton Finlay may show. Or they can simply be absurd, as in the case of the bronze plaque beside a freeway— impossible to read it from a moving car, illegal to stop and examine it. More recent (postmodern?) monuments adjust to these conditions by being unfinished and in process. An example is Jochen Gertz's monument in Hamburg on which you may write your opinion of fascism in the lead coating until it sinks into the ground, thus preserving the inscriptions as graffiti and as it were time capsule, or the same artist's field of paving in Saarbrücken with inscriptions on the lower, hidden side. See Teitz 1999: 109–10 and 230, n. 6.

[7] *Eye in the Sky* (1957) works an interesting variation on this split. A party of citizens touring the Bevatron falls victim to a malfunction of the Proton Beam Deflector which (as we learn much later) precipitates them into a kind of time warp. While they are trapped, they are absorbed into a succession of subjectivized universes projected by some of their

and grotesque (Eldritch is already a monster, so when he joins with Mayerson he must be a doubled monster), the coming together of Eldritch and Mayerson stands for the predicament of individualism in modern society. You need to be both a character and ordinary if you are to have a self and be part of society.

2. Empathetic Gestures

As the preceding summary of *Palmer Eldritch* will have suggested, Dick does retain the strong desire to invent incidents expressing what Suvin has called 'intramundane transcendence'. These incidents are expressions of an ethical hope that glimpses a way out of the prison of simulacra. The remainder of this chapter discusses a number of incidents of this kind, showing that they are commonly set outside the system, both narratively and in terms of the society of the given book, and that this gives rise to problems and thence further formal recourses in Dick's later novels. Narratologists have not reached consensus over the definition of an incident, as distinct from a scene, say, and it is true that the examples discussed are themselves made up of sets of further sub-incidents.

First, some further comments on the contents of Dick's imagined worlds. It is commonly maintained that any given invention or gizmo in SF should be subjected to sober socio-political extrapolation, explanation and testing. One cannot simply, fancifully, introduce robot psychiatrists or men with three penises into one's 'novum' without thinking through the technical, psychological and social ramifications; at least send the men with three penises along to consult the robot psychiatrists. These considerations may make light of the free play of fantasy in SF, as my facetiousness acknowledges, but what is clear is that Philip K. Dick commonly flouts them. His inventions and gizmos are offered frivolously or casually. What might be the significance of this?

It may be that the process of extrapolation and explanation would itself tie the fiction to a rational, cause-and-effect narrative coherence. Form has ideological implications. This rationalized or rationalizable narrative is not neutral, and is associated with a calculating, competitive rationality

Footnote 7 *continued*
number; the story colours each universe with the values and neuroses of the character who projects it, but it is only the unbalanced (religious fanatic, repressed, paranoid and so on) who project these universes; the 'normal' characters adjust and resist as best they can. Why is this so? Perhaps the point is that the world which the 'normal' characters collectively project is the 'real' world outside the Bevatron which, by implication, has no more ontological authority than the crazy worlds the oddballs project inside the time warp, but the text itself doesn't successfully explain why there is this difference in their powers.

that is critiqued in Dick's novels, and is also seen as lacking grounds, since the grounds of real and unreal, subject and object, are so uncertain in his novels. Narrative coherence is hard to find, and explanation of what has happened is rendered impossible or contradictory. The plot is very often about the search for an explanation, a search which is repeatedly thwarted. *Alongside* this flux, rather than rising out of it, there tends to occur a certain kind of incident that expresses ethical hope and the value of empathy or solidarity. If we see the whimsically offered future gizmo and the impulsively arriving gesture as analogous because both are free-wheeling, unjustified and unconnected, then the impulsively arriving gesture can be read as providing Dick with a way out of the problems of narrative which he had set himself by his rejection of sober extrapolation, and his departure from linear narrative.

The predicament both of the characters and of the narrative becomes more perplexing in the course of Dick's career as a novelist. In many novels, especially the early ones, we can speak of the regime of system in a relatively straightforward way. There is a totalitarian state apparatus; further, chance and the random have been made part of the ruling system or in some way minimized: this is one thing that Dick's interest in games and lotteries expresses.[8] In these circumstances a sudden impulsive outbreak can disrupt the system and set matters on a new course: so it is with the japing of *The Man Who Japed* (1956) which disrupts the rule of Morec. But system increasingly has a different aspect; it can still be seen as something imposed, but it has also to be seen as something projected, because the worlds of the novels are subjectivized. The characters, even those depicted as victims of larger powers and conditions, cannot easily disrupt what they are themselves helping to create from their deepest, often unconscious desires. (*The Man Who Japed* is unusual in Dick's *oeuvre* in expressing a positive view of the unconscious; it is Allen Purcell's unconscious which inspires and directs his japing.)

Nonetheless, impulsive and empathetic recourses are possible. One of these incidents was discussed in Chapter 8: the scene from *Clans of the Alphane Moon* in which Chuck Rittersdorf helps the alien slime mould, Lord Running Clam, to spore and thus both propagate and revive himself. This can be read as Dick's fantasy of male reproduction (one male helps another to reproduce); but it is significant that it involves such a personage as Lord Running Clam, who is an instance of the frivolous Dickian

---

[8] So it is in *Solar Lottery* (1955): the lottery is part of the solar system's political order, though the rulers cheat; *The World Jones Made* (1956): chance is eliminated by precognition as far as the increasingly powerful Jones is concerned; and *The Game-Players of Titan* (1963): the game is part of the alien rule of the vugs, and the vugs cheat.

gizmo, made sympathetic as a character, but not explicable in any serious SF fashion. In this instance, the frivolous gizmo aspect is an acknowledgment of the fragility of the empathy that is dramatized.

There are, however, a variety of scenes like this in Dick's novels, involving an empathetic or kindly gesture or word, often from an alien or outcast; for instance the robot taxi which talks ethics with Eric Sweetscent at the end of *Now Wait for Last Year* (1966) (ch. 14, 224), and the black man who hugs and consoles General Buckman near the end of *Flow My Tears*.

Again, scenes of this kind might be grouped with others. We have, for instance, the gesture of refusal, when an ordinary person balks and refuses to obey the will of the powerful. A striking instance comes near the end of *Galactic Pot-Healer*: the main character, Joe Fernwright, refuses to join his companions in becoming absorbed into the mind of Glimmung (see Chapter 7 above). Incidents embodying empathetic contact also put into question the nature of community, by asking whether a person gains self from contact with others or recognition by another.

This kind of moment of empathetic contact more and more tends to be offered as outside the stream of the plot, as a kind of coda, occurring after matters have been decided, usually for ill. Formally speaking, it is on the margins: a gesture or piece of advice that expresses a hope. By this, Dick finds one way of inserting his humanist ethic into a postmodern situation which is increasingly refusing to provide such an ethic with narratorial foundations. It doesn't always happen in this fashion, because moments of solidarity or humane exchange can occur at any time: but even taking this into account, it will be suggested that the ethical discursiveness of Dick's novels takes on a different quality in his late works, and needs to be seen in the context of a series of ambiguous experiments with the relations of postmodernism and humanism.

3. Montgomery L. Hopkins and the General

An important instance, both moving and troubling, is the meeting of General Buckman and the middle-aged black man, near the end of *Flow My Tears, the Policeman Said* (1974) (ch. 27, 194–200). The action of the novel involves a character named Jason Taverner in a series of attempts to recover his identity and his sense of meaning. (He wakes up one morning, not only without his identity papers, necessary for social survival in this world, but without his fame as a global TV celebrity.) The novel is premised on a drastic questioning of reality, because the reason for Jason's loss of identity is that he is a figment in Alys Buckman's drug trip, which has the effect of unbinding time and space, and not only for Taverner but for all who perceive him, yet fail to recognize him as the celebrity he is supposed to be. In fact, however, this loss of identity works most of the time as a metaphor for his personal hollowness as a media personality. The notion that Taverner is a person only because, and only when, people recognize him as a personality is powerfully dramatized, and part of this power stems from the fact that when he recovers his personality at the end of the novel he is as unpleasant a character as he was when he lost it (when Alys took the drug and plunged him into a time-unbound world).

General Buckman (Alys's brother and lover, the policeman of the novel's title), supposedly a powerful man in this oppressive society, does nothing effective in the course of all this and it comes to an end, with the death of Alys, without any action on the general's part. Now, as the story winds up, Buckman cannot confront Jason Taverner, though he cannot kill him, as he had intended to do, nor frame him for the murder of Alys; he cannot deal with Alys, who is dead—and as far as we have seen, he never has engaged with her effectively, even though he has been in love with her and they have had a child. He weeps, as he pilots his 'quibble' exhaustedly home, but his weeping is for some undefined general fate, not for any individual. So this moving empathetic scene with the black man happens 'outside' the novel, by way of coda, because that is where Buckman finds himself when it takes place; yet it is the scene to which the novel owes its title.

I referred above to a scene between General Buckman and 'the black man', but in fact it is the General who cannot name himself ('"I have no name," Buckman said. "Not right now"' [ch. 27, 199]), and the other who freely proffers his name and his business card. Though blacks are the victims of heavy discrimination in the novel's world, Montgomery L. Hopkins is a centred person, 'strong in his body, standing high, seeing nothing because there was nothing he cared to see' (198), with a home, a job, a wife and children. It is Hopkins who speaks for Buckman:

> 'Yes, I can tell you're feeling down at the mouth—you know, depressed. [. . .] I've had that sort of inspiration, or rather call it impulse, from time to time during my life. I'm forty-seven now. I understand. You want to not be by yourself late at night, especially when it's unseasonably chilly like it is right now. Yes, I agree completely, and now you don't exactly know what to say because you did something suddenly out of irrational impulse without thinking through to the final consequences. But it's okay; I can dig it.'
> (ch. 27, 200)

We could read the incident in terms of a blurring of boundaries: Taverner's promiscuity, the General's incest with Alys, the way Taverner becomes part of Alys's psyche through the operation of the drug, which collapses objective into subjective. Here white and black embrace, and the General both initiates the embrace and weeps. He is feminized. But it would be a mistake to use notions such as empathy or the blurring of boundaries in a formulaic way here.

It is significant that we are then given an Epilogue (205–208), taking the form of a report on what happened to the characters after the narrative drew to a close. This is standard in realist novels or detective stories, but surprising in a novel whose chief premise has been the suspension of time and place brought about by Alys's drug and its effects on Taverner.[9] And indeed the tone of the Epilogue is rather harsh and sardonic, as though Dick insults the characters, many of whom he had previously pitied, in order to be rid of them. The warmth of emotion of that scene in the forecourt of the gas station is quite lacking.

This puzzling paratextual ending can be connected to the ending of Dick's next novel, A Scanner Darkly (1977). The story, as we have seen, is extremely bleak: the predominant figure is that of a closed loop; the main character becomes a burnt-out husk. If postmodernity involves both fragmentation and homogeneity, splitting and decentring yet uniformity, then A Scanner Darkly dramatizes the condition in a fashion that is unconsoled and unconsoling—until near the end of the novel.

We again have a complicated emotional assessment and closure, followed by a more distanced epilogue, an 'Author's Note' this time. Arctor has become a vegetable, his brain burnt out by drugs. He is now an inmate of a drug rehab centre, which is also the place where Substance D is secretly made, and since he is thereby an agent in place the authorities may be on the way to discovering the secret of Substance D: but since they were prepared to let him become a vegetable in order to achieve this knowledge, we have no trust that they will use it well. Now the novel's attention shifts to Donna, Bob's girlfriend, herself not an addict as Bob had thought but yet another undercover agent, in fact Bob's minder. Earlier he imagined that he was trying to save her from ending up in a place like New-Path, but in fact she was overseeing the operation that put him in there, in order to find out if it was indeed where the stuff that destroyed him is manufactured.

Thus the end of the story. A last glimpse of Donna attempts to reinfuse

---

[9] Earlier in the text, for instance in the scene in which the nature of the drug is explained (ch. 27, 187–89), Dick underlines the incommensurability of the notion of space-time that the drug implies and the notion of space-time that the novel has to depend on in order to have a story. There is plenty of standard novelistic notation of space and time in the scene, which cannot but continue in terms of 'normal' space-time. The result is that this latter space and time—position in a room, journeys back and forth in a quibble, time of day—still pervades everything, yet is rendered null.

her with poignancy and a kind of gallantry. This is not given from Bob's point of view, because he no longer has a point of view, but from that of Mike, another agent (ch. 14, 233–37). It is a characteristic Dickian moment; nothing as dramatically defined as the embrace of Buckman and the black man, or Chuck's help with Lord Running Clam's sporing, but an image of the dark-haired girl, young, brave, somehow like a spirit.[10] It doesn't work. It ignores Donna's relation to the system and plot that has foreclosed Bob's life and reduced the whole society of the novel to a state of non-differentiation. Donna can only be in the novel if she is an addict/police agent, because that is—literally or metaphorically—how everyone gets into this novel. She cannot now be wished into being something else. (The social system of *Flow My Tears* is not supposed to permit people such as Montgomery L. Hopkins either; blacks are supposed to be non-persons.) Indeed, a final poignant image and memory, which Donna shares with the miserably disintegrating Arctor, seems to acknowledge this (ch. 13, 184–85). Donna recalls an addict she once knew who had a glimpse of some other world, a wonderful place seen through a doorway; but he could not move through the doorway, or recover the image of the doorway. What he had seen through the doorway had been a figure of a woman, which can be seen as an etherealization of Donna. An opening becomes both a blockage and a return; the 'Path' in New-Path may actually mean 'pathology'.

Flow My Tears ends with two versions of recognition: one is the recognition by others that bestows a semblance of personality on Jason Taverner, otherwise a nullity. As the effect of the drug wears off, people begin to recognize him as the celebrity he is, and he begins to recognize himself again. The other is the fuller recognition of solidarity which Montgomery L. Hopkins bestows on General Buckman—recognition across a gap, because the black man is powerless and outcast. This recognition is moving, but if the above argument is correct it is also confined to the margin of the novel. The ending of *Flow My Tears* is concerned with the human recognition that makes one a subject: in the case of Buckman and Hopkins, an image of the gaze—call it a glance of regard—that links not master and servant, but two equals in a human group.[11]

A Scanner Darkly is simpler; the images are of witnessing, or simply reception. The husk of Bob Arctor perceives the little yellow flowers from

[10] This is how Abendsen sees Juliana at the end of *The Man in the High Castle* (ch. 15, 258) —though it is hard to give Abendsen's insight much authority. See above, Chapter 6, for discussion of Juliana's killing of Joe Cinnadella. For the dark-haired girl, see the book of this title, a collection of essays and letters by Dick (1988).

[11] Relevant is Sartre's thinking on the gaze or glance as constituting a human group; see the discussions of Sartre in Jameson 1972 and Jay 1994.

which Substance D will be refined, but because he has become an 'eye' (ch. 14, 201), a camera, as he has said himself, he can do little more than receive information. There is no mind behind the eyes to interpret the information, though he does put one of the flowers in his shoe, where others may find it later. The addict in Donna's anecdote stands before the doorway and sees the figure within the doorway; he does a lot more than receive the image, but he cannot move through the doorway or even revive the image.

Now we have an Author's Note, warmer in tone than the Epilogue to *Flow My Tears*, but standing outside the novel: Dick names his friends in the counter-culture, casualties, now dead or maimed. He commemorates them and in effect dedicates the novel to them. He includes himself, by name ('Phil, permanent pancreatic damage'). It is a moving, commanding moment;[12] a moment of realism, because the effect is not to underline that the preceding novel was only a story whereas this (the Author's Note) is real; the effect is to give the author's voice such authority, coming from experience and love, that the story seems real. To put the point another way: since the story already seemed real, the story now seems a real expression of the circumstances and feelings recorded in the Author's Note. Yet if it be agreed that the story's final moments with Donna are not convincing, then the end of the whole text is ambiguous, because the Author's Note comes in as a kind of supplement to what was inadequate in the story. After all, the effective and moving rhetoric in the Author's Note is a rhetoric of naming actual names (Phil, Nick, Joanne and so on), but in the novel names were hollowed to emptiness.[13]

4. The Late Novels: Anecdotes and Visions

Subsequent novels, *Valis*, *Radio Free Albemuth*, and *The Transmigration of Timothy Archer* (1981, 1985, 1982), play in much more edgy and complicated ways with the 'real' and the fictional. The narration of *Valis* is divided between 'Phil' and 'Horselover Fat' (a Graeco-German etymological pun on Philip Dick). This is simply a device to give 'objectivity', we are told (ch. 1, 3), but pretty soon Horselover Fat breaks the rules of metafictionality —or perhaps he redoubles their application—by becoming a separate character. *Radio Free Albemuth* works a witty variation on this play with 'Phil'. The main characters are Phil and Nicholas. Phil, a science fiction writer, and his friend Nicholas, a record producer, discuss how they might

---

[12] But not everyone finds it so: 'Dick's afterword, giving the factual background of the novel, is unnecessary and superfluous' (Robinson 1984: 109).

[13] The novel's play with names, labels and signs is discussed in Chapter 10.

publish the truth about the ruling tyranny (headed by President Ferris Fremont, a thinly disguised Richard Nixon, though Richard Nixon is mentioned in the novel as the Director of the FBI). Phil suggests that he encode it in an SF novel; no, says Nicholas, no one will ever believe anything in that trash; instead they will introduce it into the chorus of one of his records. Later when they are both in a concentration camp, Phil learns that the authorities are still publishing new novels 'by' him, for their own purposes.[14]

Valis for its part prints as its coda ('Appendix: Tractates Cryptica Scriptura' [215–27]) a series of extracts from the *Exegesis*, the philosophico-theological musings of Horselover Fat, the possibly insane double of Phil, who had disappeared from the story, having been reunited with Phil into one person again, only to break loose near the end—and then to have the last word in this coda.[15] The reader has been put through many a twist in her or his assessments of what is fictional and what is (asserted by the author as) actual in the course of the novel, and so is not surprised to discover that the *Exegesis* is also an immense work by Philip K.Dick,[16] though this is not information we get from the novel, which simply prints the extracts from the *Exegesis* as by Horselover Fat.

Yet speculations by a fictional character, even a crazy one, are just as valid, or invalid, as speculations by a real person. Zarathustra is as good or as bad a thinker as Nietszche. This is also true of any passing remarks and observations made by characters in a novel—and there are many of these in Dick's last novels. When they appear in a novel, discursive remarks on the nature of suffering or the behaviour of pet-lovers or many other things are subject to a different discipline than if they appear in a moral essay or a newspaper column, but this difference does not determine our response, the way we entertain them. The narrative situation offers a context, and the character a point of view, but we can still take the given thoughts on the nature of suffering or the behaviour of pet-lovers into our own context and point of view if we choose to. Given this, it is difficult for a novel *not* to be referential, as Slusser (1987) has pointed out.

---

[14] The joke is pursued in Michael Bishop's *The Secret Ascension* (1987), in which Philip K. Dick, though dead, is the chief character, and America is, again, a Nixonesque tyranny. This Philip K. Dick is publicly known for his non-SF novels, which were mostly published after his death in our reality, and his SF novels are circulated in samizdat.

[15] The *Exegesis* has been extensively quoted and discussed earlier in the text as by Horselover Fat (e.g. ch. 8).

[16] A sample is published in *The Shifting Realities of Philip K. Dick* (1995). Chapter 12 below offers further discussion of *Valis*'s dealings with the fictional and the actual. The theological speculations are sometimes illuminating, sometimes silly; the narrator's comments on ordinary life are often wise and candid—the whole package is a disturbing one.

Dick exploits this fact, but he does it by exacerbating both the referential and the metatextual (that is, material in the text that plays with the fact that it is a text); the fantastic (messages from extraterrestrial beings: VALIS); and, in this special case, the insane (material in the text which make us wonder whether the author is right in the head). The referential relates closely to the morally discursive level, the meditations on and arguments about behaviour, virtue and so forth. A character has no reference (even when his name is Philip, the same as that of the author), but a remark about the psychology of suicide has a reference.[17] What Dick is devising here is a different way of asserting human solidarity from that whose flawed history we have been examining in those gestures of kindness in Dick's earlier novels, but one that is nonetheless highly ambiguous, given its context.

This is the best way to approach *The Transmigration of Timothy Archer*, a novel most notable for its rueful moral meditations.[18] The events of this novel, which concern the relations between Bishop Timothy Archer, Angel Archer, and others on whom he has a charismatic but usually disastrous effect, mainly serve to establish our trust in Angel Archer as the maker of these rueful, experience-rich and idealistic meditations.

In Angel Archer, the first-person narrator of the novel,[19] we have the 'dark-haired girl' seen from inside: that is, when you take Dick's fantasy figure of feminine kindness, mystery and autonomy, such as Donna Hawthorne or Juliana Frink or (a more complex case) Linda Fox,[20] and imagine her not as seen (as Other) but as seeing and thinking, this is what

---

[17] Remarks about humans and suicide are judged both in relation to the humans in the fictions and to the humans outside the fiction; on the other hand, remarks about Gethenians and suicide in Le Guin's *The Left Hand of Darkness* (1969) are judged in relation to the Gethenians in the fiction (for instance, ch. 15, 140).

[18] I do not think that it is useful to see this novel as the third in a 'VALIS trilogy', though I hate to disagree with Kim Stanley Robinson who is the proponent of this view (1984: 111–12). If there is to be a trilogy, then the trio should be *Valis*, *The Divine Invasion*, and *Radio Free Albemuth*; the last of these is another novel about the VALIS material, but certainly not a simple alternative draft of the first named. *Timothy Archer* is interesting to compare to these other novels, but that is a different point.

[19] This is unusual in Dick. Other first-person narrations are *We Can Build You* (1972) and *Confessions of a Crap Artist* (1975; alternate chapters).

[20] Complex because Linda Fox appears in *The Divine Invasion* (1980) both as a fantasy figure, a singer, goddess of the airwaves, and as a mundane person with poor skin and a tendency to belch (ch. 15, 173). Further, in this second manifestation Linda Fox is vital to the novel's ethical thinking, because in becoming involved with her the main character, Herb Asher, is revolting against God, who is using Herb to further the divine invasion by caring for another woman, Rybys—by acting as Joseph to Rybys's Mary. In his affair with Linda, Herb asserts agency; he will be kind where he decides, not where God peremptorily commands.

you get. You get someone kind, not mysterious—and not particularly autonomous either. Angel herself is strongly convinced that the events of the novel—in particular, the series of deaths that take away her friends—are determined and ineluctable. She judges herself as one who knows, even foretells, but is unable to act; and she is largely right in her self-assessment. Yet to witness and then bear witness, as she does, is humanly valuable.

One of the most striking of her meditations is that which concerns the nature of suffering, Dante, and root canal work. It is true that this passage, which is Angel's memory of a past experience, so that it is both a meditation and an anecdote, links the mundane and the textual: Angel, like the Bishop in his flightier way, is a believer in the embodied wisdom of great books. In fact Angel and the Bishop flirt with a danger that is dramatized in *Valis*, that of believing that texts have primary authority. (Angel says that the Bishop cannot love his son unless he regards him as a kind of book [ch. 9, 143].) But here the authority of dentistry and of Dante, of mundane experience and of a transcendental text, are in balance:

> So for me in a certain unusual way—for certain unusual reasons—books and reality are fused; they join through one incident, one night of my life: my intellectual life and my practical life came together—nothing is more real than a badly infected tooth—and having done so they never completely came apart again. If I believed in God, I would say that he showed me something that night; he showed me the totality: pain, physical pain, drop by drop, and then, this being his dreadful grace, there came understanding ... and what did I understand? That it is all real; the abscessed tooth and the root-canal irrigation, and, no less and no more:
> *'Three circles from its substance now appeared,*
> *Of three colors, and each an equal whole.'*
> (ch. 9, 145)

The story has become an elaborate structure for returning to something rather simple and mundane in its bases, the illustrative anecdote, though this is an anecdote of a revelation by God, that is, something like a vision.[21] An anecdote is a momentary coming together of significance, an event that has a narrative and a moral shape but seems to arrive casually and to

---

[21] There is a wonderful anecdote about dentistry (heroic extraction of wisdom teeth) in Neal Stephenson's cyberhistorical novel, *Cryptonomicon* (2000: 776–81). The passage says something significant about the body (and significantly mundane, if we think of the glorification of exotic bodily alterations in many cyberpunk novels), but there is no invocation of Dante. There is no need for it in this novel, where a grand narrative spanning histories and continents is being elaborated, as is never the case in Dick's novels.

figure as a diversion, though one with the authority of experience. (It is true because it happened to me—that it is also meaningful is treated as a lucky accident by the teller of the anecdote, though as a matter of fact meaning is easy to find in anecdotes.)

Many an incident in the earlier novels seems improvised. The discussion of gestures of empathy has attempted to define this improvised effect as a result of the resistance of Dick's humanist ideals to his insights about postmodernity. Empathy has to blossom like an unexpected bonus, or, more, like a freak of nature; it is associated not merely with marginal characters (such as the black man in *Flow My Tears*) but with whimsically invented gizmos, the slime mould in *Clans of the Alphane Moon*, the robot taxi in *Now Wait for Last Year*—personages that Dick would not bother to justify in reasoned terms, since reason is compromised in the disintegrating but over-rationalizing societies of these novels. Agency seems utopian in societies that are all system, and in societies that are all system the utopian can only be glimpsed, never systematized; so these moments of empathy are no more than glimpsed and agency is impulsive and momentary.[22]

In *The Transmigration of Timothy Archer*, which takes place in contemporary Californian society and is based on the life of Bishop James Pike (see Stringfellow and Towne 1986), the effect of the anecdote about Dante and root canal work is different, and not only because there is nothing whimsical about God or about Dante. One strength of the realist novel can be its reliance on anecdote, that is, on the way we shape casual incidents into meaningful short stories; another can be its exploitation of the referentiality of discourse about, say, common life.

These remarks on anecdotes and meditations may seem to idealize the reborn realism of *The Transmigration of Timothy Archer*. (One could then contrast it with the strong but finally stifled realism of Dick's non-SF novels of the late fifties: perceptive but repetitious.) This might not be a bad idea: it is worth trying to say how the novel's success is due to Dick's movement through the postmodern fantastic to a more measured recuperation (in both senses of the word) of the realistic. But the matter is not so simple. What happens in the novel is that Angel Archer becomes involved with the charismatic, selfish, generous and ultimately unbalanced Bishop Timothy Archer. The narrative is Angel's witness to the Bishop's life and death. His carelessness wrecks the lives of others; one of these is his son, who commits suicide. The Bishop then believes the charlatans who say that this son is communicating with him from the other

---

[22] The effect can be interpreted in Žižek's terms as a 'crazy enjoyment' (1989: 68), the moment when the subject vertiginously asserts itself in the inadequacy of ideology.

side. As often in Dick, the novel comes up against extreme phenomena that, as it may be, only an unbalanced person could believe in. (This is not an anti-psychiatric novel, like *Clans of the Alphane Moon*, in which those who are classified as insane are, at least, no more insane than everyone else.) The prospect that Timothy Archer, believing in these messages from beyond the grave, is unbalanced is disturbing for us and for Angel Archer. At least in *Valis* the messages come from some respectably unusual and emphatically fictional extraterrestrials; here, as Angel sees, we just have the pathetically banal wishes of grief-stricken and guilty parents, preyed on by shady con-artists.

What happens next is that Bishop Archer, venturing into the Judaean desert in search of the anokhi mushroom (substance of the eucharist, in his belief), but equipped only with a couple of bottles of Coke, dies of heat and thirst—and then *he* speaks from beyond the grave. At least, he appears to speak through the mouth of his mistress's son Bill, a manic depressive, who had, however, figured as one of the most sane persons in the book.[23] This manifestation, illusion or resurrection is also disturbing; it is disturbing that Bishop Archer should choose this means of coming back across, victimizing the unfortunate Bill who had previously, in a wonderful scene, resisted Archer's egoistic credulity,[24] and that Bill should believe that this is happening to him—and that Angel and perhaps Dick should be prepared to believe it too.

So much for the recuperative return to the simple mundanity of the anecdote. Though it is probable that neither Angel nor Dick *finally* believes that Archer is reincarnate in Bill, what we have while the episode lasts is a dissolving of the solidity of the casual but significant life-incident. We are back in the realm in which something can abruptly intrude into ordinary life, occupy it for a while, then withdraw. It neither leaves a new existential field in place, nor allows any authority to the old one. The new existential field would enable us to believe that there is life after death and across the boundaries of life and death—something equivalent to the faith that VALIS is real in *Valis* and *Radio Free Albemuth*; the old one would affirm that what you learn when you suffer under root canal work is definitive. We can entertain neither.

Perhaps the foregoing discussion refers too readily to ordinary life as that into which the transcendental or illusory may intrude, and implies

---

[23] Bishop Pike did come to believe in this sort of phenomenon, and wrote a book on the topic; Dick accompanied him to seances, and his notes for one of them are in the Dick papers at California State University, Fullerton.

[24] See ch. 8, 126–28: to my mind Bill handsomely wins this argument with the Bishop, though several of Angel's meditations on the nature of Bill's ailment suggest otherwise. (See Spinrad 1990: 203; Wolk 1995: 104–105, 120, n. 8.)

that suburban reality is a norm. Suburban reality is hardly a norm in *The Transmigration of Timothy Archer*, however, and still less is it so in novels such as *Valis* and *Radio Free Albemuth*. What is relevant to these latter novels is the growing power of tabloid fictionality, the infiltration of mundane reality by half-jokingly entertained transgressions of the rules assumed to underpin it: Elvis Lives! Neither Hitler nor John F. Kennedy really died, but both returned from secret retirement to help, respectively, Saddam Hussein and George Bush Sr during the Gulf War![25] That tabloid stories bring about an obvious if tacky revival of the religious, since so many are concerned with miracles and with defiance of mortality, is relevant to the theological concerns of Dick's late novels; also relevant is the erasure of the boundaries between fact and fiction that tabloids bring about. This is postmodernism at the grass roots, inventing its own literary forms, but the same phenomenon is at work in the recent book (by a Harvard professor, as the publicity insists) on people being kidnapped and ravished by aliens (Mack 1994; see Showalter 1997): what might have made an entertaining if clichéd SF novel insists on presenting itself as reportage.

This is the territory into which Dick moves with *Valis* and *Radio Free Albemuth*: the mundane social setting; the transcendental experience that disrupts the grounds of reality of the mundane social setting; the blurring of boundaries between fiction and testimony. We have an unusual combination of 'low' and 'high' postmodernism, of kitsch, if kitsch itself be defined as the incongruous mixing of the high and the low, and metatextual self-consciousness. Hence God speaking out of a crushed beer can, as *Valis* has it, and complex metafictional relations between the author and characters named Phil and Horselover Fat, with scrutiny of the unreliability of texts and messages of all kinds (books, films, recordings, radio transmissions) —a scrutiny that must reflect on the text of the novel itself.

5. The Story So Far

The term 'gesture' is intended to label a certain kind of event or scene in Dick's fiction, from his early short stories to his late novels such as *Flow My Tears* or *A Scanner Darkly*. This event or scene expresses the human warmth that is stifled or denied by the whole society and psychic system of the rest of the novel, and it has, in consequence, to be improvised, out of the blue as it were. The gesture partakes of the fantastic (consider the

---

[25] I believe I saw a tabloid headline to this effect while standing in line at a supermarket in Fullerton, California, in 1990. But I have not been able to hunt up a reference, and of what worth is personal testimony in this context?

case in *Clans of the Alphane Moon*), but also, under pressure, partakes of a complex revival of the realistic. We move from outer space and the far future to the suburbs, and the present time, but then the fantastic slips in through a back door marked 'tabloid'. Dick revives the mundanity of the anecdote, the casual but meaningful occurrence; but he does so with a twist. The late novels involve both a heightened realism and a more sophisticated play with fictionality.

The context is a general turn from the hectic to the contemplative in Dick's late novels. These novels are not dramatizations of problems and actions but discussions of them. The quality and pace of the narrative, the place of event in the text as a whole, has changed markedly. As far as genre tropes and narrative pace are concerned, the earlier novels are thrillers, with a dash of horror novel; not so the late novels.[26] *Timothy Archer* is the prime example, because what we read is a single person, Angel, remembering or foretelling or ruminating on the events of the story, rather than presenting them to us. But even in this novel, as we saw, the effect is not that of a simple recuperation of realism. Anecdotes become visions or revelations, intrusions of another reality; ruminations are so esoteric or (in *Valis*) so infatuated with authoritative texts as to part company with mundane canons of explanation.

In his late novels, then, Dick moves away from the hectically driven narrative tracing a ramifying dissolution of grounds, and replaces it with something more relaxed and meditative. The outcome is paradoxical: he both recuperates the realistic and exacerbates the metafictional. The element in the text that expresses humanity and hope is now the passage of rueful meditation. As was argued above, meditations of this kind are always more or less decontextualized: we can apply them to our own lives if we have a mind to. But if they are closely associated with the true nature of the Nag Hammadi gospels (*Valis*, ch. 4, 52), or the possibility of people speaking from beyond the grave—they do have contexts, after all—then it is likely that we do *not* have a mind to. *Valis* is a wonderful novel, but Scientology began in SF.

This book contends that the content of Dick's SF novels, the brilliantly imagined worlds that are outlined, amounts to an intuition of modernity as it turns into postmodernity. So be it; let us then analyse the formal problems that result, given Dick's persisting humanism. Yet the outcome of such an analysis in this case is that when we raise our heads, the scene has changed. Novels such as *Valis*, *Radio Free Albemuth* and *The Transmigration*

---

[26] Following Parrinder (1980), I assume that there is no such thing as a core narrative form characteristic of SF; SF, more a mode than a genre, borrows narrative forms from elsewhere —the quest, the thriller and so on.

of Timothy Archer do not have the same kind of content. The terms that were utilized in earlier chapters to analyse the relation of the novels to history seem irrelevant. The final chapter approaches the problem in its most challenging form, in *Valis*, and this time in the context of the disso-lution of the author, the ultimate (if sometimes ulterior) subject in a novel.

12. Postmodernism and the Birth of the Author in *Valis*

This chapter looks at *Valis* (1981), the best-known of Dick's late novels, relating this controversial novel to his mature works, both in terms of themes (the question of Dick's abandonment of politics for theology) and in terms of formal qualities. Here, if anywhere in Dick's work, we have a postmodernist text: not a text that treats postmodernity in a fashion that is realist and fantastic in varying—sometimes extreme—measures, but one whose form is postmodernist.

Valis concerns the activities of a group of friends in contemporary Orange County, California: they meet, banter, philosophize, engage with others. It appears that there enters into their lives a series of manifestations—messages, cures, signs. These manifestations they set themselves to explain and follow up, led by one of their number, Horselover Fat, the most credulous and ingenuous as a believer. Fat, and to a lesser degree the others, come to see the manifestations as emanating from a kind of extra-terrestrial agency with powers like those of a god: VALIS ('Vast Active Living Intelligence System'). It looks as if this entity will not only declare its own existence, and help them in their daily lives, but also reveal the oppressiveness and unreality of the fabric of their daily lives, now to be seen as something like the prison of this world, so that this novel gives a theological, and broadly speaking a Christian, form to Dick's characteristic sense of social reality as simulacrum. (And, in Dick's usual fashion, it is a simulacrum, a film, that confirms the friends' theorizing and provides them with the name Valis.) The turn to theology does give Dick the opportunity to investigate, question and above all to disseminate the simulacral in new ways. In *Valis* it is less a phenomenon to be experienced and coped with, and more a concept to be defined and speculated about. In this respect *Valis* is a more extreme departure from his earlier fiction than other late novels with similar interests, such as *The Divine Invasion* (1981) and *Radio Free Albemuth* (1985): both of these, especially the first, include a lot of theological speculation, but in both cases the SF settings also open the way to a rich experience of the simulacral.

Although the narrative of *Valis* culminates in the meeting of Fat and his friends with a child deity, Sophia, the text is less a narrative of events than a quest for knowledge—speculations, ruminations, issuing in Fat's *Exegesis*, a set of interpretations and questionings of the manifestations. *Valis* is narrated by 'Phil', who is at times a version of Horselover Fat and at times a distinct person, while both (where the word 'both' is applicable) can be related to Philip K. Dick, on whose name 'Horselover Fat' puns, and who also wrote an *Exegesis*.

It will be seen that the exact description of *Valis*'s textuality is a complicated business. Scott Durham (1988) has proposed that we see the later novels as bringing about the death of the author; I shall in the case of *Valis* invert this argument. It will be seen that *Valis*'s, and the reader's, engagement with reality is not merely problematic but disturbing. If postmodernism typically subverts prevailing assumptions about the relations between texts and social reality, this postmodernist novel practises a very strange form of subversion.

1. Wide Angle: Individualism and the End of Difference

In his 1973 article on Dick, Angus Taylor comments on the fascination of robots: since they are distinct life forms, robots may have access to a different kind of knowledge, even of the divine. We wait for them to speak this. Taylor audaciously suggests that even Asimov's robots carry this fascination, and he is right. As regards Dick's fictions, we can find it not merely in the philosophical android in *Counter-Clock World* (1967) and the taxicab that dispenses marital advice in *Now Wait For Last Year* (1966),[1] but in the 'leadies' that dispassionately debate whether to kill Nicholas St James when he ventures to the surface in *The Penultimate Truth* (1964) (ch. 12). Their curiously disciplined, taut discussion (culminating, however, not in decision but in their elimination at the hands of a third party, also a simulacrum) holds our attention because we cannot help feeling that they may know something we don't. This has not to do with robots as man-made things (foci of a warning of the spreading danger of the mechanical in our civilization), but with the autonomy that they gain when they (appear to) gain 'life'. In this they join animals and androids, gods and freaks.

When the telepathic Martian jackal rejects Barney Mayerson as 'unclean', unfit to be its prey, in *Palmer Eldritch* (ch. 13, 183–85), the rejection affects Mayerson with crushing moral force. The verdict even of a mangy scavenger has authority, when the mangy scavenger is an autonomous life form. Even Mr Tagomi in *The Man in the High Castle*, whom many readers would nominate as Dick's most humanly good character,

[1] These are Taylor's examples (1973: 36).

gains additional charisma because his gnomic Fu Manchu oriental English resembles the simplified dialect of aliens (and robots) in SF. He seems both a human and an alien. Being of us he is bewildered and hurt, being alien he has transformative power (he can make *The Gondoliers* into a source of wisdom, for instance [ch. 6, 96]).

Dick customarily establishes the humanity of his 'ordinary guy' main character by establishing his or her incompetence (for example, the opening scenes involving Joe Chip in *Ubik* and Angel Archer in *Timothy Archer*), but he is never fully satisfied with this. On the one hand, the competence and efficiency of (some) robots, and the gnomic compressed wisdom of aliens, stand for qualities humans need. On the other hand, even Dick's deities are fallible. This is obvious with Glimmung, who at one point crashes through ten floors to the basement of the hotel in which his chosen group of intersystem misfits is meeting on Plowman's Planet (*Galactic Pot-Healer*, ch. 8, 90), but true also of Palmer Eldritch: the stigmata that signify his power (flesh become steel) are also mutilations. (In rejecting Mayerson, the Martian jackal is rejecting Palmer Eldritch in Mayerson; Eldritch is very powerful, but is also parasitic, and internally split.) Further, if we tolerate the element of schlock in many of Dick's evil deities and many of his tyrants,[2] it is because we read this as the mark of humanness as well as evil.

These suggestions imply that Dick's presentations of the divine (in *Palmer Eldritch* or *Galactic Pot-Healer*) and his presentations of the android-mechanical ('Impostor' or *Androids*) are open and investigatory. Aside from early short stories in parable form such as 'Human Is' (1955, CS2), we cannot describe the android fictions as simply warning that humans are becoming mechanical, even if Dick himself described them in those terms, in his speech on 'The Android and the Human' (1972).[3] Androids threaten reduction of what makes life valuable, yet promise expansion or redefinition of it, and so do aliens and gods. But let us pursue the grimmer aspects of both androids and gods in Dick's SF.

If androids threaten humans by reducing them to the mechanical,[4] whose process is routine and whose products are replicas, deities threaten

---

[2] Stanton Brose of *The Penultimate Truth* (1964), 'the ancient sagging mass in the motor-driven chair' (ch. 13, 100); Hoppy Harrington's phocomelal handicaps in *Dr. Bloodmoney* (1965); Eldritch's stigmata; Willis Gram wallowing ludicrously in his bedsheets as he wields power in *Frolix 8* (1970).

[3] Published in Gillespie (ed.) 1975, and in Dick's *The Dark Haired Girl* (1988).

[4] In *Androids* (1968), the threat is paradoxical. Humans, notably Deckard, are in danger of becoming mechanical in their efforts to prevent androids from becoming human. This implication is not consistent in the novel, but it is very forcefully present, for instance in the Luba Luft episode (chs. 9–12).

humans by absorbing them into a unity, a state in which differentiation is cancelled. In the last analysis it doesn't matter whether this divine unity is malign (Palmer Eldritch) or benign (Glimmung).[5]

Very often in Dick's writing entropic degradation is associated with becoming merged, becoming unified. This happens, for example, in the 'gubble' passages at the centre of *Martian Time-Slip* (ch. 10), where Manfred sees Arnie, Doreen, and Jack, whom the novel has worked to differentiate in a multitude of humanly important ways, as loathsome in the same way, under the sign of ugly sexuality. As Darko Suvin observes (1976: 171), 'gubble' itself portmanteaus a string of words: rubble, rubbish, crumble, gobble. We can add 'gabble' and 'garbage'.

The horrifying passage in *Lies, Inc.* which superimposes the TV set as monstrous eye, the fake President Omar Jones who appears in it, and the cyclopean eye of the alien which thrusts itself into Rachmael's reality and which devours itself (eye becomes mouth) only to regrow before one's own eyes, works to similar effect (ch. 10, 128–30). Also relevant here are the image of a decayed eye through which an insect forces its way in the gubble passage in *Time-Slip* (ch. 10, 150), or the notion of the scanner or camera as an eye, or an 'I', to which the main character has been reduced, in *A Scanner Darkly* (ch. 14, 243; ch. 15, 266). If the eye symbolizes the observer's detachment, then the things done to eyes in these passages symbolize the failure of that detachment, a common occurrence in Dick; for instance, Deckard fails to distinguish himself from the androids he is supposed to be detachedly testing and identifying.[6]

This recurrent depiction of a failure of differentiation, if it be 'ontological' in the sense that the concerns expressed in it are taken beyond the point at which they can always be connected with specific social observation, is certainly not a departure from the political. In its grasp of the social conditions of postmodern society, *A Scanner Darkly* is Dick's most politically astute novel, and it is arguably his most unified. The last fifty pages or so,

---

[5] See Chapter 7 above. In *Valis*, God, or beings with preternatural powers from another time or space, can save, heal, or help, but can also control and absorb (ch. 9, 134; ch. 11, 166); the child Sophia is seen both as deity and as android (a computer terminal, an AI system [ch. 12, 178–79]).

[6] *Blade Runner*'s use of images of eyes is a wonderful stroke in this regard. For instance, the scenes in which a person is tested to determine whether he or she is an android focus on the eye of the Voigt-Kampff apparatus as well as the eye of the testee; we have Tyrell's big eyes with their thick glasses; the lights that resemble eyes but fail to illuminate; Deckard's dispassionate examination of enlargements of a photograph, which leads to his detection and eventual killing of Zhora. The film could be read as an allegory of the failure of ocular-centricity and thence of the notion of the distinct, detached cogito. For a magisterial survey of the modern critique of ocularcentricity, see Jay 1994, from which the pun on 'regard' is borrowed.

completing the fate of Bob Arctor, make a determination of the novel such as Dick seldom achieves elsewhere and perhaps seldom attempts. It is also a novel in which, as Durham has described, the subject is split, perhaps to the point of its 'death'.

Yet many of Dick's values are strongly liberal and humanist. He values the little guy who dissents, resists, and persists, if necessary, alone; he values the single humble act, the individual saved (Frank Frink by Tagomi), the new pot made, the embrace of two strangers in the dark and rain-spattered forecourt of a gas station.[7] But these liberal values, and hopes, are subjected to intense torsion, or distortion, in Dick's novels. Jameson (1975a) has traced this in *Dr Bloodmoney*, whose bizarre cast's weird actions he sees as Dick's response to a threatened 'leftist' belief that good and evil in history can be attached to individuals. Dick values that which is unassimilated—unassimilated into the mechanical and collective, into an oppressive society, into a single godhead, into entropy; but the urgency of assertion and defence of that value leads him to break all traditional definitions of the humanly individual. Liberal humanism, passed through this sieve, emerges as intuition of the potentially valuable in androids, gods, animals, robots: wherever and whenever life asserts a distinctness, rather than threatening it. The issue *must* be fraught with complications: vindication of the human, if it is to be be achieved, will only be effective if the human has been profoundly jeopardized. So *Hamlet*, the great play of character, throws character into thorough doubt: perhaps a person is no more than a series of disjunct actions, or a role, hardly to be differentiated from such 'non-persons' as ghosts, the mad, and actors.

What I have called differentiation and variation can, by the time *Valis* is published, be seen as a splitting: the death of the subject. It is not difficult to see *Valis* as pursuing the same risky dialectic of differentiation and unification, this time to the point where liberal humanism is not merely bent and then patched but broken and then discarded. Does not difference figure in *Valis* as an intricate web of splits: in subjects, narrator, deity? Durham has seen this disintegration not as a defeat (which is my implication, so far) but as the consummation of a process begun in the previous novels. The narrating subject cannot be exempt from the fate of the subjects it has narrated; in seeing this, Dick is appreciating the fate of 'man' in postmodern civilization. Further, *Valis* is postmodern in form—in its metatextuality, its presentation of the narrator—in a way that makes a break from novels such as *Ubik*, which go about

[7] Tagomi saves Frink: *The Man in the High Castle*, ch. 14, 228–40; the new pot made: *Galactic Pot-Healer*, ch. 16, 188–89; strangers embrace: *Flow My Tears*, ch. 27, 198–200.

the business of dissolving the grounds of truth and reality in a different way. The final section of the chapter offers an account of the fate of the narrating subject in *Valis*; the next section suggests how hazardous and embattled is the novel's postmodern flow and proliferation of textuality.

2. The Healed Infant and the Slain God

A frequent concern of Dick's late fiction is the experience of helplessly watching the suffering of another.[8] In *Valis*, Horselover Fat tries and fails to help Gloria, and then Sherri, two women bound for death in equally inexorable ways (suicide, cancer). In the interval between the two episodes, Fat tries to kill himself. This pattern is unsparingly analysed: witness and victim are seen as locked in a relationship which can only develop towards sado-masochism. Yet the analysis is offered (by Philip) with a sort of rueful authority, as of one who has been there and made the mistakes and can sum up with a kind of wise, therapeutic detachment, salted with whimsical asides and often bluntly expressed. So it is in the first part of the novel. Philip is watching helplessly over Fat as Fat endangers himself by these obsessions. Yet Philip *is* Fat; he is not detached, as the novel's sober yet pointed, distilled tone suggests, and the narration's skill with tenses (looking before and after: 'Fat had once . . .'; 'Fat would come to . . .') conveys. In addition, since Philip and Fat are the same person, his friends watch helplessly over him, powerless to heal what had begun as narrative convenience[9] and then blossomed into a case of split personality. Philip meanwhile comes to participate in Fat's obsessions and theorizing habits, the world of homoplasmates and Chenoboskion; something is gained, because the theorizings are often illuminating; but something is lost—perhaps what Philip had earlier been able to call 'the tasks of ordinary endurance' (ch. 4, 38).

This complicated set of repetitions and mirror images revolves around a simple, pure ethical challenge: the challenge to pity. Can one move from feeling something for others to doing something for others? But if this situation has an archetypal quality (like that of the traveller and the Samaritan by the roadside—not a connection that usually springs to mind when reading postmodern fiction), it also has a certain intransigence as

---

[8] For example: various episodes in *A Scanner Darkly*, such as the conversation between Donna and Mike (ch. 14, 233–37); Herb and Rybys in *The Divine Invasion* (1981) and in 'Chains of Air, Web of Aether' (1980, CS5; the Herb character is called Leo in the story); Angel Archer and almost everyone in *Timothy Archer*.

[9] 'I am Horselover Fat, and I am writing this in the third person to gain much-needed objectivity' (ch. 1, 3).

fiction. When someone is dying of cancer, there is not much scope for intrigue or manoeuvre. Then again, in reading the early part of *Valis* we can feel readily enough that the text is hardly making a fiction at all; it is reporting what must have happened to Philip K. Dick, what he did, how he messed up, what he learnt. So it is still with the later part of *Valis*, but with a very different effect.

Consider by contrast a good action in *The Man in the High Castle*: the Japanese official Tagomi rescues the Jew, Frank Frink, from the Nazis (ch. 14, 228–30). Tagomi does not pity Frink when he refuses to sign the form that Reiss puts before him. He does not know him. He despises himself for descending to the Nazis' level in shooting the assassins sent after Baynes; he also despises Reiss; he enjoys his scandalous violation of his own code of restraint when he abuses Reiss. His act of virtue is not pure, but involved with a tangle of disreputable feelings. The shooting which depressed Tagomi rescued Baynes; Tagomi has saved *two* of his fellow human beings, in ways that are to him quite dissimilar, but are similarly exhilarating to the reader, whose morals, since he or she reads for enjoyment (the enjoyment of re-enacting a gunfight, or of being righteously rude to a figure of authority), are loose but not necessarily mistaken. *The Man in the High Castle* exploits intrigue, and also coincidence (for instance the coincidence that Tagomi comes to possess the jewel that EdFrank made, sign of Frank Frink's human value) to narrate an incident which cannot easily be schematized.

Paradoxically, the result is a way out of the ontological threat which hangs over the world of the novel, the threat that everything is fake or illusion. That there are certain real things ('wu'-invested) in a world of fakes and deceits is less important than that there are certain good actions —in fact, a lot of good actions (by Tagomi, Baynes, EdFrank, the Kasouras, even Childan). In a fashion that is perhaps philosophically impure, the ethical has come to the assistance of the ontological, in a text that is free to exploit the resources of fiction. As was discussed in the previous chapter, however, Dick finds less and less room for the scenes of empathetic contact which are one way in which he expresses ethical hope in his novels. These scenes tend to get pushed to the margins of his novels, as the novels' social and existential bases are more and more inhospitable to them. Scope is still further restricted in the area of *Valis* which we are discussing. Cancer is incurable; people who want to kill themselves do kill themselves; the witness is left, helplessly regarding the sufferer, until he then becomes the sufferer, helplessly regarded by witnesses.

One might claim that what is challenging about *Valis* is that it combines play with illusions and confrontation with the irreducibly painful: it is a

Berkeleyan dialogue populated by Johnsonian stone-kickers.[10] It is just this ambition to intensify both the humanist and the postmodernist, wrapping them into a mutually exacerbating spiral, that is the most challenging aspect of Dick's fiction. But in fact *Valis* does not daringly play with textuality in a world of irreducible non-textuality. It retreats into textuality. Fat's dealings with the divine, which occupy so much of the novel, are best described as a retreat into textuality. And Fat carries Phil with him: thence the novel's particular challenge and frisson.

Consider a vital topic for Horselover Fat: whether the theophany he has experienced is corroborated by something or somebody outside himself. The first spectacular corroboration of the entrance of the divine into Fat's world is its diagnosis of the hernia afflicting his infant son (ch. 2, 14). We can say that his son is miraculously cured. This (let us accept) proves that other forces are at work than those acknowledged by the view of reality that prevails in contemporary society. One may be cured by the intervention of a being from outside the known reality.[11] Yet one may also be cured by the action of a competent doctor from inside our prevailing reality, and the text recognizes this fact. If 'healing powers are the absolute certain sign of the presence of the divine', 'Then St. Joseph Hospital is the best church in town', as Kevin retorts to David (ch. 13, 196). Yet the text also disregards this fact, reasoning as if the miraculous cure proved that 'normal' cures (admittedly, these are rare occurrences in the grim circumstances of the novel) are unreal, or less real.

The solution to this contradiction is a shift into textuality, unthreatened by comparison to events in prevailing reality (seen as 'the Black Iron Prison'). Fat speaks in Koine Greek when he is entirely ignorant of the language; this is as much a transgression of prevailing rules as is the curing of Christopher, but its human usefulness is slight. Fat and his wife receive two letters from Russia, or concerned with Russia, letters whose contents are so frightening that they cannot be divulged to the reader. Fat and his friends see the film *Valis*. Fat's text (the *Exegesis*, his cosmological speculation) is confirmed by Eric Lampton's text (the SF film *Valis*).[12] Text speaks

---

[10] The problem under discussion here is played out in the later work of Philip Roth: compare *Patrimony: A True Story* (1991, concerned with his father's death from a brain tumour) and *Operation Shylock: A Confession* (1993, postmodernly concerned with doubles, liars and lying texts).

[11] The episode is replayed in *Radio Free Albemuth*, ch. 7. The form of this novel is much simpler, however: one character, Phil, reports how another, Nicholas, received messages which led to the cure of his infant son.

[12] Dick is interested in the *folie à deux*: see *Time-Slip* (Jack and Manfred, ch. 12, 172) and *Lies, Inc.* (the danger that two of the 'weevils' might come to share a 'paraworld' [ch. 10, 121]). Clearly, if a belief is shared by a sufficiently large or sufficiently powerful social group, it is hard to classify it as delusory (see *Valis*, ch. 4, 51). The group of Fat and his friends, and Eric Lampton and his friends, is largish, but not powerful.

to text, both saying, for instance, that we humans have been educated since archaic times by members of an extra-terrestrial race related to Ikhnaton, possessors of a third eye (right in the middle of their foreheads). The number 666 comes up: usually a bad sign (ch. 9, 143). Finally, in Sonoma, members of the Rhipidon Society (as Kevin, David, Fat and Philip have named themselves) speak to members of the Friends of God (as Eric, Linda and Mini call themselves). They exchange a panoply of citations and references to a range of esoteric, not to say nutty, para-knowledge. Both parties 'shoot for the Baroque', to borrow the novel's own phrase (ch. 2, 13).

Energizing this (as it often seems) talmudic fascination with the conferring of precise names on nebulous concepts ('Form I of Parmenides', 'homoplasmate') is a postmodernist restlessness. Fat plunges into the flow of theories, terms, citations, accepting, forgetting (never refuting), collaging, stitching. It's not so much a matter of never stepping into the same river twice as a matter of never once stepping out of the different river. An example: in ch. 7 (98) we discover not only that Fat and Philip are split (one person become two), but that Fat himself is re-split. Fat and an early Christian named Thomas simultaneously inhabit his self. As the speculation is pursued (101), attention shifts to Christ ('We are talking about Christ . . . We are talking about interspecies symbiosis'), and it is determined that Christ and Elijah are one person. Attention quickly shifts to Philip.[13] Recounting a dream, he realizes that he (like Thomas/Fat, like Christ/Elijah) is split, simultaneously living as himself and his lost father.

As we read, we lose the propositions in the process. The information that Fat is really Fat/Thomas is given no chance to stagger us because it is replaced by (rather than developing into) the speculations about Christ and about Philip. Corroboration becomes corroboree.

This impulse to exceed what has previously been thought, and so to replace it while seeming to confirm it, operates in several of the 'corroboration scenes'. When Fat meets the therapist Dr Stone and discovers that he shares many of his thoughts, they exchange information about early Christianity (ch. 4, 50–54). Fat introduces the Nag Hammadi texts ('Chenoboskion'). This is a new item for us, though familiar to Stone, and it is now offered as crucial. Something similar happens when the Rhipidon Society meets the Friends of God: this time the Fibonacci Constant is the startlingly important possession which the two parties share, but which the reader has not previously heard of. Nothing is fixed or centred: that is the point conveyed by Maurice's exasperated misapprehension that Fat

---

[13] This is just after the passage Huntington (1988: 156) discusses as a specimen of Dick's habit of self-contradiction (*Valis*, ch. 7, 101).

has not read Genesis.[14] (Maurice is another therapist.) In fact he has read Genesis altogether too often, but has reinterpreted it in his own way. If you feel free to discard the account of creation in Genesis, why keep to Christianity at all (as Fat persists in doing)? Fat's version of Christianity is so decentred that Maurice falls into the mistaken belief that Fat is ignorant of Christianity.

This rhapsodic postmodernist restlessness is about to meet its end, even its nemesis. It was always vulnerable. The adventurous syncretism, ranging through Plato, Parmenides, Ikhnaton, Bruno, Paracelsus, the Rosicrucians, Horselover Fat, Eric Lampton and the Tibetan Book of the Dead, is an erasure of differences. Each of these colourfully different texts, torn out of historical context, bathed in the warm solvents of esotericism, says the same thing, although, admittedly, what that same thing is changes from speculation to speculation. And this blurring of differentiation should be connected to an underlying literalism of interpretation: the Early Christians, for instance, are found to have had some material way of attaining immortality. This material (from Jim Pike out of John M. Allegro) is what they literally consumed in the eucharist. But, paradoxically, this material, literal truth exists only in the texts that are cited and interwoven in the novel. Dick's attempts to restore 'thingness', phenomenological substance, to humble objects, are not as successful here as they were in earlier novels: the scene in which Philip secretly confers the sacraments on his son, using hot chocolate and a hotdog bun, is (in my opinion) unconvincing (ch. 12, 193). 'The first thing to depart in mental illness is the familiar', as Philip says earlier (ch. 2, 16).

It is significant that Fat is depressed by the apparent verification offered by the film *Valis*, which might have been expected to elate him (ch. 9, 139). If his theories are corroborated, he is faced with the grim prospect of conclusion. It is possible that the God whose presence is being confirmed is dangerous.

> When you know this you have penetrated into the innermost core of religion. And the worst part is that the god can thrust himself outward and into the congregation until he becomes them. You worship a god and he pays you back by taking you over. (ch. 11, 165–66)

This god who absorbs humans into himself, obliterating difference, is in earlier fictions Glimmung, Palmer Eldritch, the nameless devouring deity

---

[14] ' "You've never read the Bible," Maurice said with incredulity. "You know what I want you to do? And I mean this. I want you to go home and study the Bible. I want you to read *Genesis* over twice; you hear me? Two times. Carefully. And I want you to write an outline of the main ideas and events in it, in descending order of importance. And when you show up next week I want to see that list." He obviously was genuinely angry' (ch. 6, 77).

of 'Rautavaara's Case' (1980);[15] here it is identified with Dionysus as an insane god and a god of intoxication, poison.

Further, if the Friends of God, with whom Fat and his friends make contact after seeing the *Valis* film, are evil, then the corroboration is a trap; the members of the Rhipidon Society may be seeing in this mirror not the truth, but insanity, as they do quickly suspect. The original assumption that our prevailing reality is not just different from that confirmed by Fat's experiences, but deceptive and evil, is now flipped on its head. The disturbing quality of the Friends suggests that it is the alternative reality that is not merely different, but evil and deceptive. It is true that Sophia, the divine infant whom Fat and his friends next meet, is carefully distinguished from Lampton and his friends; but since one of them then kills her (because contact with the god had incurably sickened him), Sophia's goodness is qualified consolation. The process which began with the healing of one child ends with the death of another. Whether Sophia is a god or a machine (ch. 12, 178–79) is less important than the fact that, whatever she is, she dies. A being can only be a candidate for godhead in *Valis* if he/she can be hurt, even killed. The sado-masochism that elsewhere vitiated humans' will to help or be helped now reappears at the level of the superhuman.

The split between Fat and Philip had been healed by their experiences in Sonoma, in particular by the word of Sophia. After her death, Fat and Philip split again, however, and Fat wanders the world in search of another avatar. His friends hear news:

> 'At least he isn't dead,' David said.
>
> Kevin said, 'It depends on how you define "dead."'
>
> Meanwhile I had been doing fine; my books sold well, now—I had more money to put away than I knew what to do with. In fact we were all doing well. David ran a tobacco shop at the city shopping mall, one of the most elegant malls in Orange County; Kevin's new girlfriend treated him and us gently and with tact, putting up with our gallows sense of humor, especially Kevin's. (ch. 14, 206)

The intense poignancy of this passage comes from the fact that the pressure of Fat/Philip's insanity, and idealism (for it is both), is relaxed. People are living different lives, ordinariness ('one of the most elegant malls in Orange County') is valued because it is *not* seen in relation to the sacred, as in the unconvincing passage depicting baptism by hot chocolate.

---

[15] See Chapter 7 above.

3. Birth of the Author, Death of the Reader

In the number of *Science-Fiction Studies* devoted to Philip K. Dick in 1988, John Huntington (in his general discussion), and Scott Durham and Emmanuel Jouanne (in their remarks on the late novels) each highlight formal aspects and problems. Of these, the most relevant to the discussion here is Durham, because his argument puts the postmodernism of *Valis* in a different light from that in which I have so far set it. For Durham the late novels express Dick's recognition of the formal implications of the death of the subject he has 'staged' in his SF. The text, which demonstrates the disintegration of its subjects, can no longer emanate from an authorial subject; recognizing the logic of this, Dick's late novels abolish the author as subject, and SF as a genre is left behind in a shift into 'a liberation-theology' (Durham 1988: 186).

A topic such as the death of the subject is best approached relationally, as Durham has seen; in this discursive universe, subject, author, God, and reader circle each other in antagonistic interdependence. 'The birth of the reader must be at the cost of the death of the Author', wrote Barthes (1984), who initiated this topic with an ebullience that has not always been retained. In what follows, I modify Durham's account of *Valis* by looking at the peculiar relation set up between reader and author.

Dick is characteristically a writer who challenges the reader's capacity for belief as well as arousing his or her sympathies. Put under pressure, the reader of *The Simulacra* (1964) might ask, 'How can I believe that people in the novel could believe that they were ruled *for seventy years* by the same unageing young woman, hosting unexciting TV shows?'—and then proceed to ask: 'How could Philip K. Dick believe this? Did he give credence to it as part of his fiction, or did he toss it forth, in a kind of irritation with the absurdity of politics and the boundlessness of human credulity?' In the latter case he implicates himself, his readers and his subjects (that is, the powerless characters in the novel) in varieties of the same credulity. This example is not kind to Dick's achievement, but it does point to something important: readers and characters undergo a similar severe test of their powers of belief in the course of the novel, and readers may note that the author is (to exaggerate only a little) himself embroiled, risking disorientation, if not humiliation.

If we define the topic as the relation between the reader's, the characters', and the author's willingness to believe, then the matter is very different in *Valis*. In *Valis* the text does not offer the reader the incredible as already labelled incredible—zany or horrifying, extreme or bizarre. The incredible is offered as ordinary, as reportage. Is not this the frisson worked by this novel? Anyone reading a novel such as *Ubik* has to accept that the novel offers something visionary and phantasmagoric. Whether one then emphasizes the novel's treatment of the deliquescence of commodity in late capitalism, or, with Slusser (1988), one then emphasizes its rendition of 'historicity' in relation to an open, Emersonian event horizon, one has to pay attention to that explicit inventiveness which constitutes the shimmering portal (proportioned no doubt to Fibonacci's Constant) through which any reader gains entrance to the novel. One sign of this condition is the fact that the rules and practices of the world of the novel, which are familiar and natural to the characters if not to the readers, collapse and become strange even for the characters—and this happens very early. *Valis* is different.

In *Valis*, the von Danikenesque notion of intelligent aliens educating stumbling Terrans is inserted into a quotidian Orange County setting. The narrative is concerned with the discovery and understanding of the phenomenon—the acknowledging of it, we might say. But here what is shocking for the reader is the author's admission that he believes in VALIS, or rather, Philip K. Dick's admission that he believes in it. This is a literary effect, not dependent on the knowledge that many of the incidents to be found in *Valis* and *Radio Free Albemuth* are recounted and analysed as events in Dick's life, in his *Exegesis* and in interviews. It is an effect largely brought about by the way in which, after Philip and Fat have split, Philip begins to participate in the obsessions and textual riffs that the split seemed to have assigned to Fat rather than to the often impressively wise and blunt Philip. It is also an effect that denies textuality, because it reduces the fiction to a screen through which we look at Dick's belief in the existence of VALIS.[16]

The story (the series of illuminations or visitations, and the series of ruminations on them in which the group of friends engage) gets itself told, while the 'truth' of VALIS is left in quotation marks, and responsibility for it is placed on the shoulders of the suffering, split-off Horselover Fat. Fat for his part plunges into the hectic flow of speculation which was characterized above as a retreat into textuality, and which comes to its grim upshot in Sonoma. But the possibility that is allowed to grow, to vary and to permute, while this suspension and postponement is in place, is best defined neither as the possibility that Fat is right nor as the fact that Philip

---

[16] Relevant here is the blurring of the boundary between fictional and historical that we can observe in 'low' postmodernism, for instance in tabloid reportage (see Chapter 11 above), and also—a very different matter—the proliferation of literary and other artistic fakes and allegations of fakery, in connection with the Shoah (the Demidenko affair; the Binjamin Wilkomirski/Bruno Dössekker affair) and with indigenous authorship (Elizabeth Durack as 'Eddie Burrup'; Leon Carmen as 'Wanda Koolmatrie'; controversies over Mudrooroo Narogin and Roberta Sykes).

and Fat are the one person, but rather as the possibility that Philip K Dick believes in VALIS.

By this somewhat shocking or embarrassing tactic, the novel defeats our attempt to defend ourselves by saying that it is only a novel. In the contemporary world, the boundaries between art and life, fiction and information, have been erased in ironic fulfilment of the ambition of the avant-garde, so that (for instance) it is possible to treat news as fiction or entertainment. Dick circumvents the process by reversing it. This novel denies its fictionality, but without allowing us to recapture it for fiction by labelling the denial as a sign of its realism, a matter of mimetic style. The focus is not on reportage and/or ordinariness, as in traditional realist fiction, though the novel often works very well in this mode, but on the way the author offers his belief to validate the extraordinary (VALIS) that is set amid the Orange County quotidian. Jouanne proposes that in the late novels Dick does not merely write about simulacra but makes a sim-ulacrum—a fake (the whole fiction) presented as a reality (1988: 228). But it is the manner in which the novel is presented as a not-fake that is disconcerting. To do what Jouanne describes is indeed to follow the mod-ernist road: in response to the ever-increasing, insidious and tentacular capture of art by commodity, one makes a progressively more spikily artful and sophisticatedly fake-ish work of art. Dick is doing the reverse: it is the literalism that breaks through the reader's weariness with contemporary hyperreality and with art's attempts to exceed it.

Yet the excitement of realizing that this is not a (mere, dismissible, 'cre-ative') novel, and thence (no matter how ingenious the author is and how thoroughly he or she shreds the Subject) difficult to distinguish from the TV news, is chastened by the realization of what this means about Philip K. Dick. And, indeed, what it means about meaning. Maurice the thera-pist intuited that 'Fat had no concept of enjoyment; he understood only meaning' (ch. 6, 72); the irony of *Valis* is that Fat's quest for meaning, into which Philip and Fat/Philip's friends are swept, finds only sameness (one meaning in all the eclectic variety). VALIS offers itself as something of vast temporal and metaphysical dimensions; in the end, it is a local event that the author believes in, validated in a striking way by that return of Authority. VALIS happened or did not happen to Fat and his friends in Orange County; the primary experience that the novel allows the reader is that of reading about this phenomenon and (if my argument holds) coming to terms with Dick's belief in it.

To put the matter more simply, the reader may close *Valis* thinking, 'What do I do next?'. This response is appropriate and natural, rather than naïve and inappropriate, as it would be with most texts whose dealings with textuality were comparably complex. It is a response that marks how thoroughly the novel expresses a moment of collision: collision between ethical seriousness and a postmodernist sense of the textuality of meaning.

In *Valis* Philip K. Dick presses his sense of the threat to differentiation to extreme lengths: outwardly different people echo each other's experiences—or delusions; diverse texts and speculations are found to mean the same thing; human beings and aliens are found to suffer from similar disabilities. This takes the threat to differentiation frighteningly further than it is taken in earlier novels where, for instance, a deity (perhaps ambiguous, but nonetheless able to be defined) threatens to absorb a person (able to be seen as an individual, though an individual whose sense of identity is shaky). We can say that in *Valis* Philip K. Dick reproduces the threat to differentiation at the level of the text.

In doing this he follows the logic of postmodernism. The result is not, however, an elegant vindication of this logic. Rather, it is the record of a painful blockage. The ethical problems that the novel straightforwardly poses, such as how one helps those who need help but refuse it, are not solved. The therapist Maurice is given to saying 'And I mean this' as a way of underlining his instructions. His phrase is a reminder that meaning has an ethical dimension, and VALIS clearly has an ethical dimension if it exists at all. The achievement of *Valis* is to underline how painful it can be when pursuit of the ethical collides with the proliferating textuality of meaning. The novel suggests that if the postmodern condition poses a difficulty for its subjects (readers, characters, authors and deities alike), then this is that difficulty.

Works Cited

Works by Philip K. Dick

Note: works by Dick are listed here by date of first publication. Dates of editions referred to in this book, where these differ from original publication dates, are in square brackets.

1955 [1966]. *A Handful of Darkness*. London: Grafton.
1955. *Solar Lottery*. New York: Ace.
1956 [1968]. *The World Jones Made*. London: Sidgwick & Jackson.
1956 [1978]. *The Man Who Japed*. London: Magnum.
1957 [1979]. *Eye in the Sky*. London: Arrow.
1957 [1985]. *The Cosmic Puppets*. London: Grafton.
1957 [1969]. *The Variable Man*. London: Sphere.
1959 [1969]. *Time out of Joint*. Harmondsworth: Penguin.
1960 [1979]. *Dr Futurity*. London: Magnum Books.
1960. *Vulcan's Hammer*. New York: Ace.
1962 [1992]. *The Man in the High Castle*. New York: Vintage.
1963 [1969]. *The Game-Players of Titan*. London: Sphere.
1964 [1970]. *The Penultimate Truth*. Harmondsworth: Penguin.
1964 [1976]. *Martian Time-Slip*. London: NEL.
1964. *The Simulacra*. New York: Ace.
1964. *Clans of the Alphane Moon*. New York: Ace.
1965 [1966]. *The Three Stigmata of Palmer Eldritch*. New York: MacFadden.
1965 [1987]. *Dr Bloodmoney or How We Got Along After the Bomb*. London: Arrow.
1966 [1968]. *Now Wait for Last Year*. New York: MacFadden.
1966. *The Crack in Space*. New York: Ace.
1966 [1976]. *The Unteleported Man*. London: Methuen. (Published in revised form in 1984 as *Lies, Inc.*)
1967. *The Zap Gun*. New York: Pyramid.
1967. *Counter-Clock World*. New York: Berkley.
1968 [1972]. *Do Androids Dream of Electric Sheep?* London: Grafton. (Reprinted 1987, as *Blade Runner*.)
1969 [1987]. *Galactic Pot-Healer*. London: Panther.
1969 [1970]. *Ubik*. London: Rapp & Whiting.
1969 [1987]. *The Preserving Machine*. London: Grafton.
1970 [1973]. *A Maze of Death*. London: Pan.
1970 [1976]. *Our Friends from Frolix 8*. London: Panther.
1972 [1977]. *We Can Build You*. London: Fontana.
1972 [1975]. 'The Android and the Human'. In Gillespie (ed.) (1975).

1973. *The Book of Philip K. Dick*. New York: DAW.

1974. *Flow My Tears, the Policeman Said*. New York: DAW.

1975 [1989]. *Confessions of a Crap Artist—Jack Isidore (of Seville, Calif.) A Chronicle of Verified Scientific Fact 1945–1959*. London: Paladin.

1977. *The Best of Philip K. Dick*. New York: Ballantine.

1977 [1991]. *A Scanner Darkly*. New York: Vintage.

1980. *The Golden Man*. New York: Berkley.

1981. *Valis*. New York: Bantam.

1981. *The Divine Invasion*. New York: Timescape.

1982 [1983]. *The Transmigration of Timothy Archer*. London: Grafton.

1984 [1985]. *Lies, Inc.* London: Panther.

1984 [1986]. *The Man Whose Teeth Were All Exactly Alike*. London: Paladin.

1985 [1988]. *I Hope I Shall Arrive Soon*. London: Grafton.

1985 [1987]. *Radio Free Albemuth*. London: Grafton.

1987. *Beyond Lies the Wub*. Volume 1 of *The Collected Stories of Philip K. Dick*. Preface by Philip K. Dick, foreword by Steven Owen Godersky, introduction by Roger Zelazny. Los Angeles and Columbia, PA: Underwood/Miller. (Title of paperback edition is *The Short Happy Life of the Brown Oxford*.)

1987. *Second Variety*. Volume 2 of *The Collected Stories of Philip K. Dick*. Introduction by Norman Spinrad. Los Angeles and Columbia, PA: Underwood/Miller. (Title of paperback edition is *We Can Remember It for You Wholesale*; the story of that name is added, and 'Second Variety' is omitted.)

1987. *The Father-Thing*. Volume 3 of *The Collected Stories of Philip K. Dick*. Introduction by John Brunner. Los Angeles and Columbia, PA: Underwood/Miller.

1987. *The Days of Perky Pat*. Volume 4 of *The Collected Stories of Philip K. Dick*. Introduction by James Tiptree, Jr. Los Angeles and Columbia, PA: Underwood/Miller.

1987. *The Little Black Box*. Volume 5 of *The Collected Stories of Philip K. Dick*. Introduction by Thomas M. Disch. Los Angeles and Columbia, PA: Underwood/Miller.

1987. *Puttering About in a Small Land*. London: Paladin.

1987. *Mary and the Giant*. New York: St Martin's Press.

1988. *The Dark Haired Girl*. Willimantic, CT: Ziesing.

1991. *The Broken Bubble*. London: Paladin.

1991. *In Pursuit of Valis: Selections from the Exegesis*. Ed. Lawrence Sutin. Novato, CA and Lancaster, PA: Underwood-Miller.

1991. *The Selected Letters of Philip K. Dick 1974*. Ed. Paul Williams. Novato, CA and Lancaster, PA: Underwood-Miller.

1993. *The Selected Letters of Philip K. Dick 1972–73*. Ed. Dennis Etchison. Novato, CA and Lancaster, PA: Underwood-Miller.

1995. *The Shifting Realities of Philip K. Dick: Selected Literary and Philosophical Writings*. Ed. Lawrence Sutin. New York: Vintage.

(with Ray Nelson) 1967. *The Ganymede Takeover*. London: Arrow.

(with Roger Zelazny) 1976 [1977]. *Deus Irae*. New York: Dell.

Secondary sources

Abrash, Merritt (1995). '"Man Everywhere in Chains": Dick, Rousseau and *The Penultimate Truth*'. In Umland (ed.) (1995).

Adorno, Theodor, and Max Horkheimer (1979). *Dialectic of Enlightenment*. Trans. John Cumming. London: Verso.

Aguirre, Manuel (1990). *The Closed Space: Horror Literature and Western Symbolism*. Manchester and New York: Manchester UP.

Aichele, George (1997). 'Postmodern Fantasy, Ideology and the Uncanny'. *Para.Doxa*, 3, 3–4: 498–514.

Aldiss, Brian W. (1969). *Barefoot in the Head: A European Fantasia*. London: Faber.

—(1975). 'Dick's Maledictory Web: About and Around *Martian Time-Slip*'. *Science-Fiction Studies*, 5: 42–47.

—(1977). 'Introduction'. Philip K. Dick, *Martian Time-Slip*. London: NEL.

Amis, Martin (1991). *Time's Arrow, or The Nature of the Offense*. New York: Harmony.

Anderson, Perry (1992). *A Zone of Engagement*. London: Verso.

Arac, Jonathan (ed.) (1986). *Postmodernism and Politics*. Minneapolis: U Minnesota P.

Attebery, Brian (1992). *Strategies of Fantasy*. Bloomington and Indianapolis: Indiana UP.

Atwood, Margaret (1996). *Alias Grace*. London: Bloomsbury.

Ballard, J.G. (1995 [1973]). *Crash*. London: Vintage (with Introduction by Ballard).

Barthes, Roland (1984). 'The Death of the Author'. In *Image Music Text*. Trans. Stephen Heath. London: Flamingo (Fontana).

Bataille, Georges (1985). 'The Notion of Expenditure'. In *Visions of Excess: Selected Writings 1927–1939*. Ed. A. Stoekl, trans. A. Stoekl, Carl R. Lovitt, and Donald M. Leslie Jr. Minneapolis: U Minnesota P.

Baudrillard, Jean (1991). 'On Ballard's Crash'. *Science-Fiction Studies*, 55, part 3 (Summer): 313–20.

Bauman, Zygmunt (1997). *Postmodernity and its Discontents*. Cambridge: Polity.

Bear, Greg (1985). *Eon*. New York: Bluejay.

Bennett, Andrew J. (1992). '"Hazardous Magic": Vision and Inscription in Keats' "The Eve of St. Agnes"', *Keats-Shelley Journal*, 41: 100–21.

Berman, Marshall (1982). *All That is Solid Melts into Air*. New York: Simon & Schuster.

Bettelheim, Bruno (1990). 'Feral Children and Autistic Children'. In *Freud's Vienna And Other Essays*. New York: Knopf: 166–88.

Bishop, Michael (1990 [1987]). *The Secret Ascension or Philip K. Dick is Dead, Alas*. New York: Tor.

Bloom, Harold (1982). '*Clinamen*: Towards a Theory of Fantasy'. In *Bridges to Fantasy*. Ed. George Slusser, Eric Rabkin and Robert Scholes. Carbondale and Edwardsville: Southern Illinois UP: 1–20.

Boorstin, Daniel J. (1964 [1961]). *The Image: A Guide to Pseudo-Events in America*. New York: Harper & Row.

Breton, André (1978 [1936]). 'What is Surrealism?'. In *What is Surrealism? Selected Writings*. Ed. Franklin Rosemont. New York: Monad.

Broderick, Damien (1991). 'SF and Postmodernism'. *New York Review of Science Fiction*, 30 (February): 1–26.

Brooke-Rose, Christine (1981). *A Rhetoric of the Unreal*. Cambridge: Cambridge UP.

Brooks, Peter (1976). *The Melodramatic Imagination*. New Haven: Yale UP.

Butler, Octavia E. (1987). *Dawn*. New York: Warner Books.

Byatt, A. S. (1990). *Possession*. London: Vintage.

Carter, Cassie (1995). 'The Metacolonization of Dick's *The Man in the High Castle*: Mimicry, Parasitism and Americanism in the PSA'. *Science-Fiction Studies*, 67, 22, part 3 (November): 333–42.

Castaneda, Carlos (1970). *The Teachings of Don Juan: A Yaqui Way of Knowledge*. Harmondsworth: Penguin.

Cavell, Stanley (1988). 'A Reply to John Hollander'. In *Themes out of School*. Chicago: U Chicago P: 141–44.

Clarke, Arthur C. (1973). *Rendezvous with Rama*. New York: Harcourt, Brace, Jovanovich.

Clayton, David (1982). 'On Realistic and Fantastic Discourses'. In *Bridges to Fantasy*. Ed. George Slusser, Eric Rabkin and Robert Scholes. Carbondale and Edwardsville: Southern Illinois UP: 59–77.

Clute, John, and Peter Nicholls (eds) (1993). *The Encyclopedia of Science Fiction*. London: Orbit.

Coontz, Stephanie (1992). *The Way We Never Were: American Families and the Nostalgia Trap*. New York: Basic Books.

Coveney, Peter (1967 [1957]). *The Image of Childhood*. Harmondsworth: Peregrine.

Csicsery-Ronay, Istvan, Jr (1991). 'The SF of Theory: Baudrillard and Haraway'. *Science-Fiction Studies*, 55, 18, part 3 (Summer): 387–407.

—(1992). 'The Sentimental Futurist: Cybernetics and Art in William Gibson's *Neuromancer*'. *Critique*, 33, 3 (Spring): 221–40.

—(1995). 'Antimancer: Cybernetics and Art in Gibson's *Count Zero*'. *Science-Fiction Studies*, 65, 22, part 1 (March): 63–86.

Davis, Mike (1990). *City of Quartz: Excavating the Future in Los Angeles*. New York: Verso.

Debord, Guy (1977 [1967]). *The Society of the Spectacle*. Detroit: Red and Black.

Delany, Samuel R. (1976). *Triton: An Ambiguous Heterotopia*. New York: Bantam.

DeLillo, Don (1991). *Mao II*. London: Jonathan Cape.

Deutsch, A.J. (1960). 'A Subway Named Möbius'. In *Best SF Four: Science Fiction Stories*. Ed. Edmund Crispin. London: Faber. (First published in *Astounding Science Fiction*, 1950.)

Dews, Peter (1987). *Logics of Disintegration: Post-Structuralist Thought and the Claims of Critical Theory*. London: Verso.

Dick, Anne (1995). *Search for Philip K. Dick, 1928–1982: A Memoir and Bibliography of the Science Fiction Writer*. Lewiston: Edwin Mellen.

Dickens, Charles (1950 [1847]). *Dombey and Son*. Oxford: Oxford UP.

Dickstein, Morris (1977). *Gates of Eden: American Culture in the Sixties*. New York: Basic Books.

DiTommaso, Lorenzo (1999). 'Redemption in Philip K. Dick's *The Man in the High Castle*'. *Science-Fiction Studies*, 77, 26, part 1 (March): 91–119.

Doctorow, E.L. (1975). *Ragtime*. New York: Random House.

—(1994). *The Waterworks*. Sydney: Picador.

Donald, James (1992). 'What's at Stake in Vampire Films?'. In *Sentimental Education: Schooling, Popular Culture and the Regulation of Liberty*. London: Verso.

Donoghue, Denis (2001). 'The World Seen and Half-Seen'. *New York Review,* XLVIII, no. 3: 41–43.

Durham, Scott (1988). 'P.K. Dick: From the Death of the Subject to a Theology of Late Capitalism'. *Science-Fiction Studies,* 15: 173–86.

Eagleton, Terry (1983). *Literary Theory: An Introduction.* Oxford: Blackwell.

—(1990). *The Ideology of the Aesthetic.* Oxford: Blackwell.

Easton Ellis, Bret (1991). *American Psycho.* London: Picador.

Eco, Umberto (1990). 'Interpreting Serials'. In *The Limits of Interpretation.* Bloomington and Indianapolis: Indiana UP: 83–100.

—(1994). *Six Walks in the Fictional Woods.* Cambridge, MA and London: Harvard UP.

Ehrenreich, Barbara (1983). *The Hearts of Men: American Dreams and the Flight from Commitment.* London: Pluto Press.

Ellis, Kate Ferguson (1989). *The Contested Castle: Gothic Novels and the Subversion of Domestic Ideology.* Urbana and Chicago: U Illinois P.

Ellroy, James (1990). *LA Confidential.* New York: Mysterious P.

Ferguson, Niall (ed.) (1998). *Virtual History: Alternatives and Counterfactuals.* London: Macmillan.

Field, Norma (1998). '*Somehow*: The Postmodern as Atmosphere'. In *Postmodernism and Japan.* Ed. Masao Miyoshi and H.D. Harootunian. Durham, NC and London: Duke UP: 169–88.

Finney, Jack (1989 [1955]). *The Body-Snatchers,* repr. as *Invasion of the Body-Snatchers.* New York: Fireside.

Fitting, Peter (1992a). '*Ubik*: The Deconstruction of Bourgeois SF'. In *On Philip K. Dick: 40 Articles from Science Fiction Studies.* Ed. R.D. Mullen, Istvan Csicsery-Ronay, Jr, Arthur B. Evans and Veronica Hollinger. Terre Haute and Greencastle, IN: ST-TH Inc.: 41–49.

—(1992b). 'Reality as Ideological Construct: A Reading of Five Novels by Philip K. Dick'. In *On Philip K. Dick: 40 Articles from Science Fiction Studies.* Ed. R.D. Mullen, Istvan Csicsery-Ronay, Jr, Arthur B. Evans and Veronica Hollinger. Terre Haute and Greencastle, IN: ST-TH Inc.: 92–110.

Foucault, Michel (1978). *The History of Sexuality: Volume 1: An Introduction.* Trans. Robert Hurley. New York: Pantheon Books.

Freedman, Carl (1984). 'Towards a Theory of Paranoia: The Science Fiction of Philip K. Dick'. *Science-Fiction Studies,* 11: 15–24.

Freud, Sigmund (1985 [1919]). 'The "Uncanny"'. In *Art and Literature* (Penguin Freud Library, 14). Trans. James Strachey, ed. Albert Dickson. Harmondsworth: Penguin.

Frow, John (1991). *What Was Postmodernism?* Sydney: Local Consumption Publications, Occasional Paper no. 11.

Gans, Herbert J. (1967). *The Levittowners: Ways of Life and Politics in a New Suburban Community.* New York: Random House.

Gass, William H. (1985). *Habitations of the Word: Essays.* New York: Simon & Schuster.

Gibson, William (1984). *Neuromancer.* New York: Ace.

—(1986). *Count Zero.* New York: Ace.

—(1989 [1988]). *Mona Lisa Overdrive.* New York: Bantam.

—(1993). *Virtual Light.* London: Viking.

—(1999). *All Tomorrow's Parties*. Harmondsworth: Viking Penguin.

Gillespie, Bruce (ed.) (1975). *Philip K. Dick Electric Shepherd*. Melbourne: Norstrilia.

Gissing, George (1967 [1891]). *New Grub Street*. London: Bodley Head.

Habermas, Jurgen (1989). 'Technology and Science as Ideology'. In *On Society and Politics: A Reader*. Ed. and intro. Steven Seidman. Boston: Beacon Press.

Halberstam, David (1993). *The Fifties*. New York: Villard Books.

Harris, Robert (1993 [1992]). *Fatherland*. New York: Random House.

Harvey, A.D. (1994). *Collision of Empires*. London: Phoenix.

Harvey, David (1990). *The Condition of Postmodernity*. London: Verso.

Hawthorne, Nathaniel (1937 [1844]). 'Rappaccini's Daughter'. In *The Complete Novels and Selected Tales*. New York: Modern Library.

Heinlein, Robert A. (1957). *Double Star*. New York: Signet.

—(1989 [1959]). 'All You Zombies –'. In *The Unpleasant Profession of Jonathan Hoag*. New York: Ace.

Herbert, Frank (1990 [1965]). *Dune*. New York: Ace.

Hiaasen, Carl (1989). *Skin Tight*. London: Macmillan.

Hine, Thomas (1968). *Populuxe*. New York: Knopf.

Hoffmann, E.T.A. (1982 [1816]). 'The Sandman'. In *Tales of Hoffmann*. Trans. R.J. Hollingdale. Harmondsworth: Penguin.

Hofstadter, Richard (1967). *The Paranoid Style in American Politics and Other Essays*. New York: Random House.

Horkheimer, Max (1972). 'Authority and the Family'. In *Critical Theory: Selected Essays*. Trans. Matthew J. O'Connell and others. New York: Herder and Herder: 47–128.

Howe, Irving (1992 [1959]). 'Mass Society and Postmodern Fiction'. In *Postmodernism: A Reader*. Ed. Patricia Waugh. London: Edward Arnold.

Huhn, Thomas (1989). 'The Postmodern Return, with a Vengeance, of Subjectivity'. In *Postmodernism Jameson Critique*. Ed. Douglas Kellner. Washington: Maisonneuve: 228–48.

Hunting, Sam (1987). 'Science Fiction: Philip K. Dick'. In *Popular Culture in America*. Ed. Paul Buhle. Minneapolis: U Minnesota P: 197–204.

Huntington, John (1988). 'Philip K. Dick: Authenticity and Insincerity'. *Science-Fiction Studies*, 15: 152–60.

Ireland, David (1988 [1971]). *The Unknown Industrial Prisoner*. Sydney: Angus and Robertson.

Jackson, Kenneth T. (1985). *Crabgrass Frontier: The Suburbanization of the United States*. New York: Oxford UP.

Jackson, Rosemary (1981). *Fantasy: The Literature of Subversion*. London: Methuen.

James, Henry (1984 [1898]). *The Turn of the Screw*. Harmondsworth: Penguin.

Jameson, Fredric (1970). 'On Raymond Chandler'. *Southern Review*, 6 (Summer): 624–50.

—(1972). *Marxism and Form: Twentieth-Century Dialectical Theories of Literature*. Princeton, NJ: Princeton UP.

—(1975a). 'After Armageddon: Character Systems in *Dr Bloodmoney*'. *Science-Fiction Studies*, 2: 31–42.

—(1975b). 'Magical Narratives: Romance as Genre'. *New Literary History* 7, 1 (Autumn): 133–63.

—(1981). *The Political Unconscious: Narrative as a Socially Symbolic Act.* New York: Cornell UP.

—(1982). 'Progress versus Utopia; or, Can We Imagine the Future?'. *Science-Fiction Studies*, 9: 147–58.

—(1987). 'Science Fiction as a Spatial Genre: Generic Discontinuities and the Problem of Figuration in Vonda McIntyre's *The Exile Waiting*'. *Science-Fiction Studies*, 14: 44–59.

—(1988). 'Cognitive Mapping'. In *Marxism and the Interpretation of Culture.* Ed. Cary Nelson and Lawrence Grossberg. Urbana and Chicago: U Illinois P.

—(1993). *Postmodernism, or, The Cultural Logic of Late Capitalism.* Durham, NC: Duke UP.

—(1994). *The Seeds of Time.* New York: Columbia UP.

Jay, Martin (1994). *Downcast Eyes: The Denigration of Vision in Twentieth-Century Thought.* Berkeley, CA and London: U California P.

Jennings, Paul (1960). 'Report on Resistentialism'. In *Parodies: An Anthology from Chaucer to Beerbohm and Beyond.* Ed. Dwight MacDonald. New York: Random House: 393–404.

Jeter, K.W. (1984 [1979]). *Dr Adder.* Afterword by Philip K. Dick. New York: Bluejay.

Jouanne, Emmanuel (1988). 'How "Dickian" is the New French Science Fiction?'. *Science-Fiction Studies*, 15: 226–31.

Kermode, Frank (1967). *The Sense of an Ending: Studies in the Theory of Fiction.* New York: OUP.

Klinger, Barbara (1994). '"Local" Genres: The Hollywood Adult Film in the 1950s'. In *Melodrama Stage Picture Screen.* London: BFI: 134–46.

Krauss, Rosalind (1983). 'Sculpture in the Expanded Field'. In *The Anti-Aesthetic: Essays on Postmodern Culture.* Ed. Hal Foster. Seattle: Bay Press: 31–42.

Kubrick, Stanley (dir.) (1969). *2001: A Space Odyssey.* MGM.

Leavis, F.R. (1948). *The Great Tradition: George Eliot, Henry James, Joseph Conrad.* London: Chatto & Windus.

Le Guin, Ursula K. (1973a [1969]). *The Left Hand of Darkness.* Frogmore, Herts.: Panther.

—(1973b [1971]). *The Lathe of Heaven.* New York: Avon.

—(1988 [1985]). *Always Coming Home.* London: Grafton.

Levack, Daniel J.H., annotations by Steven Owen Godersky (1988). *PKD: A Philip K. Dick Bibliography.* Rev. edn, Westport, CT: Meckler.

Levi, Primo (1988 [1978]). *The Wrench.* Trans. William Weaver. London: Abacus.

Lewis, C.S. (1989). *The Cosmic Trilogy (Out of the Silent Planet* [1938], *Perelandra* [1943], *That Hideous Strength* [1945]). London: Pan.

Lipton, Robert Jay (1970). *Boundaries: Psychological Man in Revolution.* New York: Vintage.

Lovibond, Sabina (1989). 'Feminism and Postmodernism'. *New Left Review*, 178 (November–December): 5–28.

MacDonald, Ross (1967). *The Barbarous Coast.* London: Fontana.

Mack, John E. (1994). *Abduction: Human Encounters with Aliens.* New York: Simon & Schuster.

Mackey, Douglas (1988). *Philip K. Dick.* Boston: Twayne.

Mailer, Norman (1971 [1970]). *Of A Fire on the Moon*. London: Pan.

Malouf, David (1996). *The Conversations at Curlow Creek*. London: Chatto.

McDonald, Ian (1992). 'Fragment of an Analysis of a Case of Hysteria'. In *Speaking in Tongues*. New York: Bantam.

McHale, Brian (1992). *Constructing Postmodernism*. New York: Routledge.

Melley, Michael (2000). *Empire of Conspiracy: The Culture of Conspiracy in Postwar America*. Ithaca, NY: Cornell UP.

Miller, Walter M., Jr (1976 [1960]). *A Canticle for Leibowitz*. New York: Bantam.

Moretti, Franco (1983). *Signs Taken For Wonders: Essays in the Sociology of Literary Forms*. London: Verso.

Nelson, Cary, and Lawrence Grossberg (eds) (1988). *Marxism and the Interpretation of Culture*. Urbana and Chicago: U Illinois P.

Nelson, Thomas A. (1982). *Kubrick: Inside a Film Artist's Maze*. Bloomington: Indiana UP.

Nowotny, Helga (1994). *Time: The Modern and Postmodern Experience*. Trans. Neville Plaice. London: Polity.

Oakeshott, Michael (1983). *On History and Other Essays*. Oxford: Blackwell.

O'Brien, Geoffrey (1981). *Hardboiled America: The Lurid Years of Paperbacks*. New York: Van Nostrand Reinhold.

Ondaatje, Michael (1987). *In the Skin of a Lion*. New York: Knopf.

Osborne, Peter (1992). 'Modernity is a Qualitative, not a Chronological, Category'. *Postmodernism and the Re-Reading of Modernity*. Ed. Francis Barker, Peter Hulme and Margaret Iversen. Manchester and New York: Manchester UP.

Packard, Vance (1958). *The Hidden Persuaders*. New York: Pocket Books.

—(1960). *The Waste Makers*. New York: David McKay.

Palmer, Christopher (1996). 'Terminal Criticism: Investigating the Postmodern'. *Meridian*, 15, 1 (May): 113–25.

—(1999). 'Galactic Empires and the Contemporary Extravaganza: Don Simmons and Iain M. Banks'. *Science-Fiction Studies*, 77, 26, part 1 (March): 73–90.

Parrinder, Patrick (1980). *Science Fiction: Its Criticism and Teaching*. London: Methuen.

Patton, Paul (1988). 'Marxism and Beyond: Strategies of Reterritorialization'. In *Marxism and the Interpretation of Culture*. Ed. Cary Nelson and Lawrence Grossberg. Urbana and Chicago: U Illinois P: 123–36.

Pierce, Hazel (1982). *Philip K. Dick*. Washington: Starmont House.

Plath, Sylvia (1966 [1963]). *The Bell Jar*. London: Faber.

Pohl, Frederik (1963 [1954]). 'The Tunnel Under the World'. In *More Penguin Science Fiction*. Ed. Brian Aldiss. Harmondsworth: Penguin.

Pohl, Frederik, and Cyril Kornbluth (1969 [1953]). *The Space Merchants*. New York: Walker.

Potin, Yves, trans. Heather McLean (1998). 'Four Levels of Reality in Philip K. Dick's *Time Out of Joint*'. *Extrapolation*, 39, no. 2 (Summer): 148–65.

Pratt, Ray (2001). *Projecting Paranoia: Conspirational Visions in American Film*. Lawrence, KS: UP of Kansas.

Prendergast, Mark (1993). *For God, Country and Coca-Cola: The Unauthorized History of the Great American Soft Drink and the Company that Makes It*. New York: Scribners.

Prigognine, Ilya, and Robert Herman (1971). *Kinetic Theory of Vehicular Traffic*. New York: American Elsevier.

Pynchon, Thomas (1973). *Gravity's Rainbow*. New York: Viking P.

—(1979 [1966]). *The Crying of Lot 49*. London: Picador.

—(1990). *Vineland*. Boston: Little, Brown.

—(1998). *Mason and Dixon*. London: Vintage.

Rabkin, Eric S. (1988). 'Irrational Expectations, or, How Economics and the Post-Industrial World Failed Philip K. Dick'. *Science-Fiction Studies*, 15: 161–72.

Reid, David (ed.) (1994). *Sex, Death and God in LA*. Berkeley and Los Angeles: U California P.

Rieder, John (1992 [1988]). 'The Metafictive World of *The Man in the High Castle*: Hermeneutics, Ethics, and Political Ideology'. In *On Philip K. Dick: 40 Articles from Science Fiction Studies*. Ed. R.D. Mullen, Istvan Csicsery-Ronay, Jr, Arthur B. Evans and Veronica Hollinger. Terre Haute and Greencastle, IN: ST-TH Inc.: 223–32.

Rickman, Gregg (1989). *To The High Castle: Philip K. Dick, A Life 1928–1982*. Long Beach, CA: Valentine Press.

Robinson, Kim Stanley (1984). *The Novels of Philip K. Dick*. Ann Arbor: UMI Research P.

—(1986). 'Ridge Running'. In *The Planet on the Table*. London: Futura.

—(1988). *The Gold Coast*. New York: Tor.

—(1990a). *A Short, Sharp Shock*. Shingleton, CA: Ziesing.

—(1990b). *Pacific Edge*. New York: Tor.

—(1993). *Red Mars*. New York: Bantam.

—(1994). *Green Mars*. New York: Bantam.

—(1996). *Blue Mars*. London: HarperCollins.

Rosenau, Pauline Marie (1992). *Postmodernism and the Social Sciences*. Princeton, NJ: Princeton UP.

Rosenbaum, Ron (1998). *Explaining Hitler*. New York: Random House.

Ross, Andrew (1989). *No Respect*. New York: Routledge.

Ross, Kristin (1992). 'Watching the Detectives'. In *Postmodernism and the Rereading of Modernity*. Ed. Francis Barker, Peter Hulme and Margaret Iversen. Manchester and New York: Manchester UP: 46–65.

Roth, Philip (1991). *Patrimony: A True Story*. London: Jonathan Cape.

—(1993). *Operation Shylock: A Confession*. London: Jonathan Cape.

Sass, Louis A. (1992). *Madness and Modernism: Insanity in the Light of Modern Art, Literature and Thought*. New York: Basic Books.

Schwartz, Hillel (1996). *The Culture of the Copy: Striking Likenesses, Unreasonable Facsimiles*. New York: Zone.

Scott, Ridley (dir.) (1982/1991). *Blade Runner*. Warner.

Sennett, Richard (1970). *The Uses of Disorder: Personal Identity and City Life*. New York: W.W. Norton.

Showalter, Elaine (1997). *Hystories: Hysterical Epidemics and Modern Culture*. London: Picador.

Siebers, Tobin (1993). *Cold War Criticism and the Politics of Skepticism*. New York: Oxford UP.

Sinclair, Iain (1999). *Crash: David Cronenberg's Post-Mortem on J.G. Ballard's 'Trajectory of Fate'*. London: British Film Institute.

Slusser, George (1987). 'The "And" in Fantasy and Science Fiction'. In *Intersections: Fantasy and Science Fiction*. Ed. George Slusser and Eric Rabkin. Carbondale and Edwardsville: Southern Illinois UP: 133–70.

—(1988). 'History, Historicity, Story'. *Science-Fiction Studies*, 15 (July): 187–213.

—(1992). 'The Frankenstein Barrier'. In *Fiction 2000: Cyberpunk and the Future of Narrative*. Ed. George Slusser and Tom Shippey. Athens, GA and London: U Georgia P.

Sobchack, Vivian (1987). *Screening Space*. New York: Ungar.

Soja, Edward (1988). *Postmodern Geographies: The Reassertion of Space in Critical Social Theory*. London: Verso.

Spinrad, Norman (1975). 'A Thing of Beauty'. In *No Direction Home*. New York: Pocket Books.

—(1990). *Science Fiction in the Real World*. Carbondale and Edwardsville: Southern Illinois UP.

Stephenson, Neal (2000). *Cryptonomicon*. London: Arrow.

Stephensen-Payne, Phil, and Gordon Benson, Jr (1990). *Philip Kindred Dick: A Working Bibliography*. Albuquerque and Leeds: Galactic Central.

Stringfellow, William, and Anthony Towne (1976). *The Death and Life of Bishop Pike*. Intro. Diane Kennedy Pike. New York: Doubleday.

Sutin, Lawrence (1989). *Divine Invasions: A Life of Philip K. Dick*. New York: Harmony.

Suvin, Darko (1976). 'P.K. Dick's Opus: Artifice as Refuge and World View'. In *Science-Fiction Studies: Selected Articles on Science Fiction 1973–1975*. Ed. R.D. Mullen and Darko Suvin. Boston: Gregg Press.

—(1988). *Positions and Presuppositions in Science Fiction*. Kent, OH: Kent State UP.

Tanner, Tony (1971). *City of Words: American Fiction, 1950–1970*. New York: Harper and Row.

Taylor, Angus (1973). 'Can God Fly? Can He Hold Out His Arms and Fly—the Fiction of Philip K. Dick'. *Foundation*, 4: 32–47.

Tietz, Jürgen (1999). *The Story of Architecture of the Twentieth Century*. Cologne: Könemann.

Tipton, Steven M. (1982). *Getting Saved from the Sixties: Moral Meaning in Conversation and Cultural Change*. Berkeley: U California P.

Todorov, Tzvetan (1973). *The Fantastic: A Structural Approach to a Literary Genre*. Trans. Richard Howard. Cleveland: Case Western UP.

Tolley, Michael (1980). 'Beyond the Enigma: Dick's Questors'. In *The Stellar Gauge*. Ed. Michael Tolley and Kirpal Singh. Melbourne: Norstrilia.

Twain, Mark (1968 [1885]). *The Adventures of Huckleberry Finn*. London: Pan.

Umland, Samuel J. (ed.) (1995). *Philip K. Dick: Contemporary Critical Interpretations*. Westport, CT and London: Greenwood P.

Verhoeven, Paul (dir.) (1990). *Total Recall*. Carolco Pictures Inc.

Von Kleist, Heinrich, Charles Baudelaire, and Rainer Maria Rilke (1994 [1810, 1853, 1913–14]). *Essays on Dolls*. Trans. Idris Parry and Paul Keegan. London: Syrens.

Vonnegut, Kurt (2000 [1973]). *Breakfast of Champions or Goodbye, Blue Monday*. London: Vintage.

Warrick, Patricia S. (1987). *Mind in Motion: The Fiction of Philip K. Dick*. Carbondale and Edwardsville: Southern Illinois UP.

Wells, H.G. (1962 [1896]). *The Island of Doctor Moreau*. Melbourne: Penguin.

West, Nathanael (1962 [1939]). *The Day of the Locust*. New York: New Directions.

Williams, Paul (1986). *Only Apparently Real*. New York: Arbor House.

Williams, Paul (ed.) (1985). *The Philip K. Dick Society Newsletter*, 9/10, 1985 (cassette).

Williams, Raymond (1985 [1973]). *The Country and the City*. London: Hogarth P.

Winkler, Allan M. (1993). *Life Under a Cloud: American Anxiety about the Atom*. New York: Oxford UP.

White, Eric (1993). 'The Erotics of Becoming: XENOGENESIS and *The Thing*'. *Science-Fiction Studies*, 61, 20, part 3 (November): 394–408.

Wills, Garry (1987). *Reagan's America: Innocents at Home*. Garden City, New York: Doubleday.

Wolk, Anthony (1995). 'The Swiss Connections: Psychological Systems in the Novels of Philip K. Dick'. In Umland (ed.) (1995): 101–26.

Žižek, Slavoj (1989). *The Sublime Object of Ideology*. London: Verso.

Zwaan, Victoria de (1997). 'Rethinking the Slipstream: Kathy Acker reads *Neuromancer*'. *Science-Fiction Studies*, 73, 24, part 3 (November): 459–70.

Index